SHOTOKAN DAWN

A selected, early history of Shotokan karate in Great Britain (1956–1966)

Volume I

BY THE SAME AUTHOR

SHOTOKAN DAWN

A selected, early history of Shotokan karate in Great Britain (1956–1966)

Volume I

DR. CLIVE LAYTON

MONA BOOKS UK

55 Bridge Street, Llangefni, Anglesey, North Wales, LL77 7PN, Great Britain

First Edition 2002

Reprinted in 2007 by
MONA BOOKS UK
55 Bridge Street, Llangefni, Anglesey, North Wales, LL77 7PN, Great Britain
Tel: +44 (0)1248 723486
www.monabooks.co.uk
email: mike@monabooks.co.uk

**British Library Cataloguing-in-
Publication Data.
A catalogue record for this book is
available from the British Library.**

ISBN 978 0 9555122 0 9

DEDICATIONS

TO

RACHEL, PANDORA & CEDAR

as always

AND

TO

VICKI WINGROVE & KENNETH COOPER

who died whilst this book was in production

ACKNOWLEDGEMENTS

The author is grateful to the following people for their help during the preparation of Volumes I and II of *Shotokan Dawn*: Rachel Layton; Pandora Layton; John and Joyce Layton; Joy Macquire; Michael Randall, 7th Dan, Chief Instructor to the Shotokan Traditional Karate Organisation; Toshiko Whitcher; Walter Seaton, 7th Dan, Chief Instructor to the England Karate-Do Wado-Kai; Ronald Saunders of British Pathé News; Nicholas Adamou, 7th Dan, Chief Instructor to the International Association of Shotokan Karate; Christopher Adamou, 5th Dan; Pauline Bindra, 6th Dan, Chief Instructor to International Shotokan Karate; Cyril Cummins, 6th Dan; Richard Bygate, 3rd Dan; Andrew Sherry, 7th Dan; Terence O'Neill, 6th Dan, Editor and Publisher of *Terry O'Neill's Fighting Arts International* magazine; John Cheetham, 4th Dan, Editor and Publisher of *Shotokan Karate Magazine*; Gordon Thompson, 3rd Dan; Michael Peachey, 2nd Dan; Mrs. Joy Hackett, The Television News Archive, Independent Television News; Charles Mack, 7th Dan Judo, 6th Dan Karate-Do; Vernon Bell, 9th Dan, Chief Instructor to Tenshin-Shinyo-Ryu Jujitsu (European Jujitsu Union), 3rd Dan Judo, 3rd Dan Karate-do; Christine Bell; Terence Wingrove, 7th Dan, Federation of All Japan Karate Organizations, 7th Dan, International Ju Jitsu Federation; Vicki Wingrove; Kenneth Cooper; Hirokazu Kanazawa, 10th Dan, Chief Instructor to Shotokan Karate International; Roger Carpenter, 6th Dan; Keinosuke Enoeda, 8th Dan JKA, Chief Instructor to the Karate Union of Great Britain; Mrs. Chieko Buck, Master Enoeda's personal secretary; Roy Estabrook, 4th Dan; Roy Banerjee of the Holborn Local Studies Centre; Mitsusuke Harada, 5th Dan, Chief Instructor to Karate-Do Shotokai; Bernard Mathieu, 5th Dan, Shotokai France; Jonathan Lawrence, 4th Dan; Francis Riley, 4th Dan; Philip Moran, 4th Dan; Kingsley Avenell, 2nd Dan; Harry Cook, 4th Dan, Chief Instructor to the Seijinkai Karate-Do Association; Michael Burton, 2nd Dan, of Mona Books; Gwyn Hughes, 7th Dan, Tenshin-Shinyo-Ryu Jujitsu; Richard Tucker, manager of the Horseshoe Public House, Clerkenwell, London; Rev. Peter Challen, of the John Marshall Hall, Blackfriars, London; Ian Leonard, Syndication, *Liverpool Daily Post and Echo*.

Photo Credits: Mona Books (UK): ix, 18, 19, 20, 21, 22, 24, 25, 29, 30, 31, 32, 35, 38, 40, 41, 42, 44, 45, 46, 49, 53, 54, 59, 61, 62, 64, 71, 72, 73, 74, 75, 76, 78, 79, 81, 82, 94, 96, 97, 98, 99, 100, 101, 102, 103, 105, 112, 114, 117, 118, 121, 125, 127, 130, 131, 132, 134, 135, 136, 137, 141, 146, 147, 150, 152, 153, 154, 155, 158, 161, 164, 165, 166, 167, 168, 180, 181, 182, 183, 184, 186, 187, 189, 193, 194, 195, 196, 197, 199, 202, 203, 205, 212, 216, 217, 221, 222, 223, 226, 227, 228, 233, 235, 238, 239, 241, 245, 246, 247, 252–255, 256, 259, 261, 263, 271, 290; *Mirrorpix*: 296; *East Sussex Gazette*: 209, 211; Mitsusuke Harada: 277; Clive Layton: 80, 108, 172, 173, 178, 283, 284, 289; Rachel Layton, 311; *Liverpool Daily Post and Echo*: 179; Michael Randall: 287; *Romford Recorder*: 68, 69.

Publisher's Appeal: The publisher of this work has been unable to trace or contact a number of owners (original photographer or other) of photographs used in this book. Such uncredited persons will be duly acknowledged by the publisher in any future addition of this book upon notification of proof of entitlement.

Front cover: Vernon Bell and the first four English *karateka* – Spring, 1957.

Back cover: Master Tetsuji Murakami performing *mae-tobi-geri* on James Neal, August 1961 (*East Essex Gazette*).

CONTENTS

FOREWORD

Doctor Layton undertook a mighty task when he set about recording the first ten years of Shotokan karate in this country. I have read the two volumes of *Shotokan Dawn* and they provide a truly fair and excellent record of events. I believe that only Dr. Layton could have achieved this; he was the only one who could have written them. The amount of work involved was phenomenal, and he has given them that touch of greatness that only a deep understanding of the subject can impart. I would urge all serious and traditional *karateka* to acquire the books. I am sure that they will become famous and essential reading.

Going over all the memories, visiting the sites again after all these years, has enriched my life, spurred my individual training on, and I believe the books will have a similar effect upon all who read them.

Vernon Bell – founder of the British karate movement
24th February, 1996.

PREFACE

Before embarking upon the writing of this book, the author conducted a representative pilot study to gauge British Shotokan black-belts' knowledge of the early history of their art in Great Britain. Simple, basic questions such as, "When was karate introduced into Britain, and by whom?" and, "When did the first Japanese Shotokan instructor visit, and who was he?" and so on, showed that the level of correct answering was truly lamentable, even amongst some very senior Dan grades. If black-belts responded in this way, reasoned the author, what understanding did humble kyu grades have? Of course, virtually nothing had been written on the subject before, so perhaps people could be partly forgiven for their worrying display of ignorance.

A book on the early history of Shotokan karate in Great Britain, then, has been needed for some considerable time. The longer the project was left, the less accessible the facts and figures would have become, and dimming personal memories would have added to the unreliability by further blurring what is sometimes an already hazy picture. Additionally of course, as the years ticked by, more potential contributors would pass on, and thus deprive future generations of valuable information and heart-felt recollection.

It has been the author's intention to write this book as a kind of living record of the early days of Shotokan in this country, in the sense that, bar one or two individuals, all who have contributed still train on a very regular basis, perhaps not in karate, but in a martial art. Those who have died, trained up to the time of their death, and in one case left valuable interview material. The author felt that by concentrating exclusively on such dedicated people, whose very lives have been the martial arts, and who now rank amongst the very highest non-Japanese *karateka* and *budoka* in the world, a stronger impression might be imparted. The author has attempted therefore, wherever possible, to use the actual words from the interviewed parties, or from individuals who contributed by manuscript, to relate experiences directly. It was felt that given the focus of this self-imposed brief, such an approach would give not only greater reliability and validity, but also a certain freshness to the book, as individual characters emerged through their own reminiscences.

Of course it is quite impossible to give a complete history of the early days of Shotokan in Great Britain. One would have to consult every single trainee over the ten years covered in this book, on every single issue that arose in every single *dojo* on every single training day. Even if this was possible, and one could track down every trainee, each would have to agree to co-operate, and each would have to have a phenomenal memory. If one came across a death then the completeness one sought would be gone, and indeed a number of important individuals have died. But even if one excluded the dead trainees and relied on others' reports, how could one reliably record the tremendous diversity of personal views and the vagaries and idiosyncrasies of personal memory in a readable fashion? In addition, the wider issues outside the *dojo* would also need to be comprehensively addressed, and this would bring into play yet more people – and more unreliability. It is fairly obvious then, that the author has had to be selective, yet one would like to think that the book is certainly representative, and a fairly comprehensive picture does indeed seem to emerge.

Once the criterion for the selection of contributors was solved, the next problem that had to be addressed was geographical region. This was quite easily resolved for as Vernon Bell, the founder of British karate noted, "London was undoubtedly the most important centre for karate in the UK during the Fifties and Sixties." Essex and London were the venues for the first karate *dojos*, and it was to these *dojos* that students, later to become world famous karate instructors, would visit from all over the country, and indeed even from Europe and as far away as Hawaii. But to make the book as representative as possible, given the parameters, the author felt that it would be favourable to include more detailed information on one provincial area, and, to this effect, the North-East of England was chosen – and well chosen as it turned out.

Liverpool became an important Shotokan stronghold in the mid Sixties, and it had been the author's original intention to include a history of Shotokan karate, via selected *karateka*, of that fair city. However, despite repeated requests for information, not one Liverpudlian approached, who trained before 1966, responded to the author's appeals for a short written contribution – disappointing, not to say strange, given the genuine enthusiasm shown by others for the project.

The problem with most martial arts' histories, one imagines, is the reliance on human memory, and a dearth of literature, if it ever existed at all, from the period to be investigated. In a British Karate Federation circular dated the 3rd September, 1965, Vernon Bell wrote: "I am dedicated to guarding all the BKF records ... and documents entrusted to me since the beginning," and true to his word much has survived, though alas a substantial amount has been lost. For his partial safe keeping of these records alone, the records of the first British karate organization, Bell deserves to go down in the annals of the art. It was an act for which every true Shotokan *karateka* should forever be grateful. Histories that rely on human memory are affected by both perception and the passage of time. With many of the actual records available, one may reliably remove the distraction of time, and thus a much clearer picture of events emerges.

With such valuable information at the author's disposal, it was decided to use the actual records as the main focus of the book, to let it act as a backbone, and all other information – interview material, written contributions, facts and figures gleaned from a large array of sources – would largely embellish the existing records. Thus the book is as complete and as accurate as one is ever likely to make it.

One might think that having a significant percentage of the records made the job of writing this book fairly straightforward, but nothing could have been further from the truth. In fact, the preparation was a nightmare, an absolute nightmare. Bell alone took one and a half years to locate and sort through the material, which, unbelievably, had been stored for years in an unlocked garage, then a damp basement, and finally an attic infested with mice and birds. Then the author had to read every scrap (sometimes, literally, 'scrap') of paper, and try and make some sense of it, to order it, and then make something readable from it. If the author hadn't completed a research degree in the past, dealing with large amounts of data, it may have been the case that he would not have been able to cope with the volume of work in the allotted time. Close to one thousand grading results, all dated, for example, have been integrated into the text, which allows the reader to follow individual progress. Just to give the reader some idea of the extent of the magnitude of the task the author faced, he believes he has read well in excess of two million words in the preparation of this book. If there are errors, and of course everything possible has been done to minimise such errors, then the author apologises in advance. It has only been possible to work with the material that has survived, and any errors are made in good faith.

Although the author has concentrated on specific geographical areas with regard to interview material, all the relevant available BKF information, and more, has been put into the book. Individual membership forms which have survived, and there must be some six hundred of these, from other *dojos*, have all been included – Aberdeen, Blackpool, Bradford, Dundee, Leicester, Liverpool and Nottingham, for example. For each member, four pieces of information are provided – name, age, occupation at the time of applying to join the BKF, and date of completion of BKF membership application forms. The book thus provides valuable reference information as to who trained and when, and much can be made of the above data, now or in the future. Where interesting points are made in correspondence between Bell and a club instructor or secretary, these are always referred to. The text to both volumes of *Shotokan Dawn* is continuous; there are no chapter headings, and this is because there are no frequent, obvious divisions in the story. Events in the first ten years of Shotokan karate in Great Britain overlap to such an extent, that if chapters had been included, to do the available material justice, the author would have had to yo-yo back and forth so much, and remind the reader what had happened previously so often, as to make reading confusing and tedious. To accommodate readers therefore, and for practical and technical reasons at the typing and typesetting stages, it was decided to break the text into eleven parts, six in Volume I and five in Volume II.

Many extracts from the letters of Vernon Bell have naturally been included in this book. Bell had a penchant for very long sentences at times, and, with his full permission, the author has occasionally broken such sentences into additional sentences to aid reader comfort. Likewise, again with Bell's permission, these long sentences sometimes lacked the necessary punctuation, and the author has often added commas to aid flow and intelligibility.

All Japanese words, bar two, have been italicised for easy reference, except, of course, proper nouns. The two exceptions to this rule are 'dan' and 'kyu.' 'Dan' is to be found in most concise English dictionaries, though rank of dan is often given in Japanese, for example, *'Nidan'* (2nd Dan). 'Kyu' (non black-belt rank) is not italicised because it is met with very frequently, often in lists. 'Ju-jitsu' is written as shown, though often in quoted material 'ju-jutsu', an alternative spelling, is kept if the original spelling is as such. Sometimes 'ju-jitsu' and 'ju-jutsu' lose their hyphens.

The book is concerned with a period before decimalization took place in Great Britain, and therefore measurements are given in inches, feet, yards and miles, whilst weights are given in ounces, pounds and stones. For readers too young to remember the system, there were twelve inches in one foot, three feet in one yard, and one thousand seven hundred and sixty yards in one mile. An inch is 25.4 millimetres, a foot is 0.305 of a metre, a yard is 0.914 of a metre, and a mile is 1.609 kilometres. In terms of weight, there were sixteen ounces in a pound and fourteen pound in a stone. An ounce is 28.35 grams, a pound is 0.453 of a kilogram, and a stone is 6.35 kilograms. However, by far the most frequent calculation the reader will be required to make, should he or she so desire, is the conversion of money. The old system employed the rule that there were twelve pennies in a shilling (three pennies in threepence and six pennies in sixpence, of course), and twenty shillings in a pound. A guinea is often referred to in this book, and was twenty-one shillings. Half a crown equalled two shillings and sixpence. For conversion purposes, a shilling equals 5p, therefore £1 8s. equals £1.40; £1. 8s 6d equals £1.43 (rounded up as there are no longer halfpence). If the new values had been placed in brackets after the old values in the text, which would have been a straightforward procedure, the flow of the book, at times, would have been spoilt, and would repeatedly have taken the reader away from the past to the present, and this the author did not wish.

Finally, it has been the author's intention to record all the information available in a readable form for posterity, and it is hoped that what was previously widely regarded as the Dark Ages of British Shotokan, has now become more brightly illuminated.

August 1995
Updated February 2002

CLIVE LAYTON, M.A., Ph.D (Lond), 6th Dan

SHOTOKAN DAWN
(Volume I)

PART I

Vernon Cecil Frederick Bell was born at three o'clock on the morning of the 9th October 1922, at home at 8, Empress Avenue, Ilford, Essex, the only child of Leonard Cecil Bell and his devoted wife Elsie May (née Sapsworth). Leonard Bell had been a pilot instructor on the Sopwith Camel and SE5 aircraft for the Royal Flying Corps during the Great War, but had been declared unfit for actual combat duty due to a heart condition sustained as a youth, when he had over exerted himself in a sprint race and his heart had become displaced. Indeed, doctors told him that he would never run again, and he spent the rest of his life working quietly and methodically as a civil servant, and lived to eighty-two, passing away in 1976, followed two years later by his loving wife.

Vernon Bell (who was christened Frederick after his grandfather, on his father's side, the inventor of the photographic enlarger) recalled his early years: "My childhood was a very, very happy one, though it was also a lonely one. We lived in a house called 'Ivydene' in the Basildon Road, Laindon, and I went to a little private school situated in Laindon Road. The headmistress' name was Miss Fuller. I used to walk a mile to school and had a marvellous time there. We were like a large family and we'd play football. Allan Burlton, a friend of mine, was the son of a farmer in Laindon, and we used to play happily amongst the fields and haystacks, chase each other, and chase the pigs and cows, and watch the cars on the main Southend Arterial Road, which was at the bottom of his garden. When I was seven and a half or eight, I left this little school, this little haven, because my father changed jobs and went to work in Ilford. We moved, and I was thrust into a military environment, Palmer's Public and Endowed School, without friends. I became very lonely. We had a large house in Medina Road, in Grays, Essex. The house had a

Leonard Bell in the Royal Flying Corps – 1917

Elsie May Sapsworth shortly before her marriage – *c*. 1919

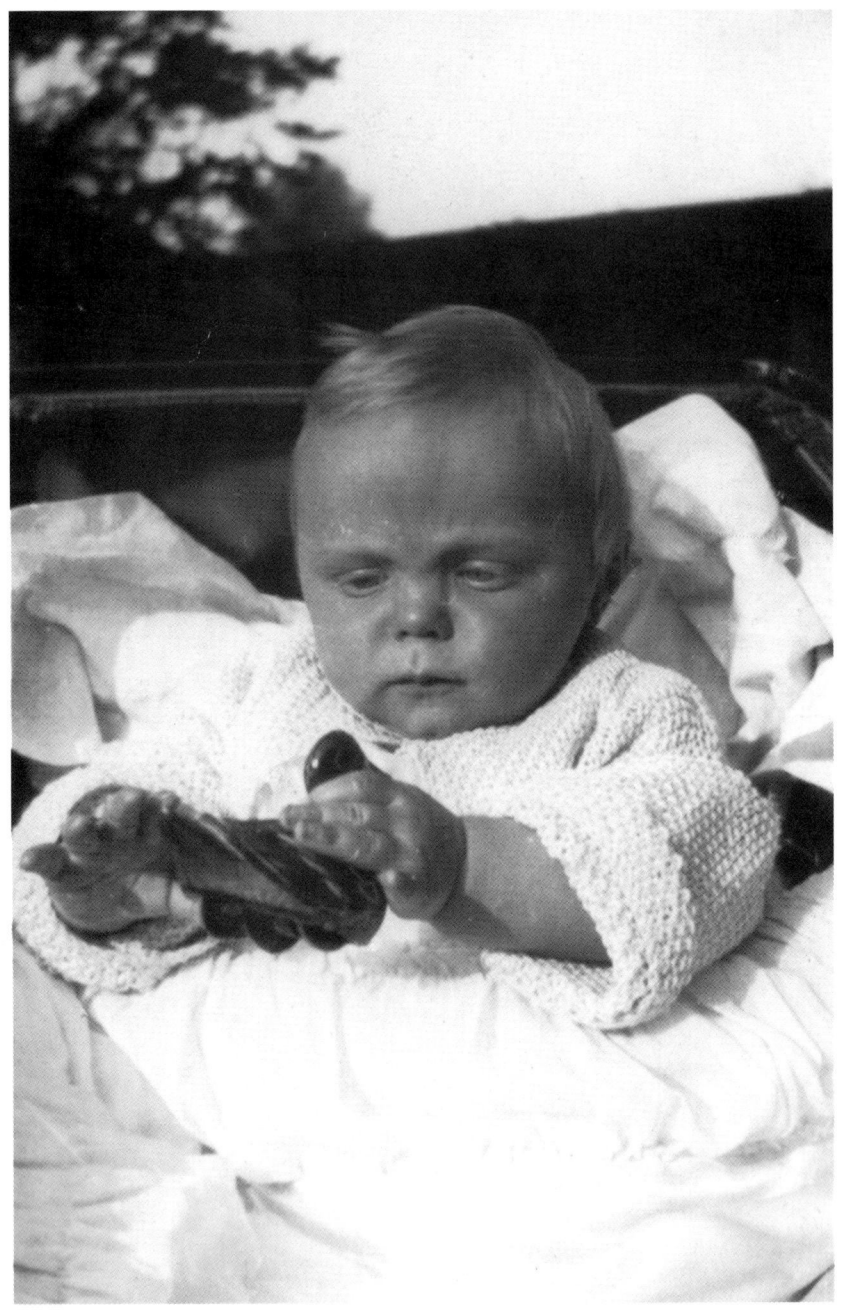

Vernon Bell aged one and a half – 1924

Vernon Bell, aged three, with his beloved dog, Rover – 1926

strange name, 'Clyst St. George.' My mother taught singing and the pianoforte from there. The garden was an acre in size, and I had a greyhound called Rover, a wonderful animal I would play with when I got home from school, but Rover passed away, and this added greatly to my loneliness. My father bought me another dog, a golden retriever, another lovely creature, which stayed with me all its life. In the garden was a tall acacia tree which I would climb and look out over the fields, and I could even see the ships coming up the River Thames at Tilbury on fine, clear days. I had nobody to play with until a family moved into a bungalow next door. A fat boy called Peter Harvey lived there. He was so fat he could hardly walk. We played together and he was a lovely friend, but all the boys at the school we went to used to play jokes on him – chalk his trousers, put things down his back, hide his shoes, tie his shoe laces together – poor devil. It took me three years to make friends at Palmer's.

"I remember the old headmaster, the Reverend Aldridge Abbot. He used to walk around with his dog collar on and wear little beady glasses. He held a cane in his hand and would whack any boy who was even thinking of doing what he shouldn't. He would expel boys left, right and centre. He was a very strict disciplinarian, a fantastic man, and so unlike my father, who was easy-going, though he had a ferocious temper. He never let me answer my mother back, which is, of course, correct. If I did, I got the boot or the strap. My punishment was to be locked in my

Vernon Bell, in black swimsuit, aged twelve, at the seaside, Essex – 1935

bedroom with my fort and five hundred and fifty-two soldiers – I remember that exact number because my father counted them for me – and eat nothing but rice pudding all day until I apologised."

As a young man, Vernon received a fine education at Palmer's. He had a love of ancient history, Latin, English grammar and biology, and was very good at sports, especially football. However, he had a deep fear of the water and avoided swimming. In fact, even the thought of entering the water brought him out in a heavy sweat. Bell continued: "When I was a young boy, my uncle, my mother's brother, Wilfred Sapsworth, a bus driver, who had a love of opera, threw me in to the water at Maldon-on-Sea, in Essex. He said he'd teach me how to swim, and carried me out into about five feet of water and just threw me in. I was scared stiff of the water after that, petrified in fact. When I came to Palmer's, everybody had to swim one length of the pool. I'd get in the water and freeze, and not let go of the bar. I got shingles very badly from the fear of it, and I'll remember that shingles to my dying day.

"I was good at cross-country and always finished either first or second in the House races. My House was Rupert Brooke, named after the famous World War I poet. But my first love was football. I could hit the crossbar from the halfway line with my left foot and was made leftwing for the 3rd Eleven. I had a form master called Spedding, Alfred Spedding, and he was a basket. He was the history and geography master at Palmer's and a Cambridge man. Spedding was the manager of the 1st and 2nd teams and he didn't like me. I never knew why, but he made me unhappy and prevented me from getting into the 1st and 2nd Eleven. I actually quite liked old Spedding because he was a disciplinarian too. But I wanted to be a professional footballer and play for Tottenham. My father had been in the Tottenham Nursery Team and I always had this ambition, even in my early teenage years. So I was frustrated in the 3rd Eleven, and as if that wasn't enough to contend with, I was being bullied by the centre-forward. He was getting hold of me, and putting me in a sort of hold, a lock, and sat on my chest. I got tired of it. I began to feel helpless, like the feelings I had in the water. The other boys began to lose a bit of respect for me, and I lost my position in the 3rd Eleven when football was my life. Anyway, the fear of water and the fear of not being in control, of being helpless in front of bigger people, greatly upset me. I left Palmer's when I was fourteen because my father moved job again, and I went to the Royal Liberty School, a grammar school, in Gidea Park, Romford, and I stayed there for three years."

In 1939, the young Vernon Bell, having failed the majority of subjects required to matriculate a second time, could not face his father, and quickly volunteered for the Royal Air Force, and undertook training as a pilot navigator. Vernon Bell remembered: "As cadets we had to jump into the deep end at the swimming pool, which of course represented the open sea, inflate the rubber dinghy and paddle two lengths. The old fears of deep water that had haunted me as a child and at Palmer's came back. It got so bad that even catching the ferry to Felixstowe when I went on leave when I was stationed at RAF Bawdsey, in Suffolk, worried me greatly. At Bawdsey I was living in a private chalet the other side of the River Deben with other men who were involved in radar. [Vernon served on aircrew duty for two years before becoming a radar operator specialising in the tracking of V1s and V2s]. A large man, much taller than my five foot seven and a half inches anyway, Ray Keene his name was, from Heanor, just north of Derby, was always taking the mickey out of me for some reason or other. I don't know why he did it, but one day I answered him back. He didn't like that at all, and threw me on the ground outside the chalet and held me down with a judo scarf hold. I felt so helpless. I panicked, but the more I tried to get out of this hold the tighter it got. Eventually he let me go, and I asked him what he did and he said he practised judo. I asked him if he would teach me, and he did. We trained in our off-duty hours and we became friends. My martial arts training started then – in 1941 that was. Ray Keene taught me several

Vernon Bell aged seventeen and a half – 1940

Vernon Bell with his first wife, Rita Meeson – 1941

throws – sweeping leg throws, drawing ankle throws, hip throws and so on, and slowly, ever so slowly, I began to lose my fears. My deep feelings of helplessness in water began to leave me and I felt that I was beginning to be in control of myself, mentally and physically. I built on that early judo training and I never looked back. I actually started a little judo section on the base and it all went perfectly. I also coached the base cricket and football teams and the CO made me station masseur as well, as I'd trained in that under the RAF educational training programme. If old Willie Sapsworth hadn't thrown me in the sea that day, and if I hadn't been bullied, I may never have taken up judo, which of course led me, later, to introduce karate to Great Britain."

When Vernon Bell left the Royal Air Force in October 1946, having attained the rank of Leading Aircraftsman Cadet, he worked for the Ottoman Bank in London. He had married Rita Meeson, whose father was a businessman of some repute, in 1941, and identical twins had arrived in 1945. Bell started up a barbell club in Upminster, Essex, and concentrated on weight-training, body-building, and so on. Bell recalled: "At this time I weighed eleven and a half stone, a weight I kept for a long time. I was an official of the Health and Strength League, and did many displays in southern England. I started incorporating judo into the demonstrations and I became the founder of the Amateur Judo Association with Captain Pat Butler, who wrote several early books on judo and self-defence. That was in 1948, if I remember correctly."

Bell left the Ottoman Bank and took a government-sponsored physical education course at the South-West Technical College in Walthamstow. As Bell recalled: "And who do you think I saw there? – old Spedding. He was a lecturer in history and geography, and when he saw me he asked what I was doing. When I told him I was training to be a PE teacher he seemed pleased and said well done. History was my subsidiary subject, so I had old Spedding again." Unfortunately, Bell was unable to complete the course due to financial pressures and became, for a short while, an encyclopaedia salesman in late 1948. But judo was Bell's life. It had done so much for him, and in February 1949, he took the plunge and became a full-time professional judo instructor. Calling his club 'Seimei Do Kwai,' his first *dojo* was his garage, which he had converted, at home at 54, Herbert Road, Hornchurch, Essex.

One early judo demonstration that stuck in Bell's mind, though he gave many, was in 1949, and involved giving a display of techniques used in the minor Humphrey Bogart black and white film, *Tokyo Joe*, that had been released that same year. The 88-minute, slow-moving adventure, not well received by critics, told of Bogart's attempts to reclaim his ex-wife and child, plus a fortune, with Bogart being dragged into smuggling and blackmail. Bell recalled: "In those days there was just judo and a little kendo. I did a demonstration in Romford, at a fete, for Gestetner. We did 'Beauty and the Beast' techniques, self-defence techniques, ju-jitsu techniques, one man against ten, and so on. The Plaza Cinema in Romford heard about me and asked if I would do a display for them, on stage. It was the biggest cinema in the area in those days and good publicity for us. Anyway, my students and I went on stage during the fifteen-minute interval between the two films, and we did scenes from *Tokyo Joe*. One of us dressed up as a Japanese guard. When the film came out there was a lot of ill-feeling towards the Japanese, especially by ex-servicemen."

This ill-feeling, disgust and indeed downright hatred, was of course based mainly upon World War II experiences in the Far East, as a result of the sadism and brutality attributed to the Japanese army. The cinema attracted large audiences, few people had televisions, and, as a mass medium, film was highly influential. Fox's black and white film, *Three Came Home* (1950), a powerful and harrowing story of life in a Japanese prisoner-of-war-camp for women in Borneo, undoubtedly fuelled this ill-feeling, and indeed justifiably brought the Japanese atrocities home in an emotional way. Based on the autobiography of Agnes Newton Keith, this critically acclaimed film by Jean Negulesco, gave Claudette Colbert one of her finest roles. The scene where a guard tortures the attractive mother-figure that Colbert plays in order to get her to sign a retraction to her accusation that a Japanese soldier tried to rape her, and then viciously kicks her in the back when she has collapsed with pain onto the floor during the torturing, is still unpleasant to watch today, and would at the time surely have been enough to make any civilised individual turn in disgust, and bring to boiling point an Englishman's blood. Indeed, the critic for the New York Times wrote that, "It will shock you, disturb you, tear your heart out."

But *Three Came Home* was not alone, and there were other films on a similar theme. *A Town Like Alice* (1956), a two-hour British Rank/Vic black and white film based on Nevil Shute's popular novel, and directed by Jack Lee, was undoubtedly one of the finest, and described the oppression and indignities suffered by women prisoners of the Japanese in Malaya. It was a considerable commercial success at the time, and starred Virginia McKenna in the lead role. One noted British critic (Leslie Halliwell) described the project as a "genteelly harrowing war film," and so it was, and the male crucifixion scene still bites.

Although judo and ju-jitsu techniques had appeared in films before, most notably in American movies, snippets of karate-like techniques were beginning to creep in during the Forties. The author does not wish to labour the point, but such films were significant in that they influenced students to take up the martial arts after the war. One of the best from this early period was *Blood on the Sun*, starring a forty-one-year-old, in-form, James Cagney. The film is particularly worthy of note, not least because it won an Academy Award for best black and white art direction (Wiard Ihnen). Made in 1945 by William Cagney Productions, and directed by Frank Lloyd, the ninety-four minute fast-paced actioner was described by one critic at the time as suitable for "those who enjoy a good ninety minute massacre" (*New Yorker*), whilst Bosley Crowther noted that it was, "Tough, hard-hitting and explosive." Certainly, for the time, the film had some very exciting fight sequences, and one 'highlight', for those so inclined, is a ritual disembowelment. The story centres on Nicholas Condon (Cagney), the American editor of the *Tokyo Chronicle* in pre-war Japan, coming across a plan by ruling warlords for Japan's world domination, and his escape from these warlords who want to silence him. There are throws and 'chops' to the neck with Cagney giving as well as receiving punishment. But there are some nice lines too. Cagney says to Sylvia Sidney (playing a Chinese patriot), "You certainly know your judo, don't you? You've had me off balance ever since you came in." But the real highlight of the film, as least as far as budding martial artists were concerned, was the two-and-three-quarter-minute hand-to-hand fight that Cagney has with the evil Sergeant Ohshima on the wharf close to the end of the movie. Ohshima punches through the locked door with his fist, and when he says, "It's as easy to kill you with these (raising his hands) as with that (throwing his pistol to the floor) – in fact I prefer it that way – Japanese fashion," you know you are in for a battle royal. There are throws, trips, strangleholds, *shuto*, front kicks and even a side-kick. Cagney mainly throws and boxes, whilst Ohshima fights with judo and the occasional karate technique. It's great stuff, and the memorable last line of the film, spoken by Cagney: "Sure, forgive your enemies – but first get even," just about sums up this tough, yet regrettably largely forgotten work.

The formula of including judo, ju-jitsu and karate-like techniques was obviously well received, for a year later Cagney was in the thick of it again in Henry Hathaway's semi-documentary, *13 Rue Madeleine*. Playing an instructor to secret agents, we see him instruct them in judo break-falls – and very nice they look too. Later, we see Cagney dispose of a soldier with the inevitable *shuto* to the neck, followed by two elbow strikes to the head, before finally strangling his Nazi opponent.

The oriental method of combat was certainly seen as effective, and this is probably best appreciated in a completely unexpected incident in Otto Preminger's famous 1944, black and white, mystery thriller, *Laura*. Described as the blackest of *films noirs*, the film won an Oscar for best black and white photography (and was nominated for three other Academy Awards). *Laura* contains a really most interesting punch for the time. Dana Andrews, in the role of an obsessed detective, Mark McPherson, is touched on the shoulder by Vincent Price, playing a parasitic playboy, after a fierce verbal exchange. Andrews spins round and, with a straight back, delivers what, to all intents and purposes, is a reverse punch to Price's heart. The sound effect for this technique is quite exceptional, and unlike any other the author is aware of from films of that period. Price keels back into a chair, stunned, and is then comforted by actress Judith Anderson. Whether the punch was an attempt at a karate movement is uncertain, but Andrews's positioning and the apparent straightness of the technique, along with the sound effect deemed appropriate, and the effect it has, strongly suggest that it was considered something a little special.

But enough about films – at least for the moment! The point being made is that in the mid to late Forties, vast western cinema audiences were beginning to be exposed to the Japanese martial arts, particularly judo, in a consistent way. It was entertainment of course, Hollywood-style, with Japanese self-defence techniques being put across as highly

Vernon Bell demonstrating *yoko-sutemi-waza* – Heath Park Girls School – early 1950s.

effective, and demand grew in the real world. Judo clubs, such as Vernon Bell's, began to spring up more readily (though of course there had been judo clubs in Britain for some decades), and the kernel of a greater public awareness in such arts was underway. This provided sufficient incentive for enterprising instructors.

All forms of self-defence and associated activities interested the young Bell, and on the 4th of August, 1950, he became a black-belt, *Shodan*, in ju-jitsu from the Anglo Japanese Judo and Jujitsu Society based at 43, Strand Street, Cape Town, South Africa. His grading instructors were Harry Johnston and Oliver Horne, though his teacher had been a Japanese gentleman named Sieshi Teppi. Back in England, and still living in Herbert Road, Bell was writing to publishers to see if they would be interested in a book he was contemplating preparing entitled, *Principles and Practice of Judo*. Bell's letters to these publishers, dated 31st October 1950, are now lost, but two replies that he received have survived. The first, dated 1st November, 1950, was from Rider and Company, of 47, Princes Gate, London SW7, and the second, dated the 9th November 1950, from Thorsons Publishers, of 91, St. Martins Lane, London, WC2. Both publishers appeared keen, with the first noting that, "We shall certainly be interested to see your

Vernon Bell demonstrating *tomoe-nage* on R. Cavender – Heath Park Girls School, 1953.

Vernon Bell demonstrating *yoko-hiza-guruma* on a moving lorry during a procession at Romford Carnival – 1954.

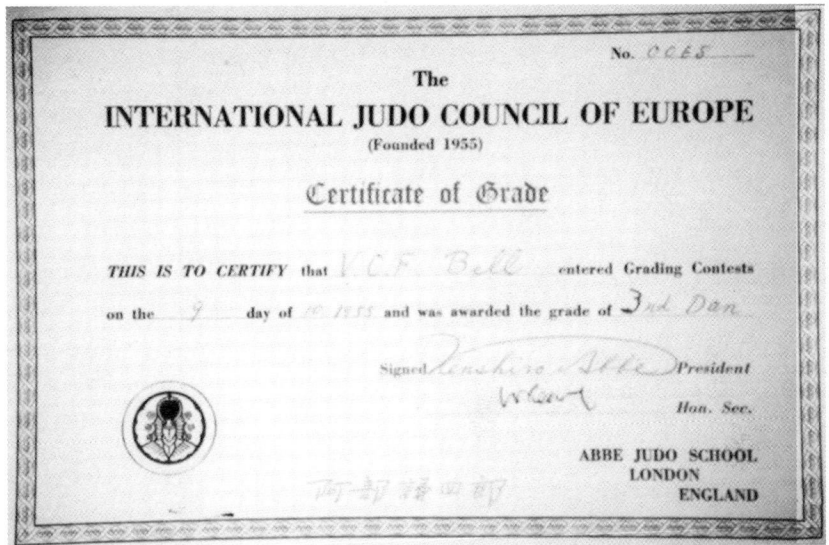

The
INTERNATIONAL JUDO COUNCIL OF EUROPE
(Founded 1955)

Certificate of Grade

No. *OCES*

THIS IS TO CERTIFY that *C.F. Bell* entered Grading Contests

on the *9* day of *10 1955* and was awarded the grade of *3rd Dan*

Signed *Kenshiro Abbe* President

Hon. Sec.

ABBE JUDO SCHOOL
LONDON
ENGLAND

Vernon Bell's 3rd Dan Judo certificate

MS. [manuscript] on Judo when completed," and the second were, "definitely interested," and welcomed Bell to call on them when he was next in town. The reply from Thorsons is interesting because L. H. Woodford, managing director, wrote, "We have handled books on judo and ju-jitsu for other publishers, and we know there is a good market for these publications..."

Under Pat Butler (who died in 1992 holding the rank of 7th Dan) and Harry Ewen, Bell graded a judo *Shodan* in 1952 and *Nidan* in 1953. Bell continued: "Judo became very popular, and by 1953 I was in charge of forty-two judo clubs in the eastern counties." Bell graded to judo 3rd Dan on his thirty-third birthday, according to his International Judo Council of Europe certificate, signed by the brilliant, and the author means *brilliant*, Master Kenshiro Abbe (see later), who had arrived in England in 1955 to teach for the London Judo Society. Bell's British Judo Council licence, however, shows a 2nd Dan for the 9th October 1955, and a 3rd Dan date of the 11th October 1958, both under Abbe.

Also on the 9th October 1955, Bell passed his ju-jitsu *Nidan* under Ewen and a S. Smith (as 1st Witness) at Ilford, through the auspices of the Mombasa Jujitsu Association, based at 75, Humberstone Gate, Leicester. At this time, Bell was self-described in an (unidentified) licence as having dark brown hair and blue/grey eyes; being five foot seven and a half inches in height, weighing eleven and a half stone, and

The photograph that launched the British karate movement

being of fresh complexion. Under 'distinctive marks' Bell wrote, "circular scar beside left eye" – an injury received in childhood. Bell's previous judo/ju-jitsu grades therefore (judo 1st Dan on the 5th August 1950) appear to have been recognised by Abbe in 1958 and stamped as such in his BJC licence.

Vernon Bell recalled how he first became aware of karate: "I came across a photograph in a magazine, of a Japanese breaking boards in the headquarters of karate in Japan. I was so impressed with this, I really was. I said to myself that I must do this, and it all started then as an idea in my head. That was the first spark, no question about it, to my bringing karate to this country. I saw Kenshiro Abbe, shortly after he came to England, break bricks, tiles and wood in a *dojo*. [It is believed that Abbe actually knew very little karate at all, though some claim that he held a *Shodan* grade. If so, it was almost certainly honorary]. I was so impressed by this and that sealed it. I was determined to find out more."

Abbe also gave a demonstration of karate at the London Judo Society's Festival of judo, held at the Royal Albert Hall, early in 1956. As recorded in *Health and Strength* magazine (March, 1956, p.8), Abbe, "broke planks of wood by striking them with the edge of his hands and feet."

Bell continued: "As a judo 2nd Dan I was quite well known in the judo world. I had a friend in Paris, Monsieur Henri Plee, who was a 3rd Dan in judo at this time, I think, and secretary to the French Federation of Judo and Assimilated Arts. Plee and I corresponded for a quite a time on judo matters and others. He sent me a programme of a Japanese master called Minoru Mochizuki who had been an early pupil of Gichin Funakoshi, the founder of Shotokan karate. Mochizuki had been invited to France and Switzerland. The year was 1955."

In fact, Master Mochizuki had visited Europe in January 1952 as part of a Japanese cultural delegation to UNESCO in Geneva. Unfortunately, the boat was late for its European docking, and with subsequent travel the delegation was unable to participate in events. However, Mochizuki travelled in Switzerland, France and Tunisia, where he gave demonstrations of judo and aikido. The French were particularly struck with Mochizuki, as they were seeking an instructor of judo and other martial arts.

An appreciation of Master Minoru Mochizuki's background is absolutely essential to the understanding of European, and hence British karate, and a brief résumé will be given here.

Mochizuki was born in Shizuoka on the 11th April 1907, and studied kendo from the age of five or six for some two years under Master Takebe in Tokyo. Moving home, Mochizuki trained every day under Master Toku, an Okinawan of noble birth, who practised karate, excelled at kendo, but taught mainly judo at the Takano *dojo*. Master Toku was certainly one of the finest *judoka* of all time. In fact, there was a saying in Japanese judo during that period that stated that before Toku there was no one, and that after his death there would be no one. He died in an American air raid on Tokyo. It may be convincingly argued that European karate began with Mochizuki's exposure to the now legendary Toku, at seven or eight years of age. (Another source, *French Judo* – February, 1972, notes that Mochizuki trained with Toku from seventeen years of age, having previously studied judo and kendo from the ages of six and twelve respectively). In an article by Andre Louka and Harry Cook entitled, *The Life and Times of Master Mochizuki* (*Fighting Arts International*, No. 55), Mochizuki recalled: "Because of the closeness to Okinawa, he [Toku] also took karate lessons. The power and the force of Master Toku meant that he quickly gained a solid reputation. He often performed impressive demonstrations in his *dojo*. He would launch himself from one corner of the room, and with his fist held out in front, would hit the central pillar. According to tradition, every student had a tablet of wood on which his name was written. As he moved up the grades, his tablet was moved ... When Master Toku hit the pillar with all his strength, all the tablets on the wall began to tremble, making a dreadful noise echoing in the *dojo* and round about, which I can still remember. For a long time Master Toku's students were proud to show visitors the marks that his *kento* [the large knuckles of the fist produced by intensive training on the *makiwara*] had left on the pillar in the course of these demonstrations." The date was about 1915, and Toku, who was probably practising either Shorin-ryu or Shuri-te, was demonstrating karate in Tokyo two years before Gichin Funakoshi's first visit to Japan from Okinawa (unless the French version is believed). *French Judo* (*ibid*.) noted that Toku "became a master of this art [karate] and when he struck wooden planks with his fist, he left a deep imprint."

Master Mochizuki gained his *Shodan* in judo in 1926 at the Kodokan (and his 5th Dan in 1935) and, in the same year, became a private live-in student of one of the greatest *judoka* of all time, the last of the judo 10th Dans, Master Kyuzo Mifune. Mifune was awarded his 10th Dan in 1945 aged sixty or sixty-one. He excelled technically, was a formidable champion, and a skilful and much respected teacher. Mifune died in 1965.

Master Jigoro Kano, the founder of judo, wanted to preserve the traditional Japanese martial arts in the form of a section within the Kodokan. Mochizuki was chosen to learn aiki-jutsu from Master Sogaku Takeda and then, later, under the mystic, Morihei Ueshiba. Mochizuki also learned Katori Shinto Ryu under Yazaemon Hayashi, kendo under Hakudo Nakayama and Shindo-Musu Ryu Jujutsu under Takaji Shimizu.

It is likely to have been at this time that Mochizuki studied with the great karate master, Gichin Funakoshi, who is credited with officially introducing karate to the Japanese mainland in 1922. Little is known on the subject of Mochizuki's association with Funakoshi, yet it is vital matter, as some authorities dispute whether Mochizuki knew any karate at all. Terry Wingrove (see later), who lived in Japan for some twenty years studying karate in particular, knew Minoru Mochizuki, and noted: "Yes, he did train with Funakoshi. There is no doubt about that – one hundred per cent ... I have a copy of a letter somewhere from Kano to Mochizuki asking him to train with Funakoshi." Similarly, Roy Estabrook practised under Minoru Mochizuki and noted: "Whilst training at the Yoseikan *dojo* in Shizuoka in 1990, I had many occasions to talk to *Sensei* Mochizuki. He could easily recall training with many of the old masters – Kano, Ueshiba, and also Funakoshi. I asked him

Students and instructors watching sparring of Yoseikan *karateka*. Kneeling, front, far left, is Master Masaji Yamaguchi, with Jim Alcheik next to him. Far right, kneeling, is Master Minoru Mochizuki.

Master Minoru Mochizuki (kicking) sparring with Master Masaji Yamaguchi

had he trained with Funakoshi, and he said, 'Yes,' and held him in great esteem, and as I recall he spoke warmly of his old teacher, although he did not train with him for long – maybe a year or so."

Unfortunately, Mochizuki became quite seriously ill with pleurisy and the idea of a new section at the Kodokan was abandoned. Mochizuki returned to the place of his birth and established the Yoseikan in 1931 (or 1933), where he taught the arts he had learned. After some seven years in China as director of the Mongolian school in Paou-to, he returned to Japan after the war and re-organised the Yoseikan *dojo*. Master Masaji Yamaguchi, a student of Kenwa Mabuni, the founder of the Shito-ryu style of karate (and a student of Gichin Funakoshi's teacher, Master Itosu), taught karate at the Yoseikan during this period. It was at this time that two Frenchmen, Claude Urvois and Jim Alcheik, trained at the Yoseikan, and attended Yamaguchi's karate lessons. They returned to France in 1952, and, within a few years, aligned or otherwise, are believed to have begun the French karate movement with Henri Plee.

Henri Plee had started his martial arts training with judo just after the Second World War, having joined the Judo Club de France, and practised under Master Mikinosuke Kawaishi. In fact, Plee was the sixteenth French *judoka* to be awarded a *Shodan* in the art, and became an influential figure in the French judo movement. After practising French Boxing, where both the hands and feet are employed, Plee saw an article in a 1948 edition (27th October) of *Life* magazine, which featured karate. This article had an accompanying photograph of two Japanese black-belts sparring – Hiroshi Kamata and Gojuro Harada, from Waseda University. Plee then acquired some Japanese textbooks on karate, which were translated for him by Rikitaru Fukuda. In the winter of 1953, Plee met Donn Draeger (1922-1982), a former Major in the US Marine Corps, who was later to become famous in martial arts circles for his books. Through Draeger, Plee acquired an invaluable early 1950's Shotokan karate film, showing Isao Obata and Masatoshi Nakayama. In 1954, Plee actually wrote the first book on karate ever to be published in Europe, entitled, *Vanquish or Die: Karate-Do*. After studying and practising alone for a number of years, and, later, including some small-scale teaching, on the 2nd March 1955 he was a founder member of the Fédération Française de Karaté et Boxe Libre, and became General Secretary. Plee was gaining knowledge all the time, and Mochizuki's visit was eagerly awaited.

Vernon Bell recalled, "Plee had two copies of this 'Draeger film.' He kept one and I had the other." This fifteen minute and forty-two second silent, black and white film is superb. It opens with a group shot outdoors, and this is followed by exercising in the splits. The action is then transferred to an old wooden *dojo* and Master Obata demonstrates the main stances of Shotokan and seventeen *ippon* defences. The old Shotokan style is lovely to watch and Obata is impressive. Next, Master Nakayama and another, unknown *karateka*, demonstrate strikes and kicks, and this is followed by *sanbon kumite*, more *ippons* featuring Nakayama, and then a group of ten students performing basics. Master Obata then demonstrates fourteen defences against being grabbed and this is followed by defences with hands tied, against a knife attack, grabbing against one person, then held by two, featuring Nakayama, *jiyu-ippon kumite,* and then freestyle with Nakayama acting as referee. To conclude, there is some tile-breaking with *shuto,* some wood-breaking with *mae-geri* and *uraken*, and finishing with some further tile-breaking with a punch and an elbow. It is a wonderful early film, the best of its kind the author has seen.

On his 1955 visit to Europe, Master Mochizuki was to spend ten days in Paris before journeying across the border to Vevey for a short stay, then returning to Paris before travelling home to his *dojo* at 5, Daiku-cho, Shizuoka. A later (grading?) card (believed to be about 1960) displayed the following information concerning the Institute of Judo, Aikido and Karate-Do, the Yoseikan, noting that the President of the Yoseikan, Minoru Mochizuki, was: 8th Dan aikido, 7th Dan judo, 7th Dan iaido, 5th Dan kendo, and, 4th Dan karatedo. In 1988, he was credited with the following ranks in the following arts, awarded in the year in brackets: 10th Dan aikido (1979), 8th Dan judo (1977), 5th Dan kendo (1956), 5th Dan jodo (1956). At the time of writing, karate is still taught at the Yoseikan.

In an uncredited, typewritten translation, of an uncredited (Plee?) article entitled, 'The Position of the Yoseikan in Japan: Interview with Master Mochizuki's Son,' in an unknown magazine (*Budo Presse?*) written about 1957, based on an interview with Hiroo Mochizuki, the following information about Minoru Mochizuki and the Yoseikan concerning karate and the other martial arts is given. Singing Master Mochizuki's achievements ("He is the only Master of Martial Arts for whom elevation of mind is primordial without any consideration of race or nationality, and consequently he is one of the few to give unreserved help to Occidentals in the study of martial arts such as karate and aikido"), and noting his expertise in a number of arts, including bo-jutsu, the author of the article states that Minoru Mochizuki only taught those arts which he had perfected, leaving specialists to teach the other arts, though in these, "he reaches a standard well above that of many

Hiroo Mochizuki performs *oi-zuki* in Henri Plee's *dojo*

experts." Regarding karate, the unknown writer notes that: "In 1924, Professor Konishi was in charge of the karate section," and later that, "At present, only the Yoseikan groups enough clubs under its wing to be considered as [the] world centre for karate..." The Yoseikan, which was closed during the American occupation after the Pacific War, certainly appears to have been a prestigious *dojo* according to the article, with names like Jigoro Kano, Morihei Ueshiba (who was still visiting the *dojo* when the article was written) and Viscount Enomoto (at one time in charge of kendo) instructing there. Admiral Takata and General Miuru were past Chairmen. Later, Bell gave copies of this translation to his students.

The Konishi connection is most interesting. Master Yasuhiro Konishi was born circa 1887, and had trained under Choki Motobu and, of particular relevance to this book, was an early and prominent student of Gichin Funakoshi. He had attended Keio University and trained under Master Aragaki. Konishi also studied under Morihei Ueshiba. Konishi founded his own school, the Shindo Shizen Ryu, in 1934. He achieved the rank of 10th Dan karate and 8th Dan kendo before his death in the early Eighties.

The fact that Minoru Mochizuki may not have necessarily perfected his study of karate, perhaps having trained under Funakoshi for only one year (though he may, of course, have trained under other karate masters), suggests why certain Japanese have dismissed any karate training he may have had, or knowledge he may have gained, as superficial. There are a number of photographs in existence that show Master Mochizuki teaching and demonstrating karate, so one assumes that he must have been fairly confident. There is, after all, documentary evidence to the effect that he was a 4th Dan, but by whom the grade was awarded is unknown. There could be many reasons why Mochizuki engaged Yamaguchi as a specialist teacher after the war. However, how good Mochizuki really was at karate does not actually overly concern us. What is important is that under Mochizuki's direction a particular type of karate was taught. If Konishi was indeed engaged at the Yoseikan teaching karate before the war, a further Funakoshi-inspired connection is obvious. This may have led Mochizuki to engage Yamaguchi in the late Forties, for his Itosu-based training is likely to have been very similar to the Funakoshi and early Konishi training that he had been exposed to as a younger man and had an affinity with. It can be readily argued (if another point, yet to be mentioned, can not be substantiated) that it was Yamaguchi's karate, Yoseikan karate, that, along with Plee's Shotokan research, formed the basis of European karate from the mid to late Fifties.

Henri Plee's *dojo* – mid 1950s

Bell recalled: "The first ever karate course in Europe was held in Plee's *dojo* at 34, Rue de la Montagne Sainte-Genevieve, Paris 5, under Plee and Hiroo Mochizuki, Minoru's son, who was then a 2nd Dan of the Yoseikan – Minoru Mochizuki's private *dojo*. [It has been reported by Harry Cook, on page 245 of his, *Shotokan Karate: A Precise History* (2001) that Hiroo Mochizuki had been a member of the JKA between 1951 to 1954, where he gained his 2nd Dan – this is the aforementioned, yet to be substantiated point]. I was there along with Jurgen Seydel, Bernard Cherix and Vladimiro Malatesti, the founders of karate in Germany, Switzerland and Italy, respectively. They're still my friends. I saw Minoru Mochizuki, but he never trained us. Anyway, I got this invitation from Plee and I decided to go. I saved up and I got on the old Skyways Autobus, a Dakota – they were used for troop carrying, and they'd vibrate all over – and I left from Heathrow. I flew to Orly airport and was met by this fat Frenchman with a car. I arrived at Plee's *dojo,* but I didn't have enough money to live in a pension, so Plee put me up in his *dojo* with a blanket. There was an old judo mat on the floor and bamboo around the walls with *makiwara* and mirrors everywhere – and old toilets. Oh! The least said about those French toilets the better! You just had to squat over them and hope for the best. You had to pull the chain and dodge out of the way and pull up your trousers before you got a wet behind.

"Anyway, the camaraderie in Plee's *dojo* was fantastic, absolutely

Hiroo Mochizuki performs *mae-empi* from the *kata Tekki Nidan* in Henri Plee's *dojo* – 1957.

fantastic. Plee was the man who really introduced karate to Europe. Plee had a section under the French Federation of Judo. On that first course he introduced me to 4th and 5th Dan *judoka*. A boxing champion

Vernon Bell at Plee's *dojo* in 1956. Left to right: Bell, Plee, Hiroo Mochizuki, unknown, Vladimiro Malatesti.

Vernon Bell and Vladimiro Malatesti at Plee's *dojo* in 1956

was also there. I thought Hiroo Mochizuki, who was twenty at the time (b. 21st March, 1936), was outstanding. He was fresh faced, curly haired, and full of life. He was dynamic. He moved like a panther and a gazelle all rolled into one. He was so fast and so smooth. You really couldn't see some of his moves – brilliant. After two days of training I did my first free *kumite*. They used to say, 'Anglais, Anglais,' and point to me. I had a white belt on at the time with a red line through it [ungraded]. I remember Cherix, and a large Frenchman whose name I cannot recall. We were a great trio. So I started down the line and learned all the moves, the *kata, ippon kata, sanbon kata, Pinan*, but interpreting these to freestyle was new to me. Anyway, my favourite techniques, which I worked out as a combination, were *gyaku-zuki chudan* followed by a reverse *mae-geri*, which later became the back-kick. Every time I came in for my back-kick to the stomach, these Frenchmen ferociously kicked my supporting leg from under me. It turned out to be my weak point. Even Plee, when I was practising with him, would go for my shins with *gedan-keri*. At the end of nearly a week of this a Frenchman lent me a walking stick, because I could hardly move. My shins were black and blue and I had real trouble standing up. I had bandages all around them. I couldn't get my shoes on and had to wear my PT plimsolls. My shins were inflamed up to the knees. When I got back to England, and I did manage to get back somehow, I was a standing joke throughout my judo clubs. 'Old Belly's been to see the Froggies and come back with his shins bruised – and him a judo man!' Abbe, who was my judo teacher, just used to laugh. Abbe *Sensei* was an eccentric and famous for wearing football socks in his King's Cross *dojo* during the cold weather. They were old Arsenal socks, red and white ringed ones. I too had to wear football socks over those bruised shins of mine when I was practising judo there. I was a standing joke. That was my introduction to karate.

"I went every few weeks over to Paris and stayed for two weeks each time. I lived in Plee's *dojo* and I always slept on the judo mats on the *dojo* floor. I wanted to educate myself, and I took to karate like a duck takes to water. I also studied aikido under Hiroo Mochizuki and Andre Nocquet. In April 1957, I was recommended to the French Federation of Judo Technical Committee for my promotion to *Shodan* in Yoseikan karate, which I took under Hiroo Mochizuki, Henri Plee and another gentleman whose name I can't remember. I took my *Shodan* in Paris after training about eighteen months to two years. As soon as I got my *Shodan*, Plee asked me to start a karate movement in Britain and arrange for Japanese experts to come. I told him I needed time to think about that. I finally felt that I had all the grounding for it. I had those

Kenshiro Abbe, Master of Judo, demonstrating *de-ashi-harai* – British Legion Hall, Upminster, 1957/58.

forty-two judo clubs under Kenshiro Abbe's guidance, and I thought what a great opportunity to start karate in Britain. Although Abbe was gracious about it, he didn't like the idea at all, not at all, but he said that as long as it did not interfere with the British Judo Council, the British Kendo Council and the Aikido Council, all of which he was Principal, then that was okay."

Kenshiro Abbe was born in 1915 and started training in judo at the age of fourteen, becoming a 5th Dan in an astonishing five years. He was the youngest ever to reach that grade, and twice winner of the Emperor's Cup (the All-Japan Championships). He came to Britain a 7th Dan, which he had obtained ten years earlier. He was also an aikido 6th Dan, having trained with Morihei Ueshiba, and a 3rd Dan in kendo.

Bell continued: "Abbe was truly a master of the martial arts. He was the greatest technician ever to come to Britain from Japan – a fantastic man, a most human man, a wonderful man. I used to travel with him to the Cambridge University Judo Club and acted as his assistant. I remember his judo demonstrations. I recall an annual BJC Budo display he gave at Crystal Palace, though I forget the exact year. He would

Kenshiro Abbe demonstrating *okuri-ashi-harai* – Upminster *dojo*, 1957/58.

wrestle a line of little children, and then take on thirty or so black-belts from 1st to 5th Dan, doing every technique in the judo repertoire. Remember there are one hundred and twenty-two throws in Kodokan judo and all the variations of them – brilliant. I remember one of his kendo displays. He took his sword and, dressed in a black *hakama*, threw a beautiful silk scarf, very flimsy, into the air. He threw it as high as possible, about eight feet, and as it came down he made a downward strike and split the scarf right down the middle. Then he followed this immediately with someone in the audience throwing up a newspaper, and he came up with the blade and split the paper. He was an expert on the sword too – the metal work. He could tell you everything – a real master. I recall how William Woods, an old friend of mine, would sit down on the floor with an apple on top of his head, with the stalk facing upwards. Kenshiro Abbe would bring the sword over and down and split that stalk and the apple to a quarter of an inch of Wood's head. You couldn't see it for it was that fast. I've never seen anything like it since. It was really out of this world.

"I remember Abbe saying to me once at his *dojo* in King's Cross, 'To be a black-belt, Bell, you must have the spirit up here in your mind

Kenshiro Abbe demonstrating *okuri-ashi-harai* – Upminster *dojo*, 1957/58.

and the feeling in your heart, here. When you become a black-belt you become teachable, and only then do you become teachable. When you become a beginner it should be made quite easy for you to reach the 1st kyu grade, but when you become a 1st kyu you must spend as much time getting from 1st kyu to 1st Dan as you spent from white-belt to 1st kyu. When you become a black-belt in your chosen art, you should have close contact with your *sensei*.'

"He was a great, great man. He was very humble. He was of noble birth and came from a long line of samurai. The Abbe family, in Kyoto, had [and still have] their own crest, which featured a beetle. He had been a senior officer, a major or maybe even a colonel, in charge of the Special Forces, the special assault regiment, the Silent Regiment, it was called. Abbe was brought over [to the UK] because of his technical prowess, his record, competition level, authenticity and lineage. It didn't matter to him if you were a young boy or an old man, a lord or a poor man; in his eyes all were eligible for training in the Budo arts. He would turn up at any time for anybody, without payment, without contract, without letters. His handshake, his word, was good enough. From the very minute he stepped off the plane in April 1955, for the London Judo Society, he was the greatest thing ever to come to these shores; far greater than the great Yukio Tani who brought ju-jitsu from Japan around 1907. Far greater than any of the karate masters, who are mostly nothing but commercialists really, that's all they are, in the western sense. Kenshiro Abbe ... I was going to re-establish Kenshiro Abbe *Sensei*'s kyushindo martial arts, including the old karate, in memory of him. I'd like to devote a work to him before I pass on.

"Anyway, I went to Abbe and told him that the British Karate Federation had been formed under my direction in liaison with the French Karate Federation, and though I still wanted to work with him my main interest would be karate and not kyushindo judo. He took it very well, did the old man. 'You karate – me judo. You karate – me kendo. We friends,' he said, and put out his hand. I shall always remember that."

In 1957, Abbe was still giving karate demonstrations. At the Amateur Judo Association's championships held on the 30th November, at the Liverpool Stadium, there was "much timber being broken with bare hands and feet" by the judo master (*Health and Strength*, 19th December 1957, p. 46).

Bell continued: "When he went back to Japan, Abbe was lonely and sad. One of the reasons why he went back was because ... certain British bastards pinched his brains, learned his techniques, and went and feathered their own nests and left the old boy alone and penniless ... Believe me when I say he was the finest *budoka* ever to come to these shores – and I've studied martial arts for fifty-five years."

The earliest known correspondence between Vernon Bell and Henri Plee, on the subject of karate, was a letter Bell wrote to the Fédération Française de Karaté, on the 21st February 1956. This letter is now lost, but Plee's reply, in French, on the 7th March 1956, has survived. Plee suggested to Bell in this letter that, "If you desire to be graded by us it is indispensable to address to us a film 8 or 16 mm in which you will execute all the movements." Plee referred to Bell's, "teaching plan," and its similarity to a Mr. Robinson in South Africa who had written a book. Plee continued, "Once we have judged and graded you, we advise you to progress and if need be, we shall procure for you a film of Japanese instructors and a teaching film as it [karate] is practised in the Karate Club of France." Plee further noted that, "The official manual of the French Fédération of Karaté does not appear for a year and nothing of worth has been edited on karate-do in French or in another language other than Japanese."

Bell replied to this letter on the 7th June 1956 (now lost) and Plee answered this letter on the 10th June, inviting Bell to a karate course in Biarritz. Plee wrote: "During this course we will be coaching beginners as well as instructors. If you attend this instructors' course, we will be able to give you an attendance certificate stating that you took part in this training course for karate masters. If you prove sufficiently capable we will give you an official Karate Master's diploma, but it will be difficult for you to learn the karate *kata* in such a short time." On the subject of Bell forming a karate organisation Plee responded so: "Creating a karate federation in Great Britain is an initiative which we strongly support, provided your initiative is not just for your own personal interests."

Plee wrote to Bell again on the 18th June 1956, in reply to a previous letter from Bell. This latter letter once again mentioned the karate summer course in Biarritz to be held that year. The course fee was two thousand five hundred Francs, plus an additional five hundred Francs for a licence. Plee wrote that, "After the course you may be examined for graduation," but Bell was unable to attend, much to his regret.

As later correspondence between the two showed (undated, but 1957), the course, which was held from the 4th to the 12th August, 1956, was not well attended, described as being "intimate" with scarcely ten participants. *News of the Training Courses* (a report written in 1957), by an unknown author, noted that: "Nevertheless, it was pleasant to feel this atmosphere of 'pioneers' of karate. Memory of the morning courses [which were taught by Hiroo Mochizuki] in the dunes, alone, followed by a dip in the waves which reached their limit at our feet during the *kumite*..."

Hiroo Mochizuki's next course was in Paris from the 15th to the 30th of August 1956. As the unknown writer noted: "From the very first day, Mr. Hiroo took a firm hold of the training course and didn't let go till the finish. Results – the thirty participants in the course, who were training morning and evening, finished up quite worn out, but pleased with what they had learnt." It was this course, previously referred to, that Bell attended.

In fact, there had been a course held at Collioure, between the 15th and 30th July 1956, when forty students attended. Hiroo Mochizuki was not there, though he was in France, arriving in Marseilles on the 12th July 1956, and had gone with a Mr. Azema to Toulon. The course organisers were expecting Mochizuki and were furious that there had been a mix-up. Plee stepped in and took the training on the course. Mochizuki did however visit Collioure on the 30th July, teaching for

Hiroo Mochizuki performs *kaishu haiwan-uke* from the *kata Heian Yondan* in Henri Plee's *dojo* – 1957.

another four days, though unfortunately most of the students had left by the time he had arrived. The unknown writer of the news item above noted: "Collioure will nevertheless remain as a nice memory of our last isolated efforts before the finally decisive instruction from the Japanese experts of the Yoseikan." The writer of the piece mentioned "experts" because Tetsuji Murakami (see later) was due to arrive in sixteen months. Murakami's intended role was to instruct the provincial French clubs, and clubs of countries abroad that followed the French direction.

Plee had, through the offices of Jim Alcheik, anticipated the arrival of a karate master from the Yoseikan named Hiyugo, a 4th Dan, but after all the formalities had been satisfied Hiyugo became ill. Murakami, also of the Yoseikan, took his place, and was sent to study, apparently at Plee's expense, at the Japan Karate Association, the style of which Plee liked the best – no doubt, readers will recall, because he had a film of JKA training, and had practised their methods. Murakami had no trouble integrating into JKA karate as we shall see, which tends, of course, to show how closely aligned the two modes of practice were. In the meantime, Hiroo Mochizuki had arrived in Paris. Plee thought that Mochizuki was very good and once noted that it was he who taught the French the *kiai*.

Bell wrote again to Plee on the 30th November 1956, noting that answers to previous correspondence had not been forthcoming. Plee wrote back on the 16th December 1956, confused as to where his letters answering Bell's questions had gone. Plee noted in this letter that the summer course had been a great success and they intended holding the following year's course in the Côte d'Azur. Plee noted that, "With your 2,500 Francs we send to you today two karate books in Japanese language ... one teacher badge (this badge shows the little straw mat on which we kick) and the Japanese sign is 'TE', mean 'Hand', and all hand techniques for karate, and defence. Also two karate badges in cloth. The full [amount] is much more than 2,500 Francs, but it is our personal gift for your efforts to diffuse karate in Great Britain." Plee continued, "If you had followed the summer course we are sure that actually you should have numerous karate pupils like other participants (some of them have seventy pupils), and [learned] how to teach and organise karate in Great Britain..." Plee considered it appropriate and, "best to come to France and arrange all for your grading, for basis for your instruction, and for organisation of the British Karate Association or Federation. Only by this way we shall be able to give you a written charter. The second solution is to send one expert to Great Britain. The two Japanese karate experts that we are expecting for our Federation must arrive about the end of February [1957]. In ... [view] ... of Suez they will arrive first in London, and one or two days after they come to France. We could arrange a meeting with you in London ... [but] if nothing can be done, later we intend to go to Great Britain for different exhibitions..."

In reply to this letter, on the 2nd January 1957, some important historical facts emerge. Bell wrote: "At your suggestion I think it advisable for me to come to France very soon to arrange for my grading and for the basis of my instruction in karate and to organise the formation of the British Karate Club. As by this method only you say you will be able to give me a written charter which is what I require mostly, as it is my first intention above all else to hurry the formation of the British Karate Club without delay, as I feel it is essential to put karate on a proper footing in this country as soon as possible, and as your official agent of the French Karate Club of Great Britain, I intend to work closely with, and under the guidance and jurisdiction of your own FFK. I suggest that I visit France early in February, well before the two Japanese karate experts arrive in London, so that we can have arranged all details, procedures, etc. ... and also to get the British Karate Club on a definite footing before I meet them." The two Japanese karate experts that Plee and Bell referred to did not come to Britain, as it so happens, on their way to Paris, and it is not known who these experts actually were.

In an extremely important letter of the 15th February 1957, Plee wrote to Bell noting: "The Japan [Karate] Federation has accepted to recognise our black-belts and sent diplomas. We have been designed [should read 'designated'] as European representatives for karate. I have explained to our committee your position in Great Britain. They have accepted to give you honorific black-belt of karate, and we accept to ask for you the Japanese diplomas of karate *Shodan*. But, for this, you have three things to do and to pay (with my apologies of course): 1) The affiliation fees to the Fédération Française De Karaté – 3,000 Francs; 2) The affiliation to the Japanese Karate Federation Yoseikan – also 3,000 Francs; 3) Your *Shodan* karate diploma – 2,500 Francs. Of course this money is integrally for Japan. If some of your karate brown-belts pupils (3rd kyu to 1st kyu) are wanted their karate diploma (officially recognised by Japan) you have to send to us their name and 1,500 Francs ... We must send the list of the diploma wanted by our Federation very soon, so if you want diploma, affiliation (you shall receive an affiliation letter) and the rest, you have to write to me by return. You certainly imagine that I have had much troubles to obtain the possibility to give you karate black-belt, and I suppose that you must not let disappear this opportunity."

Before Bell's reply is recorded, a special and important note is in order. 'Honorific' is an expression implying respect, especially, according to *The Concise Oxford Dictionary*, "of Oriental forms of speech." Vernon Bell's *Shodan* is believed not to have been honorary, at least in the usual sense, for he insists that he actually passed the *Shodan* grading under Hiroo Mochizuki and Plee, as has already been noted. Bell's Fédération Française de Karaté licence shows this historic date to be the 13th March 1957 – a date signed by Plee. No mention of 'honorary' is recorded on his actual *Shodan* diploma. Vernon Bell noted: "I remember my *Shodan* grading very well, which I did with Jurgen Seydel, Malatesti, from Florence, and, I think, Cherix, in Plee's *dojo*. I had to do the *Pinan [Heian] kata* slow motion and then fast speed. I remember doing two *ippon kata* and sanbon *kata* on both sides. I'd been training about eighteen months with Plee before I got my *Shodan*. I had visited his *dojo* many times. I started training towards the end of 1955 with him." The date of Bell's *Shodan* certificate is the 1st April 1957.

Confusing the issue further, Bell wrote back on the 21st February 1957, noting that, "It is with extreme pleasure and the utmost gratitude for me to hear that after your own personal efforts and troubles on my behalf that your FFK Committee has deemed it to authorise the award to me of Honorary Black Belt of Karate and to ask for the Japanese Federation to issue me the Japanese diploma of karate *Shodan*. I have no hesitation and I am honoured to accept this award of *Shodan*, and I will at all times do my utmost to uphold the prestige and honour of karate and the FFK both by my example and my service to the art. I assure you that I will always honour, respect and carry out in every way all the traditions, teachings and procedures of karate to the highest possible level of the FFK. My dear sir, I can assure you I thoroughly appreciate the efforts you have gone to on my behalf to obtain my karate black-belt, and I wish to convey to you my profoundest and sincerest thanks in every way, and you have made me extremely happy and honoured by this award, and I have no hesitation in accepting this opportunity to become a *Shodan*." Bell also wrote in this letter of his willingness to become the FFK British Representative should Plee consider this appropriate.

Following additional correspondence, Bell wrote to Plee on the 4th April 1957, in which mention is made of a number of bogus karate demonstrations that Bell had witnessed and heard about in Great Britain. He noted: "At the present time there seems to be in Britain a great deal of arising interest in karate by the public and there are appearing many public exhibitions of so called karate by unqualified experts at all the big public judo displays. These exhibitions of karate are performed by

Vernon Bell's Yoseikan 1st Dan karate certificate signed by Minoru Mochizuki and Henri Plee; dated 1st April, 1957.

The BKF's Affiliation certificate to the Yoseikan through the FFK – undated, but 1957.

FÉDÉRATION FRANÇAISE DE KARATÉ

34, Rue de la Montagne Sainte-Geneviève · PARIS Vᵉ · ODÉ. 12·65

CERTIFICATE OF AFFILIATION

This is to certify to all concerned that the above organisation has
duly aythorisated and authenticated official permission to establish, promote,
organise and control the British Karate Federation (incorporating the Karaté
Clubs of Great Britain) to Mr V C F Bell, of 137 Hillview Avenue, Hornchurch,
Essex, who is also authorised by F.F.K to act as official Karaté agent and
representative in Great-Britain, and to establish gradings.

The British Karate Federation will conform to the statutes and Regulations of and
work in liaison with the FFK and the YOSEIKAN (official recognised body of
Karate control in Japan).

Therefore we issue this Charter of authorisation on the 1 st April 1957.

THE PRESIDENT :   THE GENERAL SECRETARY :

The BKF's Affiliation certificate to the FFK – 1957

judo Dan grades who have no idea of what real karate is, nor of its spirit, and their crude exhibitions usually consist of feeble attempts to break pieces of wood across two chairs with the edge of the hand or foot, usually with little or no success. If it is not this it is poor attempts to demonstrate the *Atemi*, consisting mainly of kneeing to the testicles or poking of fingers into the eyes or throat. Last week I saw an exhibition in the East End of London by a so-called Japanese expert ... who calls himself a 5th Dan master of judo, and Mr. Abbe informs me he holds only honorary 3rd Dan. This Japanese confers all sorts of Dan grades in judo on his pupils up to 2nd Dan, none of which is authentic or recognised, and his Dan teachers confer all sorts of unrecognised kyu grades. At this Japanese man's display he billed Karate-Do (ways of killing) and this item comprised instantaneous death by means of arm-locks, poking fingers in eyes, chop to the neck, kicks to the knee and testicles, etc., and the demonstration was performed by two yellow-belts, and the whole lot had no idea what karate means. It now appears that in this country, at these public judo displays, it is fashionable and new to have karate on every programme, because it is new, and the demonstrations always follow the same pattern that I have already described, being performed by judo men who have never studied karate in their life, nor do they have any idea of what it is nor how it is performed, nor do they have any idea of elementary *Atemi* or jujutsu. Because of all this, the name of karate is being abused and the public are being misled as to the true nature of Karate-Do, and the whole art is being misrepresented and is suffering. Therefore, I wish to visit you in Paris as soon as possible in the next few weeks to discuss this matter fully and to get the opinions, procedures, and course I should take in dealing with these false exhibitions of karate, and also to receive your detailed advice and guidance on the best and proper ways to present true karate to the public, and to train my pupils. Also, I would be glad if your committee of the FFK, when I come to Paris, will issue me the authentic written charter to establish the true British Karate Federation, and also it will be a great help and excellent benefit to karate in Britain if (as I previously suggested) your Committee would appoint me as the official representative and agent of the FFK in Britain (with a written letter of jurisdiction), as this will give me official and correct legal standing to promote the growth and develop karate in this country properly, in the true spirit and nature of the art, and to keep the false away." In this letter, Bell also makes reference to Plee's book, *Practical Manual of Karate*, and requested back issues to *Budo* bulletin.

Continuing the theme of *judoka* practising karate, Bell wrote to Plee on the 12th June 1957. "I conversed with Mr. K. Abbe on the subject of karate and he informs me that he is a great friend of Mr. Mochizuki and that they studied karate together in Japan for many years, but, Mr. Abbe says he has never heard of Master Funakoshi, and he also says that Mr. Mochizuki is a great judo man and not a karate man. After these rather startling statements from these two eminent *judoka*, they [the author believes Bell was referring to Abbe and, possibly, Mr. Wood, the latter a 3rd Dan *judoka* and instructor for Abbe] told me that in Japan karate is very disorganised and that there are many hundreds of different experts and clubs and nobody takes karate seriously as a national sport. Finally, these two *judoka* insisted that in karate the exponents could not practice as a sport nor could they engage in friendly competition because the techniques were too dangerous and only the actions of the blows and kicks could be practised. They said there were no such things as *shiai [contest]* and that the judges awarded a point among high grades only by estimating the nearness of a blow to the opponent. After these remarks from these *judoka*, I endeavoured to explain the idea and meaning of karate to them, also the spirit and practice of the art, and I stressed to them that one could safely practise competition without injury, if suitably protected, but they refused to believe me and would not listen to my explanations even when I said I had been to Paris and had practised active contest with the French experts, and that I had experienced the true karate myself. So, Mr. Plee, you see the situation of some of the leading judo Dans in this country, and they think they know all about karate though they have never practised it, and they will not listen and just because they are judo experts they think they know all about karate. So, I wish to train hard and become proficient in karate and have many good pupils who know the real karate, to have a solid and true Federation behind me and to challenge these so-called theorists and armchair experts."

In fact, in an undated letter to Plee, much of which has been lost, but almost certainly from 1957 or 1958, Bell wrote: "I am well in the picture as I have been K. Abbe's Course Secretary and Eastern Representative, having been in close business contact with him on all his projects in the last year and know well his situation and his schemes. I am still friendly, both with Abbe and his black-belts, and have business with him, but I will have no association or contact with him, or his organisation, nor will the BKF, on any matters relating to karate."

Some years later, on the 8th March 1962, to be precise, in a reply letter to a twenty-six-year-old James Straughton of Cockermouth, Cumberland, Bell wrote: "I cannot accept your BKC [a branch of the International Budo Council] grade, as JKA, EKF, and BKF regard Mr. K. Abbe as unauthorised to grade in karate, for he can prove no evidence of his own Japanese registered grades in Dan status in karate." Bell recommended that Mr. Straughton, who had graded to 5th kyu (white belt with a red centre) in October 1961 with Abbe as examiner (though Straughton mentioned he was graded by Moss Timmons, a judo 2nd Dan and karate 1st Dan, when Timmons came to this country), attend a one-day course under Murakami (see later) held on Sunday, the 25th March 1962.

Correspondence between Bell and Plee continued, but one interesting point was the suggestion that Plee visit England for a karate course originally planned for the 6th July 1957. In a letter to Plee dated the 27th May, Bell noted: "I have got about twelve names for the course ... all these men are pupils of mine, with some karate experience. I am charging them £2 per head, which is the only way we can cover your fee, but it is extremely difficult for us to be able to cover all the expenses for your travelling and accommodation, as well as the course fee. It would appear then, that you may have to assist us by helping out with your travelling expenses. However, I will keep you informed of the situation and further developments, and I hope we can arrange enough funds to cover all your expenses, for I can not do it on my own for it is enough for me to provide your party with accommodation and meals. If I was expected to pay for your party's travelling expenses as well then it would cost me nearly £40, which is impossible for me to do alone. If we are unable to raise enough money to cover all expenses for your party, then, I suggest, you send one karate expert only to take a weekend course on the 5th July. Then, when I have raised enough money in the next few months to cover all the costs of your party of five… to visit this country in September (which is the best month in England) to give the display and take a two day course [all will be possible]. If all your party come on July 5th it has only given me two months to prepare for this very big visit, and not very long to raise all the monies required, therefore, being so early makes the entire proposition a risk."

Despite quite detailed planning by Bell, down to even providing road maps from Paris to Hornchurch, and considerable subsequent correspondence on the subject between the two of them, Plee never came to this country for the BKF, or taught karate for anyone else in Great Britain as far as the author is aware. Vernon Bell however continued to travel to Paris to train in Plee's *dojo*, and a letter Bell wrote to Plee on the 16th May 1957, conveys the problems that he was suffering with his legs, which echo his first training at Plee's *dojo*. Bell noted: "I must apologise sincerely for not having written to you before as I had promised you when I left Paris, but the fact remains that since my arrival home until now I have been very incapacitated with my legs and feet and have hardly been able to walk. Also, I have been rather ill with stomach trouble, which has not made me very active for business, and I have hardly been able to take any classes. My right shin, which I badly bruised in your *dojo* was very bad the first week home but has now healed quite well but both of my ankles have been very swollen and I have been unable to place any weight on my feet and have been unable to walk very much. Besides this ankle trouble I have been plagued with many blisters and cuts under my feet and the skin on the toes has cracked and formed sores which keep breaking resulting in my having to bandage my feet each day and so not being able to wear my shoes properly. However, the ankle swelling has gone down and my feet are healing and I can walk a little better and I hope that in one week they will be normal again. Because of all this foot trouble I have been unable to attend my judo classes very easily and it has been difficult to instruct..." Like any determined *karateka* however, Bell noted towards the end of the letter that, "I was very sorry to leave ... I enjoyed my visit very much. I look forward to returning to Paris to pay you another visit in the very near future."

In a reply letter to Bell of the 29th May 1957, Plee wrote. "I have been really sorry to read that your legs have hurt you so long. Probably [you have] not trained enough in karate, legs get strong rapidly with training ... but during this training they hurt. For you, I suppose you must have bad blood circulation and I think you must wear strong protection."

On the 12th June 1957, Bell replied to Plee, and again the subject of Bell's injuries was raised. Bell wrote: "I appreciate your sympathy regarding my legs, and it is possible that you are right in that I have not trained long enough in karate, but they will get stronger with training ... I do suffer from abnormally low blood pressure for a man of my physique and fitness and a specialist told me last year, after I had a thorough examination, that it is extremely unusual for a man of my age and my virility and fitness to have such low blood pressure, and this accounts for why I bruise easily, but I will wear strong protection in the future." It was in this letter that Bell formally asked Plee to become President of the BKF, an honorary position. However, it is not clear whether Plee accepted the invitation or not.

"I actually started my first karate class with my students in 1956 before I got my black-belt," Bell told the author. "We trained on the lawn of a tennis court at my parents' home at 'Springlands,' 12, Maybush Road, Hornchurch. My first five students were Mr. Mick Manning, a *judoka*, and the first man to obtain a 1st kyu from the Yoseikan in Britain, despite a withered right arm; Mr. Ken Elliott, a *judoka*; Mr. D.F. Clarke; Mr. Gerald Tucker, a P.E. teacher; and, the greatest expert that I've ever had in karate even to this day, Trevor Guilfoyle, from Hornchurch. He was so good, this man. He was nearly six foot six inches in height, long and lean and a racing cyclist by hobby, who got from white-belt (6th kyu), to green-belt, 3rd kyu in those days, in less than eight months, when he was nineteen years of age."

Michael Charles Manning of Corringham, Essex, was a nineteen-year-old stores checker when he started training with Bell, in June 1956, originally to practise ju-jitsu. Manning had other interests, notably angling, reading, tennis and badminton, outside his martial arts.

The first ever group shot of British *karateka* – 12, Maybush Rd, Hornchurch (Spring, 1957). From left to right: Ken Elliott, D. F. Clarke, Vernon Bell, Mick Manning, Trevor Guilfoyle.

The first ever photograph of British *karateka* engaged in karate training – 12, Maybush Rd, Hornchurch (Spring, 1957).

Kenneth Frederick Elliott, of Dagenham, Essex, was a married twenty-six year-old welder who had been a merchant seaman. He had an interest in competitive ballroom dancing, the rhythm and fluency of which he brought to his martial arts training. He also joined in June 1956.

Gerald Norman Tucker was a twenty-five-year-old who had seen National Service in the RAF. As a physical education teacher his interests, not surprisingly perhaps, were associated with sport – soccer, cricket, tennis, swimming, badminton, basketball and judo. He also started training with Bell in June 1956, and like Trevor Guilfoyle graded to 3rd kyu in less than eight months. He resigned from the BKF on the 21st July 1958, after taking up a new position at Crewkerne School in Somerset.

Trevor Patrick Guilfoyle became a student of Bell's in January 1956, when aged eighteen (born 18th April 1937), to initially practise judo. An active weightlifter and apprentice coppersmith, Guilfoyle, on anecdotal information, appears to have been killed serving with the army (see later).

Nothing is known about D. F. Clarke.

It is worth noting here that Vernon Bell was instructing in karate and gained his Yoseikan *Shodan* while Master Gichin Funakoshi was still alive, aged eighty-eight, and living in Tokyo with his eldest son Yoshihide. Although the great master was to pass away on the 26th April 1957, four days before Bell held his first grading (see shortly), it is possible that the old master knew that Yoseikan karate was being practised in Europe, especially in France, and it is not too improbable that he knew karate had reached Great Britain.

Vernon Bell continued: "Yoseikan was Gichin Funakoshi's personal club from 1924 onwards, and it was for high-ranking military, admiralty, police, and so on. It was not open to foreigners. Funakoshi taught what he called the Old Shotokan Method there, and he called it Yoseikan. As far as I can say, it means, 'The Military Ways Society.' I don't know if it's a kind of Way of Knighthood Society. It's not Bushido. I don't know its exact meaning; I've never been able to discover it. Yoseikan was not a style – it was a school." Bell had been told this in 1955 and in 1961 his views hadn't changed. In a letter to a Martin Stott (see later), who was training in Paris under Tam-Mytho, Bell wrote: "The Yoseikan ... was the private club of the founder of modern karate – Master Funakoshi – and it was at the Yoseikan that he trained the first experts of whom there were five, being – Mochizuki, Yamaguchi, Ogura, Hiyugo and Reikechi. Only these five experts have trained the present day Japanese

Ken Elliott in the process of countering Trevor Guilfoyle's *oi-zuki* – 12, Maybush Rd, Hornchurch (1957).

Ken Elliott in the process of catching Trevor Guilfoyle's *mae-geri* – 12, Maybush Rd, Hornchurch (1957).

In the foreground, Gerald tucker attacks *oi-zuki* to Trevor Guilfoyle, who is in the process of countering *gyaku-zuki* – 12, Maybush Rd, Hornchurch (July 1957).

Trevor Guilfoyle jumps in to attack Gerald Tucker on the lawn at 12, Maybush Rd, Hornchurch – 1957.

instructors, and Mr. Murakami was trained by two of these gentleman personally at the Yoseikan."

It is believed that the information contained in the previous paragraph with regard to Funakoshi is entirely incorrect, though its inclusion here is important for Bell believed it to be true at the time. The Yoseikan was not Funakoshi's private *dojo* and he never, as far as the author is aware, ever taught karate there. In the French interview of Hiroo Mochizuki alluded to earlier, 'Yoseikan' is translated as, "Association for the elevation of the mind." Master Mitsusuke Harada (see later), who has a good command of the English language, translated 'Yoseikan' for the author as, "The Hall where one grows up, is educated, in the correct manner."

Vernon Bell was training largely in isolation with a handful of students, and it was decided that for the purpose of launching karate in Britain, Hoang Nam would come over from France. Bell continued: "Mister Hoang Nam [sometimes written as Hoam Nam or Hwang Nam – the author takes the spelling used in this book from a letter by Henri Plee to Bell] had agreed with Mr. Plee and myself to take a weekend course for established BKF members. Henri Plee, my teacher, had selected Hoang Nam to come to England to demonstrate, teach and grade on behalf of the BKF. At this time Murakami still hadn't arrived in Europe. Hoang Nam was the first Oriental ever to teach karate in this country. He first came over to demonstrate for television and to publicise the new karate movement ... Hoang Nam was Henri Plee's chief assistant – a 3rd Dan Yoseikan, or old style Shotokan if you'd like to call it that."

The first mention that Bell makes of Hoang Nam in correspondence was in a letter Bell wrote to Plee on the 16th May 1957, already referred to. Plee replied on the 29th May 1957, relating to a proposed course from the 5th to 7th July (which did not materialise, but Nam came over to Britain two weeks later – see below), noting: "I shall try to send the little Indo-Chinese, but Great Britain's Ambassador has twice refused the authorisation [for Nam] to go to Great Britain (six months ago, maybe now they accept if you send a letter asking for him – Mr Hoang Nam), but he can not break wood with fist, only with elbow and sword [-hand]. If he doesn't get authorisation I send to you Mr. Bories, but he doesn't speak English (he is very effective and accepts challenges). I wait your decision, which man you prefer?"

In a letter to Plee, dated the 20th June 1957, Bell made mention of, what in correspondence terms, is the first karate grading in Britain, and of an aspiration: "Since my return from Paris, I find that my pupils have progressed much quicker and better than before, and their contest ability

Hoang Nam

and fighting spirit is getting more acute and developed, and they are progressing very well. Last week six of my pupils I graded to white-belt, and for their grading they were examined in the four movements of the first *kata*, at which they are now reasonably efficient and have been practising every week for two months. Also, they have to prove their ability in *kumite*, both with myself and with other members of the class, and two of them, Guilfoyle and Tucker, have shown excellent combination techniques with great speed of movement. I hope the day will soon come when I can develop several pupils to high proficiency and then challenge them with your own pupils, as it is my intention to have an international match with your country in the near future. I will be sending on the grading cards of these pupils for you to sign as President in the near future." (It is unclear whether Bell means President of the BKF or, much more likely, President of the FFK, to which the BKF were affiliated.)

In fact, it is likely that Bell was in error when he wrote to Plee that six of his students had graded the week before. Records show that four students had graded two weeks previously, at Hornchurch, on the 31st May 1957, and these were: K.F. Elliott, D.F. Clarke, P. Byron and M.C. Manning, all of whom were promoted to the then lowest rung of the grading scale – 6th kyu. Whilst brief details of Elliott and Manning have been given earlier, all records concerning D.F. Clarke and P. Byron are lost.

This was actually Bell's second grading – the first grading having not been mentioned in any existing correspondence. The BKF grading register clearly shows that the first karate grading ever held in Great Britain was conducted on the 30th April 1957, on the lawn at 12, Maybush Road, Hornchurch, when Trevor Guilfoyle and Gerald Tucker graded to 6th kyu. It is a date that will go down in the annals of British karate history. The grading fee was ten shillings.

In the above letter to Plee, of the 20th June 1957, Bell also mentioned that, "In the last week I have made extensive efforts to interest all the local newspapers, and also the national newspapers, in karate and the BKF, and I am pleased to say that our local newspaper is giving us a big write-up this week in the centre page and is publishing the karate photograph of the two Japanese experts which you gave me."

The following day, Friday, 21st June, 1957, the *Romford Recorder* ran what may be the first ever newspaper report on karate in this country. '—— [word(s) lost] is Bringing 'Killer' Sport to Britain,' was written by John Greenhalgh. It starts, "A short, chubby-faced Hornchurch man is to introduce a killer sport to Britain. He is 33-year old [actually 34] 'black-belt' jujutsu and karate expert, Vernon Bell, of 137, Hillview Avenue, Emerson Park. At his parents' house at 12, Maybush Road, Hornchurch, twelve students practise karate, in which each blow is meant to kill or cripple." After a brief paragraph providing three historical facts about karate, which are all incorrect (karate is three thousand years old; the Americans banned the art after the war; karate was revived in

1953), we have perhaps the first memorable statement of exaggeration of karate in this country in a newspaper: "Karate is the art which last week enabled another Japanese black-belt champion to stun a bull weighing 500 kilos with a flick of the wrist." The report is interesting mainly because of its contribution to the early history of British karate and the sense of innocence it conveys. The usual claims, benefits and precautions of practising the art today, are made to a totally uninformed public. So familiar today, but in 1957 it was of course all quite new. Vernon Bell is quoted as saying: "This form of combat comprises movements and tactics which are blows with the hands, fists, elbows, points of the fingers, knees, insteps and other parts of the body. Each kick is executed to lay a man out or break a limb. Every killer blow is so quick that you don't see it in the flick of an eye."

But Bell was making it quite clear that whilst karate was devastating, it required a high degree of individual training, and a selection process was in operation to vet each intending student. Also, he was expounding his belief that karate was the, "finest form of ... mental training." Vernon Bell had twelve students at this time with ages ranging from eighteen to thirty, and composed of members from various strata of society as reflected in their occupations – from schoolmaster to bricklayer. Lesson charges were expensive – ten shillings per two-hour session, or a guinea for a private lesson.

Bell continued in one of his many interviews with the author: "In the early days of karate training in this country, we were very fussy about who could learn this dangerous art. We had to guard it from being taught to feeble-minded individuals of low intellect. An individual had to satisfy our own internal management committee, which comprised of Mick Manning and myself, and later Terry Wingrove and Jimmy Neal. To get into the BKF, before you could do any training, you had to have a licence. You had to have a licence before you walked into the *dojo*, and a suit before you started the first lesson. You had to pay the first three months *dojo* fee at ten shillings a time before you were taken on. But above all you had to have three references to prove your psychological/spiritual, moral and financial grounding. Firstly, you had to go to your parish priest to ask for a personal reference – in other words he had to know you and your family. Secondly, you had to go to the police to provide evidence that you didn't have a criminal record, and, thirdly, you had to get a reference from your bank manager to say you were financially solvent, and that you could pay your licence and *dojo* fees towards the BKF movement, from which you were gaining vital knowledge of this new Japanese martial art.

"When these three references were provided you would come before the management committee and we decided whether you would be an asset to the promotion of Yoseikan karate. You were put on probation for three months, and if during those three months you did not attend training regularly, even though you'd paid for the training, you were out after three months. For those students who trained, they never had to be late, they had to observe all the rules and they had to practise hard. We turned a lot of people down. If we were in any doubt whatsoever about an individual in those days, we turned them down. Remember, we only took adults over eighteen, and initially only males. We believed, as the Japanese did really, that karate should only be taught to seniors. If you could not come up with two of the three references you weren't even considered. You also had to sign a kind of affidavit, which was not legal, to the effect that you would not hold anyone responsible for any injury you might receive during training. If a student didn't sign this then we didn't take them. We were all gentleman in those days. We could only appoint students we could trust to uphold the standards set by the BKF, so intending students had to be vigorously vetted. Later, when the BKF grew and we had clubs in Aberdeen, Dundee, Middlesbrough, York, Liverpool, Plymouth, Portsmouth, and so on, and we held special courses, we'd watch these individuals very carefully, especially those intending to be local officers of the BKF in their respective parts of the country. You see we couldn't afford to let it get out of hand, in the hands of commercial seeking individuals. None of our instructors ever got paid, none of our instructors ever earned a penny from training, because the BKF grew on the old ethical lines of the Yoseikan and the personal teachings of Gichin Funakoshi."

Two weeks later (Friday, 5th July 1957), the *Romford Recorder* ran another feature on Vernon Bell's karate under the title, 'Forbidden Sport Taught Here,' with a sub-heading, 'Japanese Fights Often Ended in Death,' though this is never alluded to in the text. We are treated to two photographs that accompany this report by an unknown author, though this hardly matters as the short piece largely reiterates the previous report. It is interesting that the newspaper ran the second feature so soon after the first, and one may hazard a guess and say that they had numerous enquiries from the public. One notable point however emerges from this report. Vernon Bell's pupils had to, "swear an oath to take full responsibility for any injury to themselves," a reference to one section of the documents that Bell referred to above.

The two photographs mentioned accompanying the above report, believed to be the first on karate ever published in Britain showing

Vernon Bell counters with his speciality to Trevor Guilfoyle's *mae-geri* – 12, Maybush Rd, Hornchurch (July 1957).

British *karateka*, show Vernon Bell performing *gedan kekomi*, first to counter a *mae-geri*, and then against a *mae-tobi-geri*, delivered by twenty-year-old white-belt, Trevor Guilfoyle (who, interestingly, is wearing shin pads). This second photograph has the heading, "Unarmed Combat on the Lawn." Vernon Bell, as Britain's only resident karate black-belt at the time, is quoted as saying, "Unfortunately there is no one in this country with whom I can practise properly," but that wasn't to last for long, as on 19th July Hoang Nam came to visit.

In a letter to Plee on the 20th June 1957, Bell wrote: "I am now very pleased to say that the Bank of England has authorised us permission to advance your Federation on the necessary monies in Francs for the cost of Mr. Nam's visit, and I enclose a Banker's draft for 8,000 Francs which consists of 3,000 Francs for his passport and 5,000 Francs for his

Bell counters *gedan kekomi* to Guilfoyle's *mae-tobi-geri* – 12, Maybush Rd, Hornchurch (July 1957).

course fee. Also, I enclose his travel voucher from Paris to London and return, which entitles him to 2nd Class rail and boat passage to London." Nam duly arrived on Friday, 19th July 1957, at eight o'clock in the evening, carrying six karate white-belts, one karate black belt, nine badges, a further nine Yoseikan badges, the book, *ABC of Defence*, by Lasserre, a Japanese karate film and Bell's *Shodan* diploma. The cost of these items were, in total, according to Plee (letter to Bell, 28th August 1957), twenty-five thousand, one hundred and seventy-five Francs (though in his letter he mentions an additional five hundred Francs for airmail postage for Bell's *dojo* diploma). Bell calculated that the sum was some five thousand eight hundred Francs less.

"After a meal," Bell wrote in a letter to Plee on the 26th July 1957, "he [Nam] instructed four of my senior pupils for two hours in preparation for their display on Saturday" (see below). During his stay, Nam lodged with Bell's parents in Maybush Road, where, in the substantial grounds the course was to take place. In a letter of the 12th June 1957, Bell wrote to Plee concerning Nam's visit: "He will have his own private bedroom, with proper bathing facilities, and he will eat either with my parents or at my house, which is in the next road, and he will have no expense regarding accommodation or eating as I am paying for him and he will be well looked after."

On Saturday morning, 20th July 1957, Nam took a beginners class of eight pupils for about three hours, before taking part, in the afternoon, in what is most certainly the first-ever public demonstration of karate in Great Britain – at a grand fete on behalf of the Barkingside, Newbury Park and Hainault British Legion. The fete was held at Melbourne Fields, Valentines Park, Ilford, and was opened at 2.00 p.m. by the Deputy Mayor of Ilford, the Alderman Miss A.S. Terry. The three-penny light-green programme gives the following introduction to the karate demonstrations that commenced at three o'clock and seven o'clock: "Display of karate given by members of the British Karate Federation and the first public appearance in Great Britain under the direction of V.C.F. Bell Instructor and Chairman of the Federation, also a personal appearance of Mr. Hoang Nam (black-belt in karate) and karate champion of Indo China."

Vernon Bell recalled this first demonstration so: "It was poorly attended, and people didn't understand it at all. We had a roped-off area in the middle of the park. We didn't have a microphone or anything like that. About fifty people watched, but they stayed, which was most encouraging, and they applauded, especially when Hoang Nam performed with Trevor Guilfoyle and Gerald Tucker. It seems like yesterday to me, only yesterday. I remember someone from the audience asking me why we didn't hit. They said it was only acting. What could I say? They didn't understand." In a letter to Plee dated the 26th July 1957, Bell adds to the picture: "Unfortunately it was not very successful because the rain had made the grass wet and muddy and the audience was very small owing to the weather, but Mr. Nam and my pupils gave fifteen minutes display while I compere'd, and many photographs were taken by the local press." That Saturday evening Bell, "... took Mr. Nam to the cinema and very strangely he saw a French film" (letter to Plee, 26th July 1957).

The 26th July letter noted that on Sunday, 21st July 1957, "Mr. Nam had a good class of twelve pupils for two hours on the tennis court, after

Barkingside, Newbury Park & Hainault
BRITISH LEGION

GRAND FETE

to be held at

Melbourne Fields
Valentines Park, Ilford

on

Saturday 20th, July, 1957

To be Opened at 2 p.m. by

THE DEPUTY MAYOR OF ILFORD
Alderman Miss A. S. TERRY

IN AID OF ABOVE BRITISH LEGION FUNDS

Programme - - - - - - **3d.**

The programme containing the first ever notification of a public display of karate in Great Britain.

Trevor Guilfoyle blocking Gerald Tucker's *oi-zuki* – Valentines Park demonstration, 1957.

Hoang Nam supervising freestyle practice between Gerald Tucker (left) and Trevor Guilfoyle – Valentines Park demonstration, 1957.

Hoang Nam referees sparring between Gerald Tucker, jumping, and A. Dyer. Vernon Bell can be seen to the right of the picture – Valentines Park demonstration, 1957.

Hoang Nam referees sparring between Gerald Tucker, jumping, and A. Dyer – Valentines Park demonstration, 1957.

A. Dyer attacks *mae-geri* to Ken Elliott, who blocks – Valentines Park demonstration, 1957.

Hoang Nam supervising freestyle practice between Ken Elliott (left), avoiding *ashi-barai*, and A. Dyer – Valentines Park demonstration, 1957.

A. Dyer and Ken Elliott sparring – Valentines Park demonstration, 1957.
Kneeling, far left is Gerald Tucker; kneeling, far right, is P. Brandon.

which we had a visit from the television authorities to take a karate
news film."

The result of the visit by ITN was that at 11 o'clock on the Monday
evening of the 22nd July 1957, they showed eighty-two feet of 16mm
black and white film, lasting two minutes and two seconds, on the subject
of karate. The author believes this to be not only the first karate training
ever put onto film in this country, but also, at the same time, the first
footage on the art ever broadcast in Great Britain. The ITN classified
this now truly archival material in their records under the heading,
'Sports: Karate (very violent form of judo-cum-wrestling),' and was
shot on Vernon Bell's parents' grass tennis court in their two and a half
acre garden at 12 Maybush Road, Emerson Park, Hornchurch, Essex.
The event was described in the ITN records as, "New Sport is Explained
by Teacher Vernon Bell." Because of the obvious importance of this
film, the author will give a detailed account of its contents.

The bulletin starts with Bell and eleven male white-belts exercising
under the diminutive Hoang Nam on the grass court. They form a semi-
circle around Nam so: Tucker, Guilfoyle, Brandon, Trotter (?), Elliott,
(unknown), (unknown), Pearson, Miles, Manning, Dyer and Bell, starting
from Nam's right and travelling anti-clockwise. The 'unknowns' are
probably B. Dolan and D. Blake, but the author has no named visual
references on these two. All the participants wear white *gi*, though

Pearson and Miles wear white shorts. The well-kept borders to the tennis court are evident. From the kneeling position they stretch back so that their shoulders and knees are on the floor, and then they stretch forward, whilst still kneeling, so that chests and chins are on the floor. An abrupt cut takes us to a close-up of a canvas punch bag that is fitted to the trunk of a large tree. The punch bag is struck with three *shuto*, three *urakan*, three *enpi* and three *kaishu*. The techniques are completed in rapid succession, and although we only see a hand and arm strike the bag, it is quite obviously Vernon Bell who is performing. The film then cuts to the thirty-four year old Bell striking the punch-bag, which is held by a student. Bell strikes it with three *shuto*, three *kaishu*, three *yoko enpi*, three *mawashi-enpi*, then double *shuto*, using both hands coming down simultaneously. This is followed by two *hasami-zuki* and he finishes with an upward knee strike to the bottom of the bag. Then follows a wood-breaking demonstration by Vernon Bell. Between two seats of two chairs rests a plank of wood about three feet long, three inches wide, and about three-quarters of an inch thick. The plank rests on what looks like towels, which have been neatly placed on the chair seats. Just over one-third of the wood lies between the chairs. Vernon Bell takes two preparatory 'line-up' strikes with a downward *tettsui*, before breaking the wood cleanly with the hammer-fist strike. We then see a close-up of the broken wood being held by Bell – a half piece in each hand. This is followed by twenty-three seconds of unplanned freestyle between Bell and Hoang Nam.

The students sit in a line in *seiza*. Bell begins by countering an advancing Hoang Nam with a *kekomi* off the front leg, and follows with a *mawashi-geri*, and turns, whereby Hoang Nam is given space to kick *mae-geri* to Bell's back. They then re-orientate themselves. Bell tries a jumping front kick that covers much ground, but misses. Hoang Nam covers with an *osae-uki* to a potential punch from Bell, and comes down with a counter to Bell's head, which is blocked by Bell with an *age-uke*. They part once again. Then quickly, Nam jumps in and is kicked *chudan mawashi-geri* by Bell. Bell's leg is subsequently caught by Nam and the two briefly grapple, part, and pat each other's backs. The camera angle changes, and we see Bell attacking with an abridged *mawashi-geri* followed by an evident back-kick (Nam obscures the technique) as he spins back round. Nam then attacks Bell's front leg with an *ashi-barai*, but Bell retracts his leg. The final scene in this freestyle demonstration is really rather good, and totally unexpected. Hoang Nam moves in and jumps to attack. At this precise moment Bell thrusts a *kekomi* at one of Nam's ankles in mid air, at about knee height, and

Gerald Tucker (in dark trousers) and A. Dyer practising the *1st Ippon Kata*. P. Byron assists. Note Dyer's shin pad – 12, Maybush Rd, Hornchurch, 1957.

completely turns and unbalances the little Vietnamese, who ends crumpled on the floor, upon which Bell says, "Sorry Mr. Nam." Nam gets back-up, smiling, though obviously a little embarrassed, and joins Bell who is standing by the interviewer, Hugh Trethowan, microphone in hand.

The interview lasts fifty seconds, and Bell expounds the benefits of the art – how it quickens the reflexes and increases self-confidence. "It's a great physical and mental exercise," Bell reports. He notes that the art is three thousand years old and originated in China, and has been practised for the last six hundred years; that karate was banned by the American occupational forces at the end of the Second World War, and that it had been revived and had become more popular in the last few years. Bell's concluding sentence is, "But it is the deadliest form of combat known to man."

By today's standards, of course, the karate shown in the bulletin is rather unrefined. Hiroo Mochizuki was the only Japanese *karateka* living in Europe at the time to offer instruction, and he hadn't visited these shores, so one would expect the very first karate in Great Britain to leave something to be desired in terms of technique. Bell wrote to

A blurred, but important photograph showing, from left to right: unknown, Pearson, Tucker, Hoang Nam, Guilfoyle, Miles – 12, Maybush Rd, Hornchurch (July, 1957).

A blurred, but important photograph showing, from left to right: unknown, Tucker, Hoang Nam, Bell, Guilfoyle, Pearson – 12, Maybush Rd, Hornchurch (July, 1957).

Where the British karate movement began. This original road sign no longer exists (1994).

Plee (26th July 1957) that the film was broadcast, "all over the country and Mr. Nam and my pupils all saw it. This first-class publicity on the television will do us a lot of good. I have arranged to buy the film from the TV authorities and will show it to you when I come to France next."

Karateka are truly fortunate that any film at all should have been taken from this very early period of British karate. Bell was not able to acquire a copy at the time, but the author tracked the footage down, and interested readers should contact the Television News Archive at ITN (200 Gray's Inn Road, London, WC1X 8XZ) quoting library reference number 7398/432B/5, for further details. At the time the author secured his copy on video, the charge was £55. The film is to be strongly recommended, for it will bring alive the early training.

Vernon Bell recalled of this news report: "They actually shot fifteen minutes of film [the remainder no longer exists]. I remember Hoang Nam and I demonstrated the first two *Heian* and an *ippon kata* on the lawn. It was a lovely sunny day. I wrote to the BBC and ITV – the BBC weren't interested." The author wrote to the BBC enquiring as to whether they had any film on karate from this early period (up to 1966), and deduced that they are still not interested and presumably had no footage, for he failed to receive a reply.

Rita Bell, Vernon Bell and Elsie Bell at the gate of 12, Maybush Road – *c*. 1948. It was through this gate that the earliest British *karateka* passed. The ash tree (see main text) would be to Elsie Bell's left.

The ITN footage is also extremely important because, bar a few photographs, it provides the only visual evidence of what the garden, or at least part of it, at 12, Maybush Road, looked like. Leonard Bell sold the house and garden to a developer and the old chalet bungalow was demolished and the considerable site now houses up-market, modern, four-bedroom detached homes, in a very pleasant residential cul-de-sac. A genuine shrine to the early days of Shotokan karate has been levelled to the ground, but the space is still there, and that can never be lost.

The author accompanied Vernon Bell on a pilgrimage to Maybush Road, the site of many an early training session (see later) one warm and sunny July afternoon, when all was green. Although there have been enormous changes in some forty years, and at first it was difficult to get one's bearings, Bell found a few markers which the author would like to relate, for they will prove invaluable to readers who have a genuine love of the subject and who may wish to visit the site where karate was first practised in Great Britain, albeit in the open air – but then that is somehow how it should have been in the halcyon summers of 1956, 1957, 1958 and 1959.

Maybush Road is still a cul-de-sac, and the original Number 12 was at the end. Number 10, Maybush Road is still there, though not a chalet

A photograph taken in December 2001, showing the ash tree (foreground) at 12, Maybush Road. The gate to the property would have been to the tree's right. The *dojo*/tennis court – would have been sited behind the new house.

bungalow (there are contemporary chalet bungalows, similar to Number 12, in the immediate vicinity that are well worth viewing, in order to gain a better picture in one's mind's eye), and Vernon Bell recalled the owner at the time complaining at the sound of the *kiai* from the students next door. Travelling down the road, in the front garden of the house next to Number 10, is a large ash tree (there are actually two ash trees in this garden, the author refers to the tallest tree nearest the road). This ash tree marked the end of the cul-de-sac (look for changes on the road surface), and the beginning of the Bell property. If one stands close to this tree, looking across what is now an extended cul-de-sac, one can see a path. The Bell property stood to the right of this path when viewed from the tree. Follow this very short path, which Bell said used to be of cinder, and it will take you to a metal stile where one may cross over a single railway track. As one walks up to the stile, the wall to the right marked the boundary to the Bell property. If one crosses the railway track and looks back, the fence to the left along the railway track is another boundary. The orchard (see later) ended in a line along the railway track from which it ran parallel. A large weeping willow, which one can see behind Number 10, from Maybush Road, was on the property, and the Bell family used to take advantage of its shade on hot afternoons. The lawn tennis court was not far from this tree. The old Number 12, Maybush Road, continues to haunt the author, and it haunts Vernon Bell as well.

Following filming, Hoang Nam held a grading. The grading had been delayed until after the ITN visit, as it was uncertain when the news crew would arrive and nobody wanted the grading interrupted. The following students were promoted that day according to the BKF grading register and Bell's 26th July 1957 letter to Plee, so: "Guilfoyle, 4th kyu; G. Tucker, 4th kyu; K. Elliott, 5th kyu; M. Manning, 5th kyu; D. Dyer, 6th kyu; P. Brandon, 6th kyu; B. Dolan, 6th kyu and D. Blake, 6th kyu."

Two items are worthy of note concerning this grading. Firstly, Trevor Guilfoyle and Gerald Tucker graded directly from 6th kyu to 4th kyu, and secondly, a B. Miles, who graded to 6th kyu, is recorded in the BKF grading register, but is not mentioned in Bell's letter to Plee. Apart from the fact that he was a policeman, nothing else is known of Miles, though his licence has survived which confirms he did grade that day, and that he was a BKF member on the 26th June 1957. Information on another very early BKF student, a Mr. R. Armsby, is also confined to a surviving licence, which shows that he joined the BKF on the 24th May 1957.

In Bell's own words, the following then happened on this very eventful day – the 26th July 1957. "After the grading I took the class on tactics and movement whilst Mr. Nam gave one hour's private instruction to our only lady pupil, Miss Higgins, in which Mr. Nam taught her his new ladies' *kata* for the first time, and after the lesson Mr. Nam graded her 6th kyu as he thought she had progressed very well" (letter to Plee, 26th July 1957). Miss Higgins (her first name is unknown) was the first woman to be graded in karate in this country. She graded only once under the BKF, and what subsequently became of her is a mystery. Bell's previous contention that the BKF initially did not take women students seems to have been short-lived.

Bell noted to the author: "Hoang Nam was a fantastic little man – sincere, honest, straightforward and humorous, with great humility. He could speak good English and my students understood him. He was also Chief Instructor to the All Vietnamese Boxing Association. He was All Vietnamese Boxing Champion, and he made a film about Vietnamese boxing which he showed me when he was over here later. He was wearing a green *gi*. This was taken in Paris. He defeated twenty-five people in less than a minute or two. He promised to let me have a copy of this film, but I never received it. Nam was the fastest little oriental that I've ever seen – faster than any Japanese. He was a wonderful, methodical, down-to-earth teacher. Nothing was too simple for him to explain, nothing was too great for him to demonstrate, nothing was too proud for him to do. I remember Nam bought some presents for my girlfriend, Pauline, when he first came over. [Bell divorced his first wife in 1956, and lived with Pauline Whitehead, whom he married in 1961. He had two children by this relationship – one in 1956 and one in 1958]. Nam's favourite *kata* was *Hangetsu*. He learned his karate from Plee and Mochizuki."

Terry Wingrove (see later) was practising judo and ju-jitsu under Bell in 1957, and on the Sunday was invited to take part in one karate session, as were some of Bell's other non-karate students. The sixteen-year-old Wingrove recalled: "You couldn't just decide to do karate in those days – you had to be invited. When Hoang Nam came over I'd been training with Vernon Bell for about a year, though it wasn't until 1959 that I was allowed to join the BKF. Bell was very strict on that type of thing. He'd let some of his judo and ju-jitsu students take part in the odd karate lesson, dangle the carrot if you like, and when the time came to really start you were raring to go. I remember Hoang Nam quite well. He was very polite, a very nice man – always a gentleman. He taught techniques that now, looking back, I realise had a great affinity with kung fu. Nam was a very quiet person, very well educated in the French way of life and culture. He never professed to have an understanding of karate above a certain level ... As I said, he taught more of a Chinese style. He had seen Mochizuki doing karate, and, I believe, Hoang Nam actually studied with Minoru Mochizuki when he came to Paris, but that's never been confirmed. I think Nam was in the restaurant business. Both my seniors and contemporaries only ever spoke well of him. He never hit or hurt a student and was a very patient teacher. He had soft technique. Hoang Nam kept his students, though he never had many, and always trained in the same way. He never promoted himself; there was no showtime. He was a good martial artist."

Bell continued in his letter to Plee on the 26th July 1957: "On Monday morning Mr. Nam gave two hours private tuition to myself and Mr. Elliott on the first three *kata*. On Monday afternoon I took Mr. Nam to London and showed him the West End, and we walked around the shops and he bought himself several items. In the evening he took his last class of six pupils and one lady and this concluded a very instructive and pleasant weekend for all of us. We all liked Mr. Nam very much and all my members think he is an excellent instructor, and he taught us much and we have progressed much more and our style and skill are better. We have now a much clearer idea [of what we are practising] and [a greater appreciation of the] spirit of karate. The BKF wish to thank you for your help in sending us Mr. Nam and we would like to see him again in England in November, when we would like him to take another weekend course." Nam, however, was not to return for many years.

PART II

Bell's important 26th July 1957 letter to Plee, also contains some fascinating lengthy politicking – correspondence that should be recorded for historical completeness. Readers must appreciate that it is completely one-sided of course and highly biased, but it does give the reader some insight into Bell's character, thinking, ambitions, and understanding of the judo, ju-jitsu and karate scene at that time. The author stresses that it is not the *whole* truth and does not necessarily paint an accurate picture of events, but rather one man's perception in a threatened position. Bell had begun to carve himself out a hard-earned niche, wished to promote what he considered to be true karate, and didn't want others to get in on the act. He was the one, and he wanted to be the only, as the saying goes. It may have been for the best possible reasons, but he wanted a monopoly and he wanted to be in-charge. The letter is oppressive in tone, based largely upon suspicion. The author will quote extensively from this letter, with Bell's permission. Bell wrote: "Mr. Nam informed me that you had heard from Mr. E. J. Harrison of London, who has written to you asking you to grade him and instruct him in karate, and that he will be visiting Paris on the 19th August [1957]. Mr. Nam asked my advice and opinion on Harrison, but I also promised Mr. Nam that I would write to you telling you all about it. Now, Mr. Plee, this is a dangerous situation for British karate and our Federation, and the whole situation with Harrison must be dealt with carefully and immediately, otherwise he may cause much damage to our British Federation. It is imperative, in my opinion, that you do not allow Harrison to visit France and also that you do not instruct or grade him in karate, but I would request you to have nothing to do with him, for if you do, it will cause much trouble in England for myself, for karate and our Federation. As you know, I started karate in England, and have had many pupils under my training for many months, and we have done business for a long while, and you know the efforts I have made to establish karate properly in England.

"You gave me a Charter in April to establish karate in Britain and to promote, organise and control the British Karate Federation which is affiliated to the FFK. Also, in this Charter you appointed me as the FFK official representative for karate in Britain. Also, I came to Paris to receive my diploma and to make all arrangements with you for the foundation of the BKF. Both myself, all my pupils and our Federation are one hundred per cent loyal and co-operative to the FFK, and our only wish is to have a strong Federation in Britain and all our members loyal to it, and to practice and teach the real karate.

"At present our Federation is small but united and is progressing well and strongly, and in a few months we expect to have our own large *dojo* in London and can then expand much quicker. We have had much publicity in the press and on the television, which will do us much good and show people the true karate and should make our Federation stronger. However, it is essential that there is only one federation in Britain to control karate and give grade[s] and promote the true karate of the Yoseikan, but it will do much damage if we have other associations which do not teach the true karate and are not in our Federation.

"In Britain, in judo, there are six big associations, all different and all grade differently, but none of them work together, and we do not have one large Federation which controls all judo like you have in France, and so British Budo is very much disunited and in a very terrible state. First, there is the BJA with G. Koizumi, Trevor Leggatt ... Gleeson and Palmer running it. Then there is the Amateur Judo Association run by Pat Butler, Harry Ewen and F. Ryder, with Kenshiro Abbe at its head. Neither of these two associations works together ... for Koizumi and Abbe are ... rivals for the number one Japanese in Britain. Third, there is the Anglo Japanese Judo Association run by G. Robinson and A. Morgan in North London with Mr. Otani, 6th Dan, at its head. Also in London is the *dojo* of the two Robinson brothers, Joe (6th Dan) and Douglas (5th Dan) whose father, Professor Jack Robinson, runs the South African Judo Federation and his two sons are professional instructors, who also teach wrestling and body culture in their *dojo*. Then there is the Mombasa Jujutsu Association at Leicester, which controls the Midlands of England, and finally there are the Scottish Judo Association, the Welsh Judo Association and the Irish Judo Federation. All these associations are independent of each other and control many clubs, have hundreds of pupils, with dozens of black-belts, and all teach different styles of judo, with some jujutsu. [At this point, Bell makes some derogatory comments about one particular organisation. The name of this organisation has been removed, and is replaced by dashes in the following text]. The — is the biggest ... but it is weakening in authority because its discipline is harsh and its members are not free ... The —

tries to control all British judo and infiltrates other associations and prevents its members from practising at other clubs. The ... [another name removed so as not to divulge, by default, the association that Bell speaks so negatively of] is a new body only two years old, which was formed to clean up British judo and it has over three thousand members, five hundred clubs and sixty or more black-belts ... It is getting stronger every day and it is a serious threat to the — which is getting weaker in members and support. Finally, there is the British Jujutsu Federation, of which I am President, which is independent of all these judo associations and practices jujutsu only and confers grades in jujutsu only, and its members are hand-picked and belong to no judo association and the BJ/JA [BJF] has a high standard of proficiency and ethics, and its instructors are jujutsu black-belts only.

"This is roughly the picture in Great Britain, and most of these associations teach forms of self-defence, but now ... [some are] endeavouring to teach various forms of karate, as karate in Britain is very new and little known, but it is slowly beginning to be known by name and it receives much unpleasant and wrong publicity from ... various schools of judo. Kenshiro Abbe teaches self-defence and confers defence grades and he also gives weekend courses in karate, which are just the *atemi*. The Robinson brothers teach judo, wrestling and self-defence and are now giving instruction in a certain type of karate, comprising kicks and blows, trips and locks, and the Robinsons have their own grading system, both in judo and self-defence. Recently, since I have been to Paris, ... [another association name and personal name are omitted here] is now beginning courses for women in self-defence by arrangement with the British Weightlifting Association at their headquarters in South London. In his course, Mr. [personal name omitted] proposes to teach new methods, using jujutsu, the *atemi* and karate. As I know this man well, I can honestly say he knows nothing about jujutsu or the true karate in any respect, and I am taking up this matter with him very shortly.

"Finally, I would point out that the chief danger comes from the — in the form of Mr. Harrison.

"The — until now have never been interested or concerned with either jujutsu or karate in any respect, only judo. Now that karate has been introduced into Britain, by myself, and because my British Karate Federation has been widely publicised and now that karate has been established in the correct manner by our Federation, then, the authorities of the — now think fit to infiltrate into karate and try and get control of it in every way they can (dirty or otherwise) purely because they can see by this action a method of saving their declining popularity and loss of control in ... judo.

"Now Mr. Plee, I would not say this without cause for I know this to be true, as I have ample proof, and unless a stop is made at once at the attempt by the — to dominate karate and include it as part of their judo ... [organisation], then our British Karate Federation will suffer a severe blow and weaken it considerably, for this plan by the — must be dealt with firmly and at once and opposed by the BKF and your FFK together for the sake of karate itself. Unlike you have in France, in Britain we do not have any control or help from a Ministry of Sport, who controls as to who teaches karate and who practises it by licence – in England there is no such regulation to protect us. Every sporting association in England governs itself, makes its own rules and disciplines its own members and is not subservient to the government department or ministries. Therefore, I know that the — is out to control karate for itself and to try and crush our Federation and it has chosen Mr. E.J. Harrison as its medium to do this for the following reasons: (1) He is well known as an author, journalist and linguist and the writer of many popular books on judo and as the translator from French into English of Mr. M. Kawaishi's two books, *My System of Judo*, and more recently, *My System of Self-Defence*. (2) He is the senior member and technical adviser to the — and — [another name is omitted here]. (3) He was the first white man to gain a black belt in judo at the Kodokan. (4) He is now retired and has much time to investigate karate and is free to travel in his own time anywhere so to do. (5) In Britain his is a well-known figure, both as a *judoka,* a wrestler and author on judo – though he has never done karate in his life and knows little or nothing of jujutsu. (6) He is a great personal friend of — [names omitted here], but he is over seventy years old, is very inactive, is now very feeble in his mind, but very ruthless, dogmatic, and riddled with Japanese superiority, and being such, his only desire is to visit France to use his extensive judo influence and to infiltrate into karate, not for his own benefit but for the —.

"If you instruct or grade him he will return to Britain and open his own club in London, separate from our Federation, or he will open a karate section at the — [another name is omitted here], with himself in charge, and maybe form another Federation. If he does this then all the other judo associations will do likewise and form their own karate clubs and federations and teach all different types of karate and none of them will affiliate to the BKF. The situation is grave and urgent, Mr. Plee, and as your official agent in Britain for karate, I must ask for the protection of the FFK to overcome this menace. Accordingly, I must ask you to refuse definitely to instruct or grade Harrison in karate or have anything to do with him. Also, the correct thing for him to do, if he wishes to learn karate, is to write to me as the Official Karate Instructor in Britain, and for him to join the British Karate Federation. I must also ask you to refuse to give any instruction or grading in Paris to any applicants from any British *judoka* or citizen who may approach you for such. Instead, refer them to myself and the BKF ... [so they may train], for the BKF is their proper organisation for those living in England. The only time a Britisher should visit France for karate is by arrangement with the FFK and the BKF together, mutually, for visits, courses etc., but the correct procedure should be for all British karate pupils to be instructed, trained and graded in England by the BKF which controls karate in Britain. Only in this way will it be possible for us to have one Federation in Britain to organise and control the true karate, and if our Federation is to grow strong and big, and also if the BKF is to be a credit to the FFK and the Yoseikan.

"You know and so does Mr. Nam that I, my pupils and our Federation are solidly behind the FFK and we will always do our best and teach the real karate, but ... [certain] other organizations in Britain are out to use karate as a new sport for their own benefits.

"I propose that if it is necessary and you consider it best, I will visit Paris in the middle of August, with one or two of my best pupils to go into this matter thoroughly for our own sakes and before any damage can be done, for karate in England is becoming well-known and growing quickly, and our Federation by the end of this year should be well established and strong with many members and clubs, but only if we have one true Federation and many loyal clubs in the hands of sincere and good karateists. Once again I must ask you to ignore Mr. Harrison and others like him and refuse to let them come to Paris, otherwise, there will be much trouble for yourself as well as for me and the BKF."

Harrison was indeed a *judoka* of superior credentials. In 1957 he was eighty-four years of age, and living quietly and modestly, running a boarding house that had been bequeathed to him in London. Regrettably, the sturdy, bespectacled Harrison no longer graced the mats. In 1897 he had gone to work as a journalist in Yokohama. He learned Tenshin Shinyo-ryu Jujutsu under Hagiwaru Ryoshinsai, grading to *Shodan*, and in 1904 he began his study of judo by joining the Kodokan. He left Japan in 1911, and his classic work, *The Fighting Spirit of Japan*, was published two years later. He is justly remembered as a *judoka* of great spirit, who was one of the first instructors of the art in Great Britain. He died in 1961.

After a further letter to Plee on the 10th August 1957, in which Bell requested a response concerning the Harrison affair, Plee sent Bell a telegram, which motivated Bell to write in reply on the 15th August 1957. Bell arrived at Plee's *dojo* on Saturday, 17th August, after the short flight and returned on the 20th August. During his stay Bell stayed at a cheap hotel near Plee's *dojo*, which was recommended to him by Hoang Nam. Gerald Tucker, then 4th kyu, also visited Plee's *dojo* on this occasion, but made his own way there.

The politicking continued concerning Harrison, but matters seemed to have been temporarily resolved by early the following year. In a letter to Plee on the 4th February 1958, Bell wrote: "I visited Mr. Harrison yesterday, 3rd inst., at his home and had a lengthy discussion for two hours. I explained to him the complete set-up in Great Britain and Europe of the official organisation of karate and he was much impressed and pleased to learn it ... He agrees that judo and karate must not be confused and must be kept separate and that judo and karate can and should exist separately and happily in Britain without any interference or animosity ... and that karate should be allowed to function as a separate and distinct Japanese martial art." This letter also raised some other problems that Bell was facing at this time. One was a book that Harrison had translated on karate by Lasserre, and another was a karate federation which had been set-up by a certain Mr. Barber (a Mr. Millard is also mentioned in this context), but this federation had, according to Bell, apparently completely finished. Barber had been in contact with Plee as well. Bell noted of a certain, here un-named, individual, that, "To my knowledge [name omitted here] has read many books on karate and knows the theory well but he has never practised karate and does not know the spirit, and I do not think that he will ever join the BKF as a member because he would start from the beginning and would not be equal to myself. I have several pupils who have been under my instruction for over one year and who are good, having technique, agility, style, speed and experience and a good knowledge of the art and [name omitted here] would stand little chance against them in *kumite*, even with his jujutsu knowledge and with practice. I know his ability very well and the extent of his knowledge, for he was my pupil for five years, and he knows only half of my knowledge, and has a quarter of my experience. I witnessed a display of jujutsu by him and three of his pupils last Thursday and I was not impressed in any way by what I saw, for I thought the performance was of a low standard, no technique, and lacked polish and had little effect. I say this without prejudice and in fairness, as I witness many displays of judo etc., and I organise and give many myself and have had much opportunity to compare them all."

Occasionally, Vernon Bell would have his nose put out, metaphorically speaking, unintentionally by Plee. The letter of the 4th February 1958 offers us such an incident, showing a little jealousy perhaps. Bell wrote: "Mr. Barber also said that you had sent him some karate books by Mr. Alcheik and I am surprised at this in that you have not sent me the same books, especially as I am your official karate representative in Britain. I would be glad to receive some copies of these books by James Alcheik at your earliest convenience." The book Bell was really after by Alcheik was simply entitled, *Karate*.

Certainly, a number of influential British *judoka* were interested in karate, or karate-like techniques. Harry Ewan's, *Modern Judo and Self-Defence* (Faber, 1957) showed female *judoka* demonstrating karate techniques, then classed as *atemi*, and Ewan noted the deadly effect that such blows could have. Harrison's translation, from the French, of Kawaishi's book, *My Method of Self-Defence* (W. Foulsham { 'Method' in the title of this book is sometimes written as 'System' }), already referred to, that same year, gave considerable attention to *atemi waza*, in the form of stances, punches, strikes and kicks, and training on the *makiwara*. Harrison made reference to the *atemi*, and more, in his 1953, *Manual of Judo*. Captain M.G. Harvey, in his *Self-Defence by Judo* (Nicholas Kaye, 1959), aligned *atemi* and karate practice together. Pat Butler noted that many good judo clubs taught self-defense, and that these classes were "based on ju-jitsu and judo, sometimes incorporating a little karate" (*Health and Strength*, 5th June 1958, p. 46), and he included kicking and striking techniques in his *Popular Judo* (Thorsens: 1958).

Early demonstrations of karate are clearly most important from the historical perspective. For the purpose of fullness and accuracy, the author will provide details of all the demonstrations he has acquired information on for the period 1957 to the end of 1958, that Vernon Bell and the BKF gave.

On Saturday, 14th September 1957, came a second public demonstration at the Autumn Fair of Hornchurch Grammar School organised by the Parents' Association. On the cover of the sixpenny white programme, with blue lettering, appears the school emblem bearing the school motto, 'A good name endureth.' Vernon Bell and members of the BKF are mentioned and thanked in the introduction, 'Good Afternoon,' by L.C. Brand, the secretary to the Autumn Fair Committee. The official opening was at 2.30 p.m. and the karate display was given

Autumn Fair programme – 1957

at 3.45 p.m., following on from a performance, in the open air theatre, of excerpts from *Androcles and the Lion*, given by the school's Second Year dramatic society. The programme notes: "A demonstration of karate, the deadly system of Japanese self-defence. This is the first performance of its kind to be presented to the public by the British Karate Federation – (See page 6)." Well, we know, of course, that it was not the first public demonstration of karate (in Great Britain), so there was confusion after only a couple of months! The fifteen-minute display was followed by a performance of the Rainbow Puppets.

The boxed write-up on page six of the programme referred to above is worthy of inclusion here. Under the heading, "Exhibition of Karate," the following was written: "Exhibitions of karate and Karate-do by members of the British Karate Federation under the auspices of the International Karate Federation, featuring demonstrations of the formal *kata*, *kumite* contents, tactics of attack and defence and methods of deadly combat. The exhibition is one of the first ever to be given in this country of the true karate (Japanese killer sport of unarmed combat) and is given by permission of the European karate representatives of Yoseikan (in Japan) – the French Karate Federation. Organised and arranged by V.C.F. Bell (black-belt of Yoseikan, National Coach of the British Karate Federation and the only official karate representative of the FFK and Yoseikan in Britain). It is pointed out that the British Karate Federation is the only officially appointed, controlling and governing organisation of karate in Britain, as appointed by the Yoseikan in Japan, of whom the French Karate Federation are the official European body, and the FFK have appointed by charter, Mr. V.C.F. Bell their official karate representative and controller in Britain to establish the true karate, as practised in Japan."

Two weeks later another first occurred for Vernon Bell and members of the BKF. The British Olympic Weightlifting Championships were held at King George's Hall, London, W.C.1, on Saturday, 28th September 1957. As Vernon Bell noted: "This was the first ever national public display of karate in this country." The white, one-shilling programme, noted that proceedings commenced at 4.00 p.m., and the "Karate and Judo – Demonstration of the Deadly Japanese Arts" featured third in a ten item programme. Coming between the Featherweight and Medium Heavyweight classes, the demonstrators were: "Messrs. V.C.F. Bell, T. Guilfoyle, G. Tucker, K. Elliott, M. Manning – Members of the British Karate Federation."

On the 1st October 1957, Bell conducted a grading after a week-long course, held between the 18th and 24th August 1957, at 12, Maybush Road. In the BKF grading register, two people are listed – a Mr. Anderson, who graded to 6th kyu, and L. Pearson, for which there is a blank. Perhaps Pearson failed the grading; then again, he may not

BRITISH OLYMPIC WEIGHTLIFTING CHAMPIONSHIPS

(FEATHER, LIGHT-HEAVY & MED.-HEAVYWEIGHT CLASSES)

Presented by

B.A.W.L.A. UNDER B.A.W.L.A. LAWS

AT

KING GEORGE'S HALL   LONDON W.C.1

Saturday, 28th Sept. 1957   at 4 p.m.

OFFICIALS

Organizer - - - - - -	H. C. FRANKLIN-CRATE
Publicity Officer and M.C. - - - - -	JIM MASON
Stage Manager - - - - - - -	D. SHELL
Asst. Stage Manager - - - - - -	G. HART
Clerk of Scales - - - - - - -	W. BONNIFACE
Loaders - - - - - -	T. INSKIP & P. COLEMAN
Recorder - - - - - - - -	F. COPE
Scoreboard - - - - - - -	E. PEPPIATT
Box Office - - - - - -	Mrs. PEPPIATT
M.C.'s Messenger - - - - - -	H. CLARK
Stewardesses and Programmes	- Ladies of the London Olympiads, under the direction of Oscar State

PROGRAMME - - - - **PRICE ONE SHILLING**

FELLOWES, PRINTERS, MIDDLESBROUGH

The British Olympic Weightlifting Championship programme which featured a BKF demonstration – 1957.

Trevor Guilfoyle countering *mae-geri* to a chair-wielding Vernon Bell – 12, Maybush Rd, Hornchurch (1957).

have graded. In another, typed first page copy of the register, Pearson's name again appears, but once again there is a blank.

Bell received a letter from the President of the French Karate Federation, E. Sirvent, dated the 7th October 1957, inviting him to the "first karate tournament" which was to be held at the Sports Hall of the Association Sportive de la Préfecture de Police, 16 rue du Gabon, Paris, on Friday, 25th October 1957, commencing at 8.00 p.m. The event was to be a showpiece for karate and other martial arts with demonstrations in French boxing, judo, free boxing, kendo, iai-jitsu, kumi-tachi, stick fighting and bo-jitsu being given, as well as karate of course. Additionally, two days of instruction under Hiroo Mochizuki was scheduled for Saturday 26th and Sunday 27th October, "so that our friends from far away should derive greater profit from their trip to Paris and may give their clubs in return the most authentic techniques."

Trevor Guilfoyle in the process of performing *yoko-tobi-geri* upon a sword-wielding Vernon Bell – 12, Maybush Rd, Hornchurch (1957).

An interesting administrative aside to the above letter is that Monsieur Sirvent noted: "We remind you that membership goes from September to September, a period during which the Mutuelle Nationale Sportive (sports insurance) insures our members in case of accident."

On page 15 of an unknown newspaper of the 10th October 1957, reporter Dez Marwood, wrote a piece on Vernon Bell's karate under the heading, 'Secret "Sportsmen" Train to Kill', and noted that the art of karate was, "much more violent than judo, and as different from it as is football from cricket." The twelve students are again mentioned, but on this occasion their ages are given ranging from seventeen to thirty-five. Much that has gone before is repeated, but this report focused more on the effects of karate and the reasons for learning it. "Mr. Bell explained,"

Trevor Guilfoyle countering *gyaku-zuki* to a sword-wielding Vernon Bell – 12, Maybush Rd, Hornchurch (1957).

wrote Marwood, "that karate is a deadly form of combat fighting using the techniques of the arms, feet and hands with every blow aimed at a blood vessel, joint or nerve centre in such a way as to render an opponent incapable – or even kill him." Vernon Bell demonstrated a jumping kick on a student, and noted, "Delivered in full force that would have crushed his rib cage and collapsed a lung." Asked why he thought such a "sport" would catch on in Britain, Bell replied, "Because it's the answer to the thug's broken bottle." What is interesting however, is the fact that Vernon Bell estimated that, training for two hours, twice a week, it would take the average pupil three to four years to attain a black-belt. At ten shillings a session, Dez Marwood calculated that to attain such a grade the financial cost would be between one hundred and fifty and two hundred pounds. We know training wasn't cheap, it encouraged

Protective padding worn by early BKF members – October 1957

only the dedicated, but it does seem, perhaps, a strange way to end the report?

In this Marwood piece, we also have a bordered comment near the centre, from Geoffrey Gleason, British Judo Association national coach. Under the title, 'Street Fighting – says Judo Chief,' Mr. Gleason's

In the famous 'no trousers' shot, Mick Manning holds the kick-bag for Gerald Tucker – October 1957.

comments reflect the feelings of many *judoka* about karate at that time. Noting that he did not want karate to be confused with judo, he is quoted as saying, "Judo is essentially a sport – karate is pure street fighting and is just designed to cripple. It is primarily an OFFENSIVE method of fighting – not DEFENSIVE." He also commented that judo had a more advanced and dangerous type of training, but this was only taught to trusted individuals once black belt was reached.

Three photographs accompany the above article. The first shows Vernon Bell breaking a wooden board with a right-handed downward *shuto*, much as in the ITN news item, though Bell used a hammer-fist on that occasion. The other photographs are more interesting. One shows the protective pads worn. With a caption, "To avoid breaking bones during their secret practice sessions, pupils wear an assortment of pads," we see shin pads, forearm pads, shoulder pads and pads to protect the heart and lungs. This will no doubt come as quite a surprise to many who believed that protection did not come to be used until much later. The other photograph shows schoolteacher Gerald Tucker performing a flying back-kick (as in the *kata Unsu*) on a suspended bag held by a

Competitors awaiting freestyle competition at the First French Karate Championships – 25th October 1957. Note the bamboo chest protectors.

Henri Plee performing *tameshiwari* during a demonstration at the First French Karate Championships – 25th October 1957.

Henri Plee assists Hiroo Mochizuki's performance of *tameshiwari* during a demonstration at the First French Karate Championships – 25th October 1957.

Hiroo Mochizuki leading a class before the 1957 championships. Hoang Nam is to be seen front row, far right.

fellow student, at solar plexus height, in the orchard of 12, Maybush Road. The fascinating and humorous point about this photograph is that whilst Gerald Tucker is nicely caught in full flight, he hasn't any *gi* trousers on – or any other trousers for that matter! The author is reliably informed however, that Tucker was actually wearing shorts at the time.

On the 25th October 1957, Bell attended the first national French karate tournament held in Paris at the sports hall of the police headquarters, Coubertin. As has been noted previously, it was the first tournament of its kind held in Europe. The following day, at the headquarters of the French Karate Federation, the Fédération Internationale De Karaté was formed, as a non-political organisation with no distinction made of race or religion; with the aim of bringing *karateka* together throughout the world; to co-ordinate the activity of karate in all nations; to set down the technical and organising rules; to organise and supervise international events; to represent karate in the international sports organizations, and so on. The signatories to the creation of the FIK were Messrs: Vladimiro Malatesti, representing Italy, as President of the Fiorentino Centre of Karate, via Laura 50, Florence; Vernon Bell, representing Great Britain, as Chairman of the British Karate Federation, 137 Hillview Avenue, Hornchurch, Essex; Jurgen Seydel, representing West Germany, as head of the Karate Lehrgruppe Bad Homburg, Urseler Strasse 19, Homburg; Henri Plee, representing France, as Vice-President of the French Karate Federation, 34 rue de la Montagne Sainte Geneviève, Paris V; and Hiroo Mochizuki, representing Japan, as delegate for Europe to the Yoseikan, 5 Daiku-cho, Shizuoka-shi, Japan.

In a letter to Bell dated the 4th November 1957, Jurgen Seydel wrote: "I am utmostly glad to have made your acquaintance, and I would be very pleased to see you again ... My chaps are keen on contacting your boys. A couple of them want to take a British comrade in their family during the holidays, winter or summer." In a letter to Bell dated the 29th January 1959, the founder of karate in Germany wrote: "I would be very honoured to welcome you to Bad Homburg as my guest. We don't know each other too much, but I was very impressed when we met in Paris, and I think it was not merely by chance that we understood each other so well." These two letters marked the beginning of a long and friendly correspondence between the two men.

The 3rd November 1957 is an important date in European karate. Master Tetsuji Murakami arrived in Paris one month before he was due, having suffered badly from seasickness on his voyage. Murakami had been specifically recommended to Plee and contracted for the Paris

Jurgen Seydel at a wall-mounted *makiwara*

dojo for one year. Readers will recall that Plee had, by virtue of previous recommendation and availability of material, a preference for Japan Karate Association training. Although Murakami came to France a 3rd

Dan in karate from the Yoseikan, he had also studied at the JKA prior to his departure to Europe. Murakami was also a 2nd Dan in kendo and a 1st Dan in aikido. He also knew well, by all accounts, the techniques of kyudo (the Way of archery).

In a typewritten translation of an uncredited and undated news item entitled, 'Master Murakami (3rd Dan of Karate – 2nd Dan of Kendo) has Arrived! He will Stay in France for a Few Years' that appeared in *Budo Presse*, the writer (Plee?) noted: "We were very curious to see how much better he could be than Master Hiroo Mochizuki who is a 2nd Dan. Now we understand. It seemed impossible, but he is still faster. And when we say fast, we do mean fast." The unknown writer also provided some further facts about Murakami's age (thirty-four), height (5 ft 5 ins) and weight (9 stone). The article appears to have been in error concerning the master's age. Assuming the piece was written in late 1957 or early 1958, Murakami was, in fact, thirty years old, having been born on the 31st March 1927. The writer of the article also wrote: "Thin, wiry and capable of jumping to an incredible height, surprisingly strong for his build, he is an example of what a man with unassuming physical appearance can achieve with karate." This important news item continues with the fact that Murakami had studied karate daily since being eleven years old, and Shotokan for about ten years. He had also studied the old form of karate, which the writer likened to the graceful Chinese boxing. It was further reported that Murakami, "never refuses an invitation in *ju-kumite*," and that he can easily break boards and, remarkably the writer notes, seven Japanese tiles. Murakami was light and fast, and the speed of his *kata* was something to behold, apparently. The French were impressed all right – very impressed.

Masters Sugiyama and Kondo had also been sent by the Yoseikan to teach karate in Italy and Switzerland, respectively, in 1958/1959. Little is known of these instructors in Great Britain, as they never visited these shores. Jurgen Seydel wrote to Bell on the 6th June 1959, noting: "I have been to Switzerland for two weeks ... The Swiss Budo Union has a Yoseikan teacher, Mr. Kondo, who makes some fine work in judo, kendo, aikido and karate. The Budo Union is affiliated to the Yoseikan and all diplomas are given by Mr. Kondo or Mr. Murakami, who also visits them."

Bell held a grading at 12, Maybush Road, on Saturday, 21st December 1957, for the more senior members of the BKF. It had been five months since their previous grading under Hoang Nam. Trevor Guilfoyle and Gerald Tucker were both promoted to 3rd kyu (thus becoming the first two *karateka* to reach that grade in this country under the BKF); Mick

Manning and Ken Elliott were graded to 4th kyu, D. Dyer and D. Blake to 5th kyu, and P. Byron to 6th kyu (either Byron failed his grading or Bell made a mistake, for Byron passed 6th kyu under Bell on the 31st May 1957. Given what Bell wrote below, it seems that Byron passed to 5th kyu). In a letter to Plee on the 4th February 1958, Bell gave the above results and what was required for the gradings. Bell wrote: "For these gradings they had to perform the first three *kata* correctly and efficiently on both sides, demonstrate eight techniques of *shuto*, six techniques of *hiji-ate*, eight techniques of *kento*, eight techniques of *ashi-waza*, eight combination tactical *kumite* techniques, and have a three minute *kumite* with each of the other members. Finishing [was] with karate self-defence and demonstrating... [one's] favourite techniques in a free tactical *kumite*. All pupils gained a high standard and marks were high in spite of a rigid marking system and all gained over eighty per cent."

Although Bell quoted the above grading results to Plee, the BKF grading register does not reflect these. The register quotes Guilfoyle, Tucker and Elliott only as grading that day, though Manning did grade separately under Bell on the 19th January 1958, at Hornchurch. No mention is made of Blake, Byron and Dyer.

Also, a B. J. O'Connor was apparently graded by Bell at Hornchurch on the 13th January 1958. But he appears to have failed, for there is a blank under the "New Grade" section. Later, in a letter to Plee dated 12th August 1957, O'Connor is referred to as ungraded.

Bell, reminiscing, recalled: "I wrote to the judo clubs as I was well known in judo circles, letting them know that karate had been established in April 1957, under charter from the French Federation, which authorised me to promote and examine in Yoseikan karate. I let them know that the Yoseikan had also granted me a charter to promote karate in Great Britain. I had a good response from the judo clubs and they wrote back saying that they would be interested in learning the new system of Japanese boxing – karate. So I opened a *dojo* at the British Legion Hall in St. Mary's Lane, Upminster, which had been my judo *dojo* for many years, and, during the years that followed, I invited all the people to either come down themselves or send their representatives to attend seminars. I ran these seminars for many weekends. The karate sections were formed within established judo, aikido and kendo clubs. I must make that quite clear. Each had a charter to establish a karate club within the framework of the BKF, and a person was appointed as local district officer for karate and the BKF. The appointed person would take it upon himself to establish, finance and promote karate, and to

St. Mary's Hall, Upminster – now a Royal British Legion club – in 1994

bring myself or Mick Manning, or later Jimmy Neal or Terry Wingrove, to take weekend courses. The St. Mary's *dojo* was the first *dojo* in Britain where karate was ever practised."

The British Legion Hall is still standing, though there have been some minor alterations to the building. The surrounding environment has changed particularly, no doubt reflecting that in 1958 the population of Upminster was barely thirteen thousand, a fraction of what it is today. As one enters the building there are ladies and men's lavatories to either side, where in the Fifties the *karateka* used to change. The hall proper is entered through double doors. The original hall used to measure some forty-five feet in length by thirty feet in width, and this is unchanged except that at the far end there is now a bar and a small extension beyond, which is perhaps more noticeable from the rear of the outside. In the Fifties, a partition at the end of the hall concealed stacked tables and chairs. The light parquet flooring is original, and one cannot but recall the many famous *karateka* to have trained on it (see later). On the surrounding site, where patrons' cars can be parked either side of the building, there used to be grass. At the rear, where the British Telecom building is today (built in 1968) there used to be a cornfield that extended down the left side of the building when viewed from the front. The porch at the entrance to the hall is not original. The asbestos roof and the plain brick from which the building is constructed, and which may be compared with the rear extension, are original. A bricked-off door to the right of the building is more recent. The outside paintwork, today, is brown; in 1958 it was emerald green. The Masons Arms public house across St. Mary's Lane, where the students would refresh themselves after training, is still there.

In a letter to Plee dated the 8th February 1958, Bell mentioned that he started training in karate at St. Mary's just after Christmas, 1957, and that lessons were held on Saturdays between 4.00 and 6.00 p.m., and on Sundays between 10.00 a.m. and 2.00 p.m. A beginner's course was held at the *dojo* for the first time on 19th January 1958, which attracted ten pupils, all of who were progressing nicely three weeks later. The names of eight of these students are known: R. Armstrong, P. Clarke, P. Conlon, B. McCarthy, A. Pearson, H. Rayner, J. Russell and J. Sen.

At the time of joining the BKF, Reginald Armstrong was a twenty-four-year-old driver with the Merton and Morden Urban District Council, with a keen interest in a wide range of sports. Paul Clarke of Barkingside, Essex, joined as a nineteen-year-old 'box lad,' and had additional interests in reading and film. Peter Conlon was a twenty-two-year-old engineer and Barry McCarthy a seventeen-year-old laboratory technician. Alex Pearson was a twenty-eight-year-old fitter with the Metropolitan Water Board, from East London, with interests in motor cycling and swimming. Henry Rayner was a nineteen-year-old from Cricklewood, who worked as a packer with B. Elliott and Company of Willesden, manufacturers of machine tools and engineering equipment. He also had wide interests in sports, including boxing, which he did. James "Monty" Russell, aged thirty-nine from Hayes, was a flooring contractor by trade, with an interest in weightlifting. Joseph Sen was nineteen when he started karate, and worked as a clerk for the Anglo-Dutch Cigar Company in London, NW11. He was keen on music and motorcycling.

It is believed that the two remaining students were Brian O'Connor, an eighteen-year-old laboratory technician from Sydenham, who had interests in canoeing, mountaineering and skating, and Edward Revill, a twenty-one-year-old driver with interests in parachuting and the Special Air Services (SAS). He had been in the army, and listed a number of sports interests on his BKF membership application form, including tennis, cricket, skating, swimming and basketball.

In a letter to Jurgen Seydel dated the 23rd April 1958, Bell noted with regard to these beginners, "some ... come from thirty to forty miles away," and that the course would end in June with a grading for white-belt. Bell continued in this letter: "From our old original members on the first course, we have only three left out of one dozen who started eighteen months ago, and these three now form our Committee of whom two are 3rd kyus and one 4th kyu. The others only gave up because of family commitments, work, etc., and not because they wanted to, and all of them were 6th or 5th kyus and may one day, very likely, continue their studies. So you see we are few in number but very keen, and karate, being a specialised subject, we are not interested in large numbers ... It appears that karate in Britain is now consolidated and will progress slowly but surely, but we do experience some opposition and jealousy from the judo associations, but there are many *judoka* who wish to learn karate, and some have left judo for karate, which is a good sign."

In the above letter, Bell gives us the grading syllabus for both 6th and 5th kyu, which are as follows:

"6th kyu – ten minutes gymnastics and preparatory exercises; the kowtow [*rei*] and *dojo* etiquette. Eight techniques of toughening on the *makiwara* including the fingers, heel of hand, fist, back of hand, knuckles and elbow; eight techniques of *kento*, eight techniques of *shuto*, eight techniques of *hiji*, three techniques of *ashiwaza*; 1st *kata* as *uke* and *tsuki* on both sides, first slowly then quickly; three minute conventional *kumite;* Three minute *kumite shiai* for one point under contest rules. To pass, an overall 70% [on] theory and practical [was required].

"5th kyu – similar to 6th kyu, except for five more techniques of *ashiwaza*, the second *kata*, eight combination techniques of leg and arm and more contest ability, style and skill in combat, and, elementary karate self-defence."

Bell remembered 'Monty' Russell in particular: "There was this old chap, nearly forty, Russell his name was. We used to call him the battleship. He was as fat as he was tall and his karate was crude but every move was made with one hundred percent effort."

In his letter of application to Bell and the BKF Committee (4th January 1958), Russell tells of an incident that led him to enquire about karate: "Last summer I had a kitchen to tile for a woman living just near to me. I began at 9 a.m. A few nail heads were sticking above the surface, so I began to knock them down. It would have taken about ten minutes to have gone all over the floor, but I had just started when I heard someone shouting and swearing. I went out and it was the fellow in the next house in his back garden. He told me to stop banging, as he was a night-worker. He said he would hop over and attend to me. I invited him over, but instead he went into his shed to get an axe. His wife and mother-in-law were all arguing with me and the woman I was doing the job for, so I left them and finished banging the nails down and went out and told them they could stop as the banging was finished. Later in the morning when I had completed the job, the fellow (a Polish chap) came out and apologised. But I thought from that day one needs a good form of self-defence."

Bell continued: "St. Mary's already bore the strong spirit of martial arts training as judo, aikido and ju-jitsu had been practised there many years beforehand. It was my personal *dojo*, and we even made films there – including a bojitsu film. I felt that I should make St. Mary's the official *dojo* of Yoseikan karate in Great Britain. It was a beautiful *dojo*, modern, heated, airy and well lit, with a highly polished parquet floor. There were separate changing rooms for men and women, and somewhere where you could make a cup of tea. It was on the main bus routes to all parts of Essex and Kent and also on the District Underground train line to London. It had all the facilities, but, above all else, the main reason for commencing karate at Upminster was because other martial artists who practised there could see it.

"Anyway, we began to expand slowly, gradually, and I only let other *bona fide* martial artists train. I didn't let people come in off the street and practise, like people responding to an advert; we didn't do it like that. They used to come to us from all over England, through the police, through libraries, through societies, and slowly the spirit came and karate began to be integrated into the martial arts in this country. On Sundays, we had a beginner's class, an intermediate class, self-defence and *kata* training. Tetsuji Murakami was the first Japanese karate instructor to come to the *dojo* and he taught aikido as well. In 1958, we had our very first female *karateka,* the very first woman to train in Great Britain. Her name was Doris Keane, from Romford. She trained for a few months at the St. Mary's *dojo*, but it was too much for her, too hard."

Readers will no doubt recall that a Miss Higgins had been graded by Hoang Nam on the 21st July 1957 – if the contents of Bell's 26th July 1957, letter to Plee are to be believed, and there is no reason to doubt them, especially as Hoang Nam could have disputed the contents on his return to Paris. On this basis, Doris Keane does not have the distinction of being the first woman *karateka* in Britain. Yet Bell is fairly insistent that Keane was the first, despite the evidence. Some forty-five years is a long time for distortions in the memory to occur, and it must be said that Bell had no recollection of a Miss Higgins at all. Strangely, perhaps, as we have seen, Miss Higgins does not appear on the ITN news item, yet she was apparently there and, according to Bell's letter of the 26th

Doris Keane is flanked on her left by Trotter and Bell, and on her right by Dyer and Brandon – 1957/58.

July 1957, she trained with Hoang Nam and six other BKF students the following day, and watched the news in the evening.

Also, a 'Higgins' does not appear in the BKF grading register for the 21st July 1957. The grading results were not entered into the register by Bell until the 16th September 1957. Perhaps Miss Higgins stopped training, and her name was omitted on that basis. Perhaps Miss Higgins wasn't registered as having graded because she didn't take the full grading, remembering that Nam had taught her his special ladies' *kata*, but if this is the case why did he grade her to 6th kyu, for it would have seemingly demeaned the entire grading in the eyes of the men?

However, there may be an answer. It is remotely possible that Higgins was Keane's maiden name. The author says 'remotely' because it is most likely that Bell would have known if she married. The only photograph of Keane shows her in the garden of 12, Maybush Rd, alongside white-belts, Dyer and Brandon. There is no photographic or written evidence to suggest that Dyer and Brandon successfully continued training into 1958, so the photograph, on this basis, is probably from 1957. To confuse the issue further though, immediately to Keane's left stands Trotter, wearing a coloured belt. The first mention of Trotter in the BKF Grading Register is March 1959, and he became a red-belt in July that year, so unless he was wearing a judo graded belt at an earlier time, the whole episode is an intriguing mystery.

Bell continued: "We never took children in those days, nor students under eighteen and those not working. We were responsible individuals you might say. The atmosphere at St. Mary's was martial, it was Japanese, and it was also English heritage. A learning atmosphere pervaded more than anything else though. I remember old man Smith, fifty-one years of age, with white hair, who used to train, and the old doctor who used to come on his Velocette motorcycle all the way from North London, from Hampstead. Wonderful people came to that *dojo*; they were all wonderful people. All the famous Shotokan instructors trained as beginners in the early days there – what more can I say? The British Legion members called us the "week-evening people" and the "weekend people." We were at that *dojo* for about fifteen years, if I remember correctly, and the end came very suddenly. We had no warning. The British Legion cut all rentals out, all private organizations. They wanted a central focusing point for the entire region. We had one month to get out. We stored all our equipment in the loft there – *makiwara*, judo mats, kendo *katana*, bojitsu sticks, everything. We had to pack it all in and move."

An early student at the St. Mary's *dojo* was Ernest Hughes. A former Russian interpreter with the armed forces, Hughes joined the *dojo* as soon as he had completed his Bachelor of Arts degree from the University of Cambridge, in 1958, having studied oriental languages and Russian. As a university student, he recalled having read widely on the martial arts and of coming across karate. Whilst at Cambridge, Hughes had been a member of the University's Japan Society and a former secretary to the weight-lifting club. His hobbies and interests at the time included linguistics, especially Chinese, Mongolian, Russian and German. Another interest was Far Eastern history. His membership form to the BKF is dated the 22nd June 1958, when he was twenty-three years of age. He noted: "At that period there was considerable hostility to the spread of karate in judo circles, and I came to hear of Mr. Bell and his karate club as a result of this clash ... At that time references were needed to join and I remember approaching one lecturer for this chore ... I vividly remember travelling by underground to train on Sunday mornings. I also remember visiting Hornchurch to practise in the grounds of ... Bell's parents' house.

"Through the mists of time the karate men of that period seem unusually dedicated. With the Pacific War not far away in time, a sort of Budo militarism prevailed, with instructors regarded as deities ... The first system taught was not classical Shotokan and had self-defence elements ... Bell was continually in France training and there was much talk of Mochizuki, Murakami and others."

Hiroo Mochizuki demonstrating *yoko-tobi-geri* on the top of a building during a FFK course – *c*.1958.

Bell's 4th February 1958, letter to Plee is important for another reason also, in that it is the first letter, in English at least, that is known to have survived, in which the name of Tetsuji Murakami appears. (Murakami's first name was mostly spelt 'Tetsugi' in the early days. The use of the 'j' instead of the 'g' is actually correct, and has been used throughout this book). Bell wrote: "My Federation most certainly wishes to arrange a visit to this country by Mr. Murakami as soon as possible, but I regret that after consultation ... [the money] we can raise will not be enough to cover the total cost that an official period of residence of some two to three months by Mr. Murakami in this country [would entail] ... [It] is not at the present stage possible, nor safe. However, the position governing this proposal may change quickly in the very near future, because karate is growing and getting more known and publicised in Britain, and if I can publish one of your books our organisation will grow immensely. So then in some three months we may be in a much better position to make Mr. Murakami a far better offer to reside here for a long period. Rest assured there is nothing we would all like more than to have him with us at once for a long stay in England, but we must face facts. However, we would like him to come here in the first place for a short stay for one week's instruction from the 1st to the 7th July [1958] and would be glad if you will book him for these dates ... If we can have him for two weeks I will let you know as soon as possible, and believe me honestly and sincerely when I say that we would give anything to have this Japanese master with us for a long period, but the very high cost of living in England makes things very difficult." As it turned out, Master Murakami was not to visit England that year, but would be engaged by the BKF for the first time the following July (see below).

The problem, in Bell's mind, of Harrison's translation of Lasserre's book, already referred to, dragged on. Harrison and Bell had corresponded (letters now lost) on the subject, but matters raised their head again when Bell received a letter from Plee, dated the 28th January 1958. Plee wrote: "Foulsham is publishing a karate book written by Harrison. It will appear next month." Plee also mentioned that, "Mr. Koizumi has written to the Yoseikan to ask not to send Japanese karate expert to London."

Bell wrote to Plee on the 26th February 1958: "I feel it is imperative that a strong course of action should be taken regarding the publication of Lasserre's works in Britain, for if my Federation is unable to include its details in the front of Lasserre's book, it is likely that, on publication, British people will regard Lasserre's work as being the *bona fide* authority on karate, and will accept his teachings. Also, being the first book on karate in the English language, it is likely to sell many copies and prove successful, in which case it will give Harrison and Lasserre an open English market to translate to the public all the other works by Lasserre in England. In the opinion of our Committee, this action would do the English karate movement much harm, and retard its progress some years as much time would have to be spent in re-educating the British public as to the true nature of the real karate. Also, the publication of Lasserre's works in England would undo the hard work and success that the BKF has built up so far in England for the karate movement. Accordingly, I suggest that you do your best in Paris to suppress the publication of Lasserre's works in English by approaching Foulsham's agents in Paris to acquaint them with the true situation of Lasserre's status."

At this time, Bell had had Plee's book, *Conquer or Die*, translated into English (though in a later letter to Plee, dated 2nd June 1958, Bell mentions that he is having it translated by an English teacher who can speak French fluently), and at the time of the above letter was having translated Plee's, *The A.B.C of Karate* (the translation being completed in May 1958). Bell genuinely believed that Lasserre was not a *karateka* and had no business writing a karate book. On the other hand of course, Bell had much to lose from the publication. As Bell wrote, quite openly to Plee, in the letter of the 26th February 1958: "I feel that if I can publish your books in England before Foulsham's publish Lasserre's books, then much good will be done for the British karate movement, and so help to overcome this mess regarding Harrison. I would also like your permission to write a preface in the front of your book about the British karate movement and will send you a copy of it in due course."

In a letter dated the 8th March 1958, Plee replied to Bell giving his, "official permission to proceed with, and handle all arrangements for, the publication of *The ABC of Karate* in English," and Plee wondered if Bell intended including *Pinan Shodan* in the translated version (Bell did – letter to Plee dated 2nd June 1958). Plee's final okay was, naturally, to be given once he knew the conditions of the contract. Another letter from Plee to Bell dated 18th March 1958, noted that: "You have delayed too long. The book should have been published a year ago when I told you so. Now you must hurry. On top of it all the first *Pinan kata* should be translated from Mr. Alcheik's book. Thus all English *karateka*s would have to buy the book."

Plee's 8th March 1958 letter is important for another reason also. Plee noted that there was to be a karate course in Paris from the 16th to the 31st August 1958, that he would be there, and that Bell could sleep in the second *dojo* (third floor) as long as he brought a "pneumatic mattress and enough to cover you." Plee noted that no cooking was allowed in the *dojo*. But the important information concerned Master Murakami. Plee noted that Murakami charged two thousand Francs for a one-hour private lesson, and fifteen thousand Francs for ten private lessons, and recommended that Bell take them.

In a later letter to Plee (22nd April 1958), Bell noted that he would, "like to study with Mr. Murakami privately for ten lessons, having one lesson each day, so please arrange this for me with him. I am hoping to bring with me one of my committee members, Mr. G. Tucker, 3rd kyu, so please reserve him a vacancy on the course, and I will confirm his attendance at a later date." In fact, as a later letter (12th August 1958) to Plee showed, students, R. Armstrong, 5th kyu, and P. Clarke and B. O'Connor accompanied Bell, both of who were ungraded. Gerald Tucker did not attend. Bell wrote in this later letter, in which he also enclosed a banker's draft for twelve thousand Francs, the course fees for the four of them, "as your old friend and colleague I would be glad if you can arrange for me to sleep in one of the small cubicles or rooms above the second *dojo*, where I slept last time, for I would like a little privacy as I am a light sleeper and have some baggage containing personal and karate

Master Tetsuji Murakami in Bad Homburg, Germany – 1958

records that I must keep near me and safely. I also have a rubber Lilo mattress which I do not wish to inflate each day, which would be necessary if I sleep in the *dojo*, so I would appreciate your kind indulgence in this." Unfortunately, Bell and students had to leave the course early.

Group shot of students under Master Murakami in Paris – 16th–31st August 1958. Bell stands to Murakami's left, Plee to Murakami's right. To Plee's right is Szpirglas, French and European karate champion. The British students who travelled with Bell are in black *gi* (left to right – J. O'Connor, J. Clarke, R. Armstrong). Tam Mytho is second from left, kneeling, and to his left is a Swiss karate delegate.

"Nobody regretted it more than I," wrote Bell in a letter to Plee on the 29th September 1958, "but as you know it was unavoidable due to lack of finances, but I learned enough during my nine days to teach to my members for sometime to come." Bell continued: "It was as well that I returned early for one of the BKF Committee, Mr. Guilfoyle (3rd kyu), was mobilised for the RAF the next week after my return, so I had time to teach him for a whole day all the postures, defences and 1st *Pinan* that Murakami had taught me, for in Guilfoyle we lose our oldest and best member for two years. Also, the next week, Mr. O'Connor, who you remember was with me on the course, was mobilised for the Royal Marines."

Bell's work of trying to suppress the translated version of Lasserre's book appearing in English was further motivated by the fact that he was trying to get a karate book published also. In a letter to Plee dated the 2nd April 1958, we learn that: "With reference to my own book, this is not yet settled, and Messrs. Stanley, Paul and Company are only considering it. They are dubious about the marketability of my book, as they do not think that karate is sufficiently developed in Britain yet to fulfil the need for a book. I have given them a thorough report of British karate and have expressed the desirability of publishing a book, an authentic book, in English, on karate. I now await their decision."

Bell also noted to Plee in the letter of the 2nd April 1958: "I approached Messrs. Rider and Company in the first place with the prime view of publishing your own book, *The A.B.C. of Karate* ... but at my interview with them they said that they would prefer to have an official karate book written by an Englishman which would be the authentic manual of our British Federation, and they stressed this point strongly. Hence, I went ahead and planned the details of the book. As yet no definite arrangements have been made to publish my own book and I have not started to write it, as first many difficulties with Rider and Company must be overcome and I await their final decision. My feeling is that it will not be published, at least not for some time, so in the meantime I wish to go ahead with the publication of your own book as soon as possible, and for this I would like to act as official agent."

In a letter to Plee, dated the 22nd April 1958, Bell wrote: "Regarding my own book, I regret that negotiations with Messrs. Rider and Company have fallen through and the book will not now be published, which may be just as well and for the best." Bell's planned book was never actually started, let alone published. There was no further news concerning the Lasserre book, and Bell wrote to Plee: "Believe it or not, Mr. Harrison has sent me a new pupil who had written to him after reading his book, *The Fighting Spirit of Japan*, as to where he could learn karate and Harrison recommended my Federation, which is a sign of goodwill." In fact Bell had a fondness for Ernest John Harrison, "I liked the old boy," he told the author.

The letter of the 22nd April 1958 is also important because it provides confirmation of Murakami's first planned visit to Britain, between the 15th and 30th January 1959, but more of this later.

The problem, as Bell saw it, of English *judoka* visiting Plee continued. In the letter of the 22nd April 1958, Bell wrote: "I would like to point out that Kenshiro Abbe is sending two of his black-belts to Paris for one week, I believe on Friday next week, 2nd May, to visit and study judo at several French clubs ... It is my opinion and belief that these two *judoka* [one a 3rd Dan, the other a 2nd Dan] may attempt to visit you for the purpose of studying karate and making some form of contact on Abbe's behalf ... The British Karate Federation has in no way any wish to be associated with the activities or purposes of K. Abbe and in no way wishes to do business with him or recognise his ideas. Your kind co-operation and understanding in this matter will greatly help our British karate movement and our Federation by taking a firm line with these black-belts of Abbe's..." (the rest of the letter is lost).

Plee replied to Bell on the 25th April 1958, noting that: "<u>You may be sure</u> that any British men wanting to learn karate would not be accepted by me if they are not members of your Federation." Plee mentioned that an exception to this rule would of course be British men living in France.

Bell wrote to Plee on the 2nd July 1958, concerning the latter's book. "After the failure of negotiations with Stanley Paul and Company, to publish your book two months ago, I have arranged with Messrs. Putnam and Company Limited, of London (who published the complete Kano *Jujutsu*) to take your book and they are very interested and are considering it for publication. At present a copy of your book is being studied by them and I am seeing Mr. Huntingdon, the Director, this week to open business negotiations regarding percentage, and will let you know immediately I know the arrangements, so please tell your editor immediately to stop any of his negotiations for, as I originally told you, I will handle this properly and correctly to the end. I fully intend to get your book published in England and will keep my promise as I always do, but these things cannot be hurried and it takes time to find a good publisher and arrangements cannot be made in a few weeks, so both you and your editor must be patient. I definitely do not wish you to negotiate the book from France as I have definite arrangements now for its publication. Also, you must understand that I have spent much time in the last few months trying to get your book published and I have done it very seriously and honestly. Therefore, as I promised you, I would act as your official agent for this book in England. I fully intend to carry out my promise and proceed seriously with it until it is published, but I must have complete freedom to act for you in all respects to get this book published. In England these things take time and publishers will not be hurried, but now we have at last got positive results here to publish your book, so leave everything with me and tell your editor to do nothing as this book, publication in English, is definitely and safely in my hands and will soon be published. I am doing everything in my power to hasten Messrs. Putnam and Company's publication of it."

It was in the above letter that Bell asked for Plee's opinion concerning the promotion of Trevor Guilfoyle to 2nd kyu before Guilfoyle's entry into the RAF. Bell wrote: "We expect to lose our best karateist, Mr. Guilfoyle ... he is a Committee member and oldest member. He can demonstrate expertly the five *kata* of kyu grades and also *Pinan Shodan kata* as good as some French black-belts, and his *kumite* is first-class. I

Trevor Guilfoyle countering an attack by a sword-wielding Vernon Bell – 12, Maybush Rd, Hornchurch (1957).

Trevor Guilfoyle countering with *empi* on Vernon Bell – 12, Maybush Rd, Hornchurch (1957).

wish to grade him to 2nd kyu. What do you think? Please let me have your opinion. Mr. Manning, another Committee member, I have graded this week to 3rd kyu after one and a half years at karate, for he gives very good exhibition of the first four *kata*, combination techniques and has good *kumite*, ability and techniques."

Guilfoyle, as it turned out, wasn't to grade further. Michael Manning was graded to 3rd kyu on the 1st July 1958, by Bell, at the St. Mary's *dojo*, in what appears to have been a solitary grading. According to the BKF grading register, Bell appears to have conducted another solitary grading on Ernest Hughes, in London, that same day. A blank appears in the "New Grade" section of the register, so presumably Hughes failed. The same fate seems to have befallen C. Musgrove a month earlier, when Bell had apparently failed him on the 1st June 1958, again in London. Where exactly in London these two isolated gradings took place is unknown, though it seems likely to have been at 'private' judo club gradings.

Quite a number of letters between Bell and Plee ensued with regard to the publication of Plee's book. Much of this information is confidential, in that it is financial in nature, the details of which have little to do with the remit of this book. However, in one undated and hand-written letter, Plee makes an important comment – and not to do with the book: "Here karate progresses seriously. Yesterday we had the first *shiai* for *Shodan* for eighteen men – no one has got the black-belt."

In another undated hand-written letter, Plee makes it quite clear, in plain terms in fact, that he is tired of waiting for a publisher for his book in England. He wrote: "It is one year and a half that I told you to translate immediately *The ABC* ... and put it to Foulsham. My dear Bell, you are always a little too slow ... For instance, I told you and wrote to you twice that you had to give a date to have Mr. Murakami. You take your time now for this Japanese expert, but Mr. Murakami's calendar is full till the end of '58. I am sorry but the other clubs have been more decisive."

Plee also made another important point to Bell in the above letter: "Writing a book is a good idea, but now it is too early. You are not able (excuse me but we are between pupil and teacher) to understand exactly the good and the wrong techniques, and two or three years after, your book would be against you." Plee was being blunt, but one feels that he was being truthful. Plee's letter finished on a friendly note.

Plee received a letter from John Huntingdon, dated the 10th June 1958, in which Huntingdon noted: "This morning I had a pleasant meeting with Mr. Bell about your book, *ABC of Karate-Do*. We are very interested indeed about the possibility of publishing the book in English and I hope to give you a firm decision shortly." However, photographs were required to replace the existing line drawings. In subsequent letters, much talk was of percentages and the book's format. However, some interesting facts emerge from these letters. A little information will be given now; other information is dispersed.

Bell had offered his services for the photographs for the Plee book to save Plee coming to London for the photos, but Bell noted in a letter to Plee dated the 3rd July 1958, probably in response to the hand-written letter by Plee, where plain speaking had been the order of the day, that: "I understand now why it is not possible for me to pose for the photographs and agree with you that it would not be wise, for at my stage I am technically insufficient for the purpose."

If Plee's earlier letter hadn't been sufficient to put Bell in his place (if that's the way you wish to view it), two comments made by Plee in his letter to Bell on the 16th June 1958, certainly would have done. Plee wrote: "No, you can't be included in some of the photos of the book. Meaning no offence, in spite of your research and your extreme good will, you are still quite far from real karate" (Plee had wanted Murakami and Mochizuki for the photos), and, "I obtain for you a first Dan with official recognition from Japan, long before it is due." This last comment must have depressed Bell greatly. However, if Plee genuinely felt this, it surely begs the question as to why Plee recommended Bell for the grade in the first place?

Details exist for a number of karate demonstrations performed during 1958 by Bell and his students. The first of these was on Friday, 23rd May, at 7.30 p.m., at the YMCA Red Triangle Club, Lambourne Hall, Western Road, Romford. The event, compere'd and organised by Vernon Bell, as Eastern Area Representative of the British Judo Council, marked the 2nd Annual Eastern Counties Judo Championships of the BJC, in association with the BKF. The great judo master, Kenshiro Abbe, 7th Dan, President of the BJC, was in attendance, acting as referee and taking part in a number of judo displays, including "Match of the Century – K. Abbe will accept the challenge of an unknown guest in a Judo contest (NO FALLS barred)" and, "1 man versus 10 – K. Abbe will take on in succession 10 (or more) high grade *judoka* in the shortest time." After the introductions, a judo display got under way with *randori* (informal practice) and *ukemi-waza* (break-falling), then followed an explanation of contest rules, actual contests commencing with semi-final heats of the East Area kyu grades, and displays. Of the twenty-five items, "Karate and Karate-Do (demonstrations by members of the

British Karate Federation)" was item fifteen, and followed a ten-minute interval.

The karate display was begun with group exercising under 3rd kyu Gerald Tucker, and included *araku* (walk) – *gedan-barai* (guard), and *judanka* (stance) and *gedanka* (stance) demonstrated by 3rd kyu Trevor Guilfoyle. Then followed a wood breaking demonstration by Vernon Bell, and, "toughening exercises on the *makiwara*." *Kento* (fist), *shuto* (hand-sabre), *hiji-ate* (elbow) and *ashiwaza* (foot) techniques were demonstrated by T. Guilfoyle (3rd kyu), J. Sen (6th kyu), G. Tucker (3rd kyu) and T. Guilfoyle again, respectively. The performance of four *kata* by the above followed, with the addition of H. Rayner (6th kyu). Combination techniques followed on, demonstrated by the two 3rd kyus, and the display finished with three versions of *kumite* (sparring): "conventional – practice of certain movements for specialisation of techniques," "Free – informal practice to develop skill of attack/defence under combat conditions," and *Shiai*. Three pairs – J. Sen and H. Raynor, M. Manning and G. Tucker, and, R. Armstrong and H. Rayner, demonstrated the *kumite*, respectively.

On the bottom of the back page of the programme, which cost sixpence, under, "Exhibition of Karate," the following was written: "Exhibitions of Karate and Karate-Do by members of the British Karate Federation are under the auspices and statutes of the European Karate Union and International Karate Federation and the Yoseikan of Japan, to which the BKF is affiliated and responsible. It is pointed out that this display is one of the first to be given in Britain of the TRUE KARATE-DO (deadly Japanese sport of combat) and is staged by permission of the European Karate Union and the IKF, and is arranged by V.C.F. Bell (SHODAN of YOSEIKAN, Japan, National Coach of Yoseikan in Britain). The EKU and IKF have appointed by official Charter, Mr. V. Bell their official agent, representative, and controller for Britain to form and establish and develop the true KARATE of Yoseikan, as practised in Japan, in the name of the British Karate Federation."

Three days later Bell and his students were part of the Grand Whit-Monday Fete on behalf of the Ilford and District Spastics Society, held at the Gordon Fields, Gordon Road, Green Lane, Ilford. The sixpenny programme showed that the fete was declared opened at 2.30 p.m. and karate was at 6.00 p.m. and scheduled for half-an-hour, between the Alan Airs Concert Party and Skiffle Band and a tug-o-war contest between youth clubs. A number of celebrities were to attend the day's events including Dr. Desmond Morris, the well-known zoologist, and Dickie Henderson, the comedian. Four sentences were given over to

LEICESTER Y.M.C.A. GYM. SECTION

presents

A DISPLAY

of

PHYSICAL CULTURE

at

THE Y.M.C.A. THEATRE, EAST ST.

LEICESTER, on

SATURDAY, JUNE 28th, at 7 p.m.

JOHN LEES . 1957 Mr. UNIVERSE

N.A.B.B.A. EAST MIDLANDS PHYSIQUE CONTEST

(Under the auspices of the National Amateur Bodybuilders Association)

MISS VENUS of the Midlands

(Ladies' Open Figure Contest)

SYD BAKER . MAN IN BRONZE

OSCAR HEIDENSTAM

THE LOUGHBOROUGH GYMNASTS

TONY CARROLL

AND THE FIRST APPEARANCE IN THE MIDLANDS

A Special Demonstration of KARATE

The New Japanese System of Self-Defence

Tickets & Entry Forms from the Y.M.C.A. Office
Granby St., Leicester   Tickets at 6/-, 4/6, 3/6

LAKIN & FENNELL, LTD., 41 WELFORD ROAD, LEICESTER

A Display of Physical Culture poster featuring a BKF demonstration – 1958

karate in the programme conveying the usual notes on authenticity and what spectators would see, including wood-breaking.

Another display was given in Leicester on the evening of Saturday, June 28th 1958. The Leicester YMCA Gymnastic Section, presented, "A Display of Physical Culture" at the YMCA Theatre, in East Street. Bell had written to Plee (22nd April 1958) concerning this planned display and noted that, "This should be a good opportunity to establish karate in the Midlands." The orangey-pink posters noted that the karate demonstration would be the first appearance in the Midlands of this new Japanese system of self-defence. The audience had paid six shillings a ticket for the best seats, though others were available at four shillings and sixpence and three shillings and sixpence. The cream-coloured sixpenny programme showed that compere, Oscar Heidenstam, opened proceedings by introducing Vernon Bell and students of the British Ju-Jitsu Federation, who gave a display. After eight further displays of bodybuilding, gymnastics, weightlifting and so on, the karate demonstration followed on from, "Syd Baker – Fabulous Man in Bronze." Billed as "Karate – The Deadly System of Japanese Self-Defence," Bell once again was able to get a separate section explaining the new art. Under the heading of, "Display of Karate and Karate-do," it read: "By the British Karate Federation (under the auspices of the European Karate Union and International Karate Federation), including exhibitions of gymnastics, wood-breaking, *kata*, *kumite* (free practice), arm and foot techniques and self-defence. Programme arranged and devised by V.C.F. Bell, *Shodan* in Karate-Do of Yoseikan of Japan, National Coach of BKF."

In a letter to Plee dated the 3rd July 1958, Bell noted the Leicester display, "was a good success and from it we have been asked to promote one further north in Nottingham in September on the occasion of the Northern Physical Culture Display, before two thousand people. Also, we have been asked to give a display at the West of England Judo Championships in October, and we hope to give a display in September in Manchester at the BJA Championships. We feel these last two displays will do much to promote better understanding and liaison between the judo organisations and our karate. Also, we feel that these displays do karate much good in getting it known to the public as a sport and physical culture, and it is now beginning to be known quite well by name and by our displays we hope to differentiate it completely from judo ... and to show that the two arts can function quite separately, without prejudice or jealousy. To date, we feel that we are achieving our aim and karate is now being very well received by the public and sporting organisations, who find our displays very enlightening." It was also in this letter that Bell congratulated Plee on being promoted to 3rd Dan. Bell wrote, "I think you deserve it for your service to karate over many years, [and that] I only hope I can do as much for karate in England as you have done in France."

Bell and his students were busy on the 5th July 1958, for they attended two functions that afternoon. The first was at an Annual Police Show

★ ANNUAL POLICE ★
SHOW & FAIR

(By kind permission of Captain F. R. J. Peel, C.B.E., M.C., B.A., the Chief Constable of Essex)

at

WINTRY PARK FARM, EPPING

(By kind permission of Mr. J. Foulds)

on

SATURDAY, 5TH JULY, 1958

Official Opening 2.30 p.m.

★ROYAL MARINES BAND
★QUEEN'S OWN
  CAMERON HIGHLANDERS BAND
★6 COMMAND WORKSHOP R.E.M.E.
  JEEP DISPLAY TEAM
★METROPOLITAN POLICE
  MOTOR CYCLE TEAM
★PARADE OF VETERAN MOTOR CARS
★PARADE OF MODERN MOTOR CARS

★EPPING SILVER BAND
★CHELSEA PENSIONERS
★"SCARRI" FAMOUS TRICK
  AND COMEDY CYCLIST
★DISPLAY OF KARATE AND
  KARATE DO
★"BUSTER SID"
  AND HIS
  WILD WESTERN RODEO

EXHIBITIONS by the ROYAL NAVY, ARMY, ROYAL AIR FORCE and ESSEX FIRE BRIGADE
TRADE STANDS ★ CRIME EXHIBITION ★ GIGANTIC FLORAL EXHIBITION
GEORGE PRINT'S MAMMOTH FUN FAIR

● SPECIAL BUS SERVICES FROM HARLOW, ONGAR AND LOUGHTON ●

GATES OPEN 12 NOON. REFRESHMENTS AVAILABLE ALL DAY. LICENSED BAR (being applied for)

Admission: ADULTS 1'6. CHILDREN 6d. CARS 2'6. MOTOR CYCLES 1'6. CYCLES 6d.
SOUVENIR PROGRAMMES 6d EACH.

THE SHOW OF ALL SHOWS—WHATEVER YOU MISS DON'T MISS THIS

(This show is presented by the Harlow Police Divisional Sports Club, Police Station, Harlow)

Annual Police Show and Fair featuring a BKF demonstration – 1958

and Fair held at Wintry Park Farm, Epping, on behalf of the Harlow Police Sports Club. Bell had written to Plee earlier (letter dated the 2nd June 1958) that ten thousand people would attend the Essex Police Show, "And this should do karate much good, for we are trying to popularise it as a sport."

The Essex police had been interested in Bell's karate for some time. In the letter to Plee of the 4th February 1958, Bell had written: "Our Federation has been fortunate in securing the genuine interest of the local Police Force and we have been honoured with a proposed visit by the Chief Constable of Essex and the local Chief Superintendent, who wish to visit our *dojo* to witness karate as they think it will be good for it to be taught to the police. I have been requested to write an article on karate for the Official Police Gazette and for this I would like your official permission to refer to sections of your book, *A.B.C. of Karate-Do*."

The official opening of the Police Fair was at 2.30 p.m., and for an admission cost of one shilling and sixpence for adults and sixpence for children, quite a show was provided, according to the advertising poster. Among the displays to be seen were the Royal Marines Band and the Queen's Own Cameron Highlanders Band, parades of veteran and modern motorcars, a demonstration by the Metropolitan Police Motor Cycle Team, displays by Scarri the famous trick and comedy cyclist, and Buster Sid and his Wild West rodeo. There were exhibitions by the Royal Navy, the Army and the Royal Air Force. The sixpenny programme showed that the "Display of Karate and Karate-Do," came after "Charlie Delta's Impersonations," and before, "The Mighty Atom – Strongman Tony Carroll of Northampton." One of the interesting features of the fourteen programmes featured was, "To the Death!" – a sabre fighting demonstration.

The second display that day was a gala held at the B.D.V – Raleigh Athletic and Social Club, in Essex. It was a long day, with the novelty races and tug-o-war heats commencing at two-thirty in the afternoon, to dancing in the marquee finishing at ten o'clock in the evening. There was an archery display, a dog training demonstration, a Miss Gala Day competition, and so on, plus Punch and Judy and a funfair to keep the children amused. The "Karate – Japanese Boxing" demonstration was thirty minutes in length, commencing at 6.15 p.m., having preceded a boxing display and followed by the tug-o-war final. The threepence programme gives no further details of events, but interested parties could contact the team manager, Vernon Bell, for his address was given.

Both of these karate demonstrations went well, and Bell received letters from a Superintendent of the Essex County Constabulary and the secretary of the B.D.V. – Raleigh Athletic and Social Club, noting: "Thank you and your colleagues for a very fine performance which the karate team gave in the centre ring," and, "We were very pleased with the demonstration that you staged ... [and] sincere thanks for a very interesting and unusual display," respectively. The BKF performed another demonstration for the Harlow Divisional Sports Club the following year, and received a letter from the honorary treasurer, Inspector H.N. King, on the 30th March 1960, who commented upon, "The first class display" that Bell and the BKF had given.

With regards to the St. Mary's *dojo*, Upminster, Bell noted to Plee in his 13th June 1958, letter that, "The beginners course [already referred to] finishes on the 29th June 1958, with gradings after six months, and all but one is still there."

According to the BKF grading register, the above grading was held on the 28th June 1958, (but this may be inaccurate – see below), at the St. Mary's *dojo*. It was the first of many karate gradings to be held there. Bell promoted the following students: 5th kyu (from novice) – J. Sen, H. Rayner, J. Russell and R. Armstrong; 6th kyu – P. Conlon. Other students recorded in the BKF grading register on that date were: A. Pearson, P. Clarke and F. Fox, but no new grades are recorded, so one must assume that they failed.

In a letter to Plee dated the 13th July 1958, already referred to, Bell wrote: "The BKF held an official grading on Sunday, 29th June 1958, at the completion of the first six months beginners course. After a three-hour examination of the seven [there were actually eight] out of the ten who finished the course, four were graded to 5th kyu and one to 6th kyu. Each man had to demonstrate (a) preparatory exercises with the class for three minutes, (b) eight techniques of *kento*, eight techniques of *shuto*, eight techniques of *hiji-ate*, five techniques of *ashi-waza*, (c) 1st *kata* – attack, 1st *kata* attack and defence with partner, first slowly and then quickly, plus conventional *kumite*, free *kumite* with brown-belts and five one-minute *shiai* each. We think the standard was good and the results well merited."

In a most important letter to Plee, dated the 13th June 1958, Bell mentions the very first *dojo* in Great Britain specifically hired for the purpose of teaching karate and that had, to the best of everyone's knowledge, no previous martial arts heritage. Bell noted that: "We are opening our first London *dojo* situated at 42, Kenton Street, Russell Square, London, WC1. *Dojo* hours are 10.30 a.m. to 1 p.m. every Sunday, beginning 13th July 1958, and we hope this new *dojo* will greatly facilitate the spread of karate in London and the provinces, for many more people can then visit us. We still have our country *dojo* in Upminster." Bell had in fact been looking for such a *dojo* for some time. In a letter to Plee dated the 2nd June 1958, already alluded to, Bell

Members of the BKF Wheatsheaf *dojo*. From left to right, standing: Armstrong, Musgrove, O'Connor, Revill, P. Clarke; kneeling, from left to right: Sen, Hughes, Bell, Raynor, Fox – 1958.

wrote: "We hope to have a London *dojo* very soon, but it has been very difficult to negotiate for the cost is high..." Bell noted that the BKF would be pleased to welcome any French *karateka* to the *dojo* who may be in the country, but none ever came.

This pioneering London *dojo* was the Wheatsheaf pub. Vernon Bell recalled: "It was a family *dojo*. Of the twenty or so members that we had there, all knew each other well. There was a happy atmosphere, very personal – a nice *dojo*. Everyone threw themselves into learning the noble art of Karate-do. There was a piano in one corner and we had to remove all the chairs and tables to one side before we could start, and we had to replace them after training because Christian Scientists used to meet there. Ballet was also taught above the pub. We practised on old, smooth, pink and white lino, on a wooden floor. We'd look out onto the street below, from the first floor, and we could see the people passing by and they all heard the bangs, thuds, *kiai*, and so on. We used to laugh our heads off because this had never been done in England before, never before had people heard *kiai* walking along a London street. As I recall, we trained two evenings a week there and Saturday afternoons [though Sunday is mentioned above]. I remember

Breathing practice at the Wheatsheaf *dojo* – 1958

Raynor demonstrating a kick on Musgrove at the Wheatsheaf *dojo* – 1958

in particular Armstrong, Sen, Pearson, Russell, Revill, Rayner and Clarke."

Information on Armstrong, Clarke, Conlon, McCarthy, Pearson, Rayner, Revill, Russell and Sen has already been given, when they joined

Mae-geri practice at the Wheatsheaf *dojo* – 1958

Side-kick practice at the Wheatsheaf *dojo* – 1958

the St. Mary's *dojo* in January 1958. Other students who trained at the Wheatsheaf, for whom information at the time is available, were: Francis Fox, a thirty-three-year-old of unknown occupation, who also had an interest in sports, including hiking; Clifford Musgrove, a thirty-six-year-old waiter who applied to join the BKF on the 1st June 1958; Gordon Izzard, a twenty-four-year-old labourer who applied for BKF membership on the 4th September 1958; Keith Richardson, a twenty-two-year-old car salesman with an interest in judo, who applied for BKF membership on the 16th October 1959; and John Lydon, a thirty-one-year-old coach painter who applied to join the BKF on the 14th April 1960.

Terry Wingrove remembered Reginald Armstrong as a, "very capable *karateka*. One of the things I recall about him, apart from the fact that he was outwardly a milkman, but in reality was in the [Territorial] SAS – he had to take a job where he could get straight away when called – was the tattoo he had on his right forearm of a man punching a *makiwara*. You always saw this tattoo when he blocked *ude-uke* or *uchi-uke*."

Bell continued: "Joe Sen was the only Chinese we ever had who couldn't speak a word of Chinese." The parting between Sen and Bell a year later was unfortunate and rather acrimonious to say the least, judging by the correspondence. But an interesting quote of how Bell saw his position and responsibility to the development of karate in Great Britain is given in a letter to Sen dated the 23rd July 1959, in reply to a letter sent by Sen on the 21st July. Bell wrote: "As founder of karate in this country, I am personally liable and responsible for everything that happens and develops in Britain for this art, and it is my sole duty, both to the Yoseikan, to the EKU and our own Federation to do everything in my power to see that karate is run and taught properly and only to responsible and loyal supporters of these bodies."

"Revill was in the paratroopers," Bell recalled, "and he came to us to learn karate for his para training. He drowned himself in the Serpentine, Hyde Park. He committed suicide because of a broken heart from a love affair. [His death was reported in the *News of the World* newspaper (21.9.58). Curiously, one might say, he was found dead wearing swimming trunks]. Rayner was the most beautiful stylist we had at the Wheatsheaf *dojo*. He perfected every movement. He emigrated to Australia and we lost touch with him. Then there was the best looking bloke of the lot, six foot tall with black curly hair. I can't remember his name. Then there was old Fox, an Italian waiter, with a big white face. He was so nervous you daren't look at him. Then there was Gibson, the butler – strange fellow. He would come into the *dojo* and wouldn't speak to anyone except me. He would only speak to me. 'You are my *sensei*,' he'd say, 'I'll tell you anything.' He told me about losing his lodgings, how he hadn't got any money. One evening we had a whip round, half-a-crown each, to help him pay his next week's rent. He had a cast in one eye and was about forty years old. He was a lovely man, totally honest. Then we had the chap who never bought a *gi*. He was the tallest bloke

P. Clarke and Raynor sparring at the Wheatsheaf *dojo* – 1958

in the class, and he always practised stripped to the waist. He had two very great nipples with hairs on them and all the blokes used to tweak these for him. He had these little pair of white trousers, which he had borrowed from a friend, a chef, who he brought up, but who would never train. This friend would just sit and watch every time. These were the principal students at that *dojo* and I can see their faces now. There am I in the front in my black *gi*. We're doing *mae-geri*, then a swinging kick, and then *yoko-geri*. The room was so small that twelve blokes training were enough. The lino was all torn up and I allowed them to train in slippers sometimes. They were the keenest students I ever had I think, and I remember this *dojo* the clearest. We practised the *ippon kata*, which they practised in France – one attack, one defence, done on both sides in four seconds. The first attack is an *oi-zuki* to the face, parried with a *jodan uchi-uke*, followed by a sweeping *gedan keri* to the ankle region. Well, if you do it too hard you can sweep both your opponent's feet from under him. The sole of your foot sweeps the inside of the ankle. I had to tell these students to always cut their toe nails before practice and take the bunions from underneath the feet otherwise they'd scar. The Japanese, when practising this kick, trained against a concrete pillar. If they had done the technique to anyone they'd have taken all the skin and muscle away from the ankle – that is actually true. This had to be performed in four seconds, attack and defence on both sides if you can imagine this! To get your black-belt you had to do three

Shuto-uchi practice at the Wheatsheaf *dojo* – 1958

Punching practice at the Wheatsheaf *dojo* – 1958

Empi practice at the Wheatsheaf *dojo* – 1958

Kicking practice at the Wheatsheaf *dojo* – 1958

of these *kata* plus two *sanbon kata* – three advances and what they used to call a parade – and the last one you did whatever counter you wanted to. You also had to know the five *Heian*, or *Pinan* as we called them then, to show their Chinese origin. But we didn't think about gradings in those days. We just enjoyed each other's company. We had a lot of

Bell leads *Mae-geri* practice at the Wheatsheaf *dojo* – 1958

fun with good discipline in a confined area. Downstairs the customers were sipping their drinks and the ceiling would vibrate to our movements upstairs. The landlord of the Wheatsheaf was always joking with us. I remember his great round face. 'You blokes aren't sitting on the pot upstairs are you. You're just jumping around kicking the hell out of each other. What you see in all this sort of thing I don't know. You must be Japanese orientated. Bring your blokes downstairs and we'll get you a round of drinks.' We'd all go down to the bar afterwards and sit and talk about what we'd been doing, how it was done in Japan, how it came here, what they were going to do when they got their black-belts, and so on. It was a happy family-type time, which has never existed in any other *dojo* I've ever known in the last fifty years. I can honestly say that."

On the 18th February 1964, Monty Russell contacted Bell again requesting a meeting, and noting how he missed the old times. Bell replied on the 7th May 1964, the delay being due to Russell's letter going to Bell's former address. This letter is interesting because Bell wrote: "We have got a very strong karate movement going now and have some very fine exponents, but I still feel that the present-day ones are nowhere near as keen or devoted as the older ones in your time."

It was at the Wheatsheaf that black *gi* were worn for the first time. The purpose of this was, as Bell explained, "To show that we weren't *judoka*." In the last page of the letter to Plee of the 13th June 1958, Bell wrote of his decision. "The BKF have decided to adopt the new Japanese style *keikogi* in black and our suppliers are already manufacturing several of these, and we now have our regular firm who supply all our needs."

Bell noted to Plee in his letter of the 13th June 1958, that, "The BKF has many large displays during this summer, both in London and the provinces and we now do a set programme for all these displays ... We also hope to appear on television again shortly [they didn't], for with our London *dojo* we can progress rapidly."

PART III

etters between Plee, Bell and Putnam's continued. In a letter of the 25th July 1958, from Rome, where Plee was holidaying, Plee wrote that the Italian version of the *ABC of Karate* had been prepared, and the title was to be, *First Karate Manual by 'l'image'* (to use Plee's own words). Plee noted that, "I suggest you change the title too because with so many photos it is not an ABC but a basic manual."

Replying to Plee's Rome letter on the 12th August 1958, Bell proposed the English edition be titled, *The First Basic Manual of Karate-do*.

Information concerning a demonstration that Bell and his students gave at the Seventh Annual Rosicrucian Rally at the Victoria Halls, Bloomsbury Square, London, WC1, on Saturday 6th September 1958, at 9.15 p.m., provides us, for the first time, with the BKF display format that Bell had noted to Plee in his letter of the 13th June that year. Under the heading of, "Karate and Karate-Do – Demonstration by members of the British Karate Federation," the following took place:

A. 1) Preparatory group exercises under V.C. Bell (1st Dan)
    2) *Araku* (walk) – *Gedan Barai* (guard) *Judanka* (stance) *Gedanka* (stance) under T.Guilfoyle (3rd kyu)
B. Breaking of wood with naked hands to show blow power – V. Bell
C. Toughening exercise on the *makiwara*
D. Techniques of *Kento* (fist)   J. Russell   (5th kyu)
E. Techniques of *Shuto* (hand-sabre)   J. Sen   (5th kyu)
F. Techniques of *Hiji-ate* (elbow)   M. Manning   (3rd kyu)
G. Techniques of *Ashi-waza* (foot)   T. Guilfoyle   (3rd kyu)
H. *Kata* (basics of Karate-Do) being formal attack-defence on both sides.
    1) 1st *kata* (2 hand 2 foot techniques) – J. Sen & H. Rayner (5th kyu)
    2) 2nd *kata* (2 hand 2 foot techniques)
    3) 3rd *kata* (2 hand 2 foot techniques) – M. Manning and
    4) 4th *kata* (2 hand 2 combined techniques) -T. Guilfoyle (3rd kyu)

    5) 5th *kata* (2 hand 2 combined techniques)
I. Combination techniques – M. Manning, T. Guilfoyle.
    (being 8 combative tactical movements for contest).
J. *Kumi-te* – (Conventional) – J. Sen, H. Rayner.
                (practice of certain movements for specialisation of techniques).

K. *Kumi-te* – (Free) – J. Russell (5th kyu); P. Conlon (6th kyu).
(Informal practice to develop skill of attack-defence under combat conditions).

L. *Kumi-te* – (*Shiai*) contest: R. Armstrong (5th kyu) H. Rayner (5th kyu).

M. *Kumi-te* – (*Shiai*) 1 man v the rest – T. Guilfoyle (3rd kyu) takes on rest of team half-minute each.

N. Karate Self-Defence (being techniques against common assaults) V. Bell (1st Dan).

On the back of the programme, the usual pronouncement that the karate was official, and so on, was given. In a letter to Plee, dated the 29th September 1958, Bell noted that this display "was much appreciated."

The Victoria Halls demonstration was the last karate display that Trevor Guilfoyle ever took part in for the BKF. In a letter to Bell dated the 29th August 1958, Guilfoyle wrote: "I wish to tender my temporary resignation for the approximate period of two years owing to my call up for services in HM Forces as from 1st September 1958."

Bell recalled: "Guilfoyle went and joined the SAS and we never heard from him again, never again. He disappeared from the face of the earth and I believe he is dead. His resignation from the BKF was temporary. He was so good, so keen, so strong. He would have come back, or at least he would have let us know that he wasn't coming back. No, he's dead all right, but I wish I knew what happened to him. All we've got is the memory and the photographs. British karate really lost somebody the day he died."

A week later, on Saturday, 13th September 1958, Bell and his students were in Nottingham giving yet another demonstration at the Co-Operative Arts Centre in George Street. It was the Annual East Midlands Strength and Physique Show, and the sixpenny programme showed that events commenced at 7 p.m. For an admission fee of 7s. 6d., 5s. or 3s., one could see fifteen events, of which the karate display was the second. The advertising poster stated, "Display of Karate and Karate-Do – Deadly System of Japanese Self-Defence Arranged by V.C.F. Bell, *Shodan* in Karate-Do of Yoseikan of Japan, National Coach BKF." The general events were much the same as for other such exhibitions: posing, muscle routines, strength displays and so on, and specific details will not be given here. The karate demonstration given was identical to the one presented at the Victoria Halls. In a letter to Plee, dated the 29th September 1958, Bell noted that the display "went down very well and gave us good publicity."

Contracts were sent to Plee by Bell, who readers may recall was acting as his agent, for a modest percentage, concerning the *ABC of*

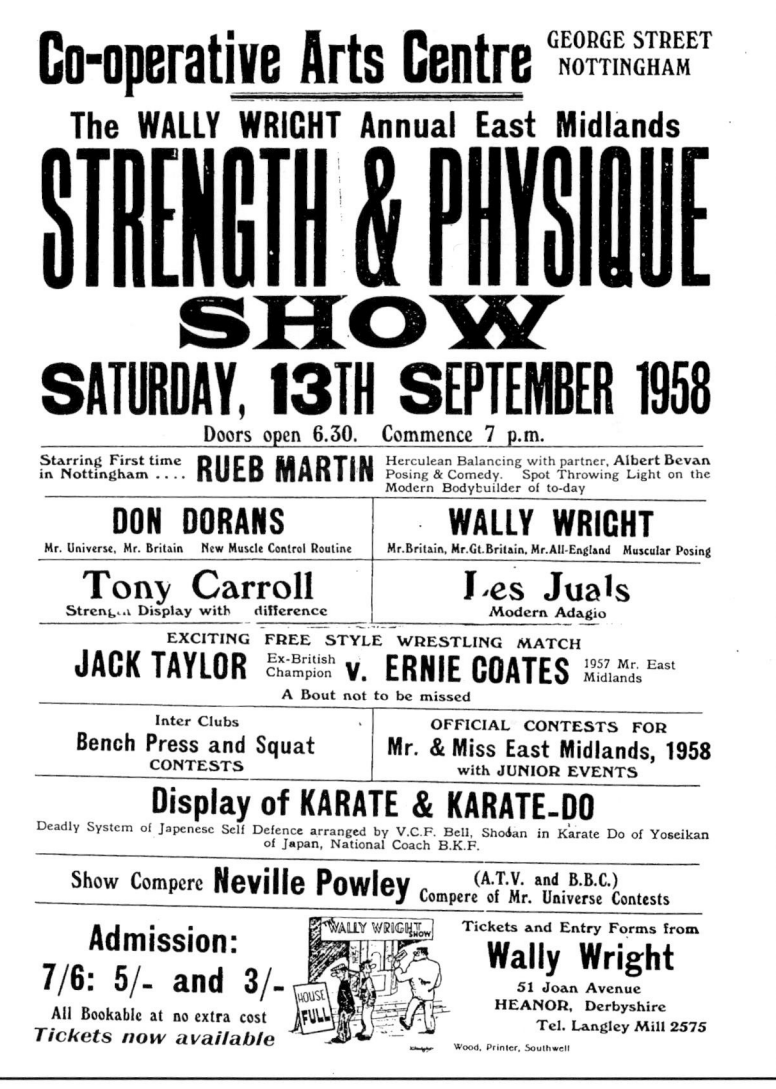

A Strength and Physique Show poster featuring a BKF demonstration – 1958

Karate-do, on the 13th September 1958 – though other contracts were sent later, and it wasn't until 29th September that Bell wrote to Plee noting, "I am very pleased to tell you that Messrs. Putnam and Company have confirmed officially that they accept your book for publication." At Putnam's, a Mr. Brown was in charge of the book. The book's translation had been re-typed and checked. Brown informed Bell that the book would be distributed in Canada, USA, Australia and New Zealand, Hong Kong, Singapore, Malaya, India, Ceylon, Pakistan, Burma, South Africa, West Indies and other Commonwealth countries and colonies. In this letter, Bell noted that, "I am pleased to say there has been no more news or developments from Foulsham's or Harrison regarding the proposed publication of Lasserre's book on karate, and it has probably been forgotten."

Bell's letter of the 13th September 1958 is interesting for some other historical points, and vital for another. Firstly, Bell noted that, "The karate movement in Britain is still progressing well, though fairly static. We have lost three men to the Armed Forces, one is deceased, one is marrying and one has left the district, and at present we have only ten active members. We are holding a grading on the 21st December 1958, when five expect to get their orange and three their white-belts." The vital information referred to above comes as a postscript. On the August course Plee had shown a Japanese karate film and Bell wanted to purchase a copy. The postscript read: "Can you give me the address of the Japanese Karate Association in Tokyo." It is the first time the JKA is mentioned in Bell's correspondence.

The next important demonstration was much further afield at the Colston Hall in Bristol. The Western Amateur Judo Association held the Western Counties Individual Judo Championships and Display on Saturday, 4th October 1958, commencing at 7.30 p.m. Of the eighteen items on the programme "Karate and Karate-Do" was listed eleventh, after the inter-club team contest semi-finals, and once again followed on from a break – this time of fifteen minutes duration. The demonstration was the now familiar format, but included two notable additions. Five *kata* were shown including, "1st *Pinan* (*Shodan*) *kata* (23 moves), a *kata* of tactical combat against seven imaginary assailants in turn," and proceedings concluded with Vernon Bell taking on the four-man team for half a minute each.

It is also worthy of note that Vernon Bell gave two other demonstrations at the same event. The first was in ju-jitsu with M. Manning (Vernon Bell was Chairman and Senior Coach to the British Jujutsu Association), and the second in aikido, with three assistants (Bell was Founder and National Coach to the British Association of Aikido). Once again the display given was identical to the Victoria Halls demonstration, though Trevor Guilfoyle was no longer named of course, and Bell had taken his place. There was also some minor switching of roles.

Despite the fact that Putnam's had apparently accepted Plee's book, at least as far as Bell was concerned, a letter from a John Buchanan-Smith of the 15th October, shows that there were still problems concerning the translation of the book, and who would pay for it.

Bell wrote to Plee on the 16th October and informed him of this. However, this letter is important because it provides the reader with some further interesting historical facts. Bell wrote: "I was pleased to receive the printed notepaper of the International Karate Federation, upon which you wrote your letter, but I am very disappointed to note that Great Britain is not included in the list of countries printed at the bottom of the notepaper. I am very surprised at this omission and wonder why you have left my country out, especially as we are third in the International Federation, next to Japan and France, and are the second country to start karate in Europe after France. Will you please correct this and include Great Britain in all other printed notepapers, as this error can cause much inconvenience and wrong thinking by people who see the notepaper and it will not do our BKF much good."

Plee replied to Bell's letter two days later and wrote, "A terrible omission..." Readers might like to know that the countries listed at the bottom of the said notepaper were, in order: Japan, France, Germany, Italy, Switzerland, Canada, Belgium, Portugal, Tunisia, Morocco, USA, Spain, Panama, Uruguay and Argentina.

Further interesting facts emerge from Bell's letter of the 16th October 1958. Bell wrote: "I enclose a copy of a letter I sent last week to Mr. C. Michelmore, Producer of the BBC television programme, *To-Night*, which is shown every evening at 6.45 p.m., for three-quarters of an hour and is a topical programme of news from all parts of the world. On the 8th October last, a Japanese film taken in Tokyo was shown for three minutes showing many Japanese karate black-belts practising in an Instructors class in a *dojo* in Tokyo. The film showed the BBC commentator, Mr. A. Whicker, in this *dojo* giving an account of karate as different from judo, and this Mr. Whicker interviewed a Welshman, who was practising in this *dojo*, and who demonstrated exercises on the *makiwara*. Mister Whicker is travelling throughout Japan making films for the BBC on Japanese culture and customs. This Welshman's name was not mentioned, but he comes from Cardiff, and he stated on the film that he was a judo black-belt studying at the Kodokan on a two year course for the British Judo Association and was visiting this karate *dojo* to practice. Mister Whicker asked him about karate in Britain, and this Welshman said that karate was unknown in Britain and there was no karate in Great Britain at the moment and that he may be starting it when he returns from Japan. To my mind this action by the Welshman is complete sabotage ... [the next part of the sentence makes little sense] and may cause much embarrassment to the BKF. I have written to the BBC for an explanation and my letter is enclosed herewith, but I have as yet had no reply. I intend to write to the Yoseikan about this matter requesting their advice, but meanwhile perhaps you can tell me what *dojo* in Tokyo this film was taken at and would [you] approach the Yoseikan on behalf of the BKF to investigate this false statement. Hence you can see how urgent it is for the name of Great Britain to be included on your notepaper, for the sake of the karate movement. I would like your immediate advice on the matter and the course of action you think I should take. When you reply please send me the name and address of the Japanese Karate Association in Tokyo..."

The President of the French Karate Federation, E. Sirvent, wrote to Bell on the 20th November 1958, informing him that the next grading for black-belts, including a competition test, would be held on Thursday, 27th November 1958, at 7.30 p.m. at the Karate-Do Kwai of Hoang Nam, at 12 rue Pestalozzi, Paris. An instructors' meeting was to follow between 9.00 p.m. and about midnight, to establish refereeing rules for national and international competitions. The letter also notified Bell of the National Karate Tournament, to be held in the police headquarters in the rue du Gabon (same location as for 1957) on Monday, 15th December, and invited competitors. It is perhaps interesting to note that in this competition, competitors would be required to wear body and chin protectors.

Plee wrote to Bell on the 12th December 1958 – any intervening letters have been lost. Plee noted: "About the Lasserre book, I can not tell you 'all' information, because 'one' has asked me to keep secret, but I can tell that the book will not be published..." No doubt this came as a great relief to Bell at the time, but a great shame for future karate historians – in a sense! *The Manual of Karate*, by E. J. Harrison, was however published by W. Foulsham and Company Limited in 1959, thus becoming the first karate book ever to be published in England, predating the first edition of the famous American Shotokan publication by Hidetaka Nishiyama and Richard C. Brown, *Karate: The Art of 'Empty-Hand' Fighting*, by one year. The Director of Foulsham's, Mr. S. Belasco, noted in a letter to Bell, dated the 15th March, 1960, that, "*The Manual of Karate* is a good book, but it is not selling all that fast and we are wondering whether or not the judo enthusiasts are ready for this new approach to the science." Of course E. J. Harrison was a *judoka*, a 4th Dan, and had, by his own admission, "limited knowledge of karate culled from printed and oral testimony" (Preface to *The Manual of Karate*). The book was based on two previous Japanese publications – *Karate-Do Nyumon* ('Introduction to the Way of Karate') a book sponsored by the Society for Study of Japanese Karate (not to be confused with Gichin Funakoshi's book of the same title), and to a lesser extent Reikichi Oya's, *Karate no Naraikata* ('Methods of Study of Karate'). *The Manual of Karate* became a famous book. It was reprinted and revised, with the last edition appearing, the author believes, in 1974. There are still a few copies available for those prepared to search, and the author will not go into this book further, except to mention one notable quote that Harrison makes in its preface. Harrison wrote that, "Perhaps the operation of "vested interest" will interpose an insuperable obstacle to the eventual integration of both these arts [karate and Judo], which I have reason to believe the followers of karate, both Japanese and non-Japanese, regard as a consummation 'devoutly to be wished.'" It is, in the author's mind, an extraordinary statement. Yes, "vested interest" was undoubtedly present, but the thought that judo and karate could somehow merge seems baffling today. It would no doubt have seemed baffling in 1959 too, had Harrison actually ever practised karate.

The end of 1958 saw another demonstration at the Ilford Baths. The Ilford Gymnastic Club had organised an "All-Star Christmas Carnival of Sport" on the 18th December with activities commencing at 2.30 p.m. The karate display was on at 2.50 p.m. and lasted fifteen minutes and followed the usual format given earlier. The display, in the Grand Centre Ring, followed on immediately after the march of the Band of the 1st Battalion The Queen's Own Cameron Highlanders, and was followed by Scarri the trick and comedy cyclist. Unfortunately, the show ran half-an-hour late, and the karate demonstration was shortened. The BKF was often paid fees and expenses for these demonstrations. The honorary secretary of the IGC, a Mr. K. Popplewell, wrote to Bell on the 3rd January 1959, noting, "our most grateful thanks to you and your team for putting on such a wonderful act of karate and jujutsu at our show. I am sure everyone enjoyed your demonstrations, I for one did." A fee of £7, no small amount, was paid to the BKF for this display.

One demonstration that Vernon Bell and members of the BKF gave in Scarborough was notable in that it introduced the north-east of England to karate (this is particularly relevant to this book). The Scarborough Ippon Judo and Boxing Club presented, for the first time, a series of displays and "sporting contests." The venue was the Gaiety Theatre, Aberdeen Walk, and was scheduled to start at 7 p.m., on Thursday, 22nd January 1959. Tickets cost ten shillings for ringside, and then six

First indoor public demonstration of karate – Ilford Public Baths, 1958

First indoor public demonstration of karate – Ilford Public Baths, 1958

shillings, four shillings and two shillings, depending on one's seat. The souvenir programme, priced at one shilling, noted the order of events. Boxing opened proceedings and there were five bouts with some good boxers mostly from the north-east, but Toma Hansom, the Tripolitania and North African Champion was also there, fighting Don Robinson, an ex-R.A.F and Yorkshire Champion. Then followed item six, "Japanese

First indoor public demonstration of karate – Ilford Public Baths, 1958

First indoor public demonstration of karate – Ilford Public Baths, 1958

Boxing and Karate – V. Bell assisted by R. Armstrong (4th kyu) and J. Trotter (3rd kyu)." (The posters advertising the karate had included the caption, "As seen on T.V."). Then followed Leeds man "Reg Park – World's Best Developed Man," a Mr. Universe, Mr. World and a Mr. Europe, who gave a demonstration of body culture. An interval followed and then there were a series of judo displays and contests.

On the 4th February 1959, Bell wrote to Plee and mentioned this display. Bell wrote: "On January 24th [which is an incorrect date], I took three pupils two hundred and fifty miles to north-east England to give a fifteen minute karate exhibition at Scarborough at the North-East Judo Championships of the AJA. It was a great success and we had much praise." In this letter Bell met two *judoka* who planned to go to Paris to learn karate and, under a president with influence, start a rival karate federation when they returned after studying for one month! Bell wrote: "This is all very hard for our karate Federation, Mr. Plee, and must be stopped ...we do not want karate to get like judo in Britain with about six associations. The BKF has done much hard work to popularise karate in Britain, and we do not want a lot of untrained and unqualified people to interfere with our karate movement." Bell requested that Plee have nothing to do with these gentlemen, but asked him to pass them on to the BKF. Bell continued: "I ask you to do this as my friend and as my tutor for the sake of British karate." Bell further noted that: "I have had requests from all over England for karate knowledge ... even the BJA have sent enquiries. We are going to circularise all British Judo clubs to encourage friendly co-existence." Also in this letter Bell mentioned that, "Kenshiro Abbe no longer teaches karate."

In a letter to Plee dated the 4th March 1959, Bell made it quite obvious that he was going to make the most of the publication of Harrison's book. Bell wrote: "I am drafting out a long circular about British karate and sending it to over five hundred judo clubs in Great Britain and will use the publicity from Harrison's book for our own good." This letter is also interesting for the following: "As karate is growing quickly now in Britain, and will [do] more so after publication of the Harrison book, it would do a great deal of good for the BKF if you would see your way clear to grant my promotion to 2nd Dan in karate, for I could then grade my own pupils to 1st Dan."

The contract on the *ABC of Karate* was finally signed, and the agreement between Putnam and Plee was dated 23rd December 1958. It was hoped to actually publish the book in the autumn of 1959, but other problems seemingly arose and the book was actually never published in England, at least to the author's knowledge. However, in 1962 Foulsham's did publish Plee's, *Karate by Pictures*, which was, '*The Science of Self-Defence by the Empty-Hand Lucidly Explained and Illustrated.*' It is a most interesting book from the historical perspective, and the photographs, mostly of Plee and his students, are mainly taken in Plee's Paris *dojo*. There are additionally some equally fascinating photographs of Japanese. At the left-hand side of the yellow front cover, for example, a black and white photograph shows an unknown Japanese performing a vicious *jodan mawashi-geri*, whilst the back cover shows the same Japanese *karateka* performing a *yoko-tobi-geri*. Noting the pioneer nature of the book really, Plee, in the preface to *Karate by Pictures* wrote that: "You must consider the documents which follow as a basis given in a friendly way, so as to help you, by men [and a woman actually] who are making progress but who do not pretend to be perfect." The subjects for the photographs in the book were Messrs. Loi, Morgand, and Chouk, all 1st Dan; and, Messrs. Maquin and Szpirglas, who were 2nd Dan. Plee at the time was 3rd Dan, and the woman, Mrs. Delmas, a 1st Dan. All these *karateka* were known to Bell. There is also one other particularly relevant quote from *Karate by Pictures*. Plee wrote that, "statistics indicate that in karate circles there are about 20% former *judokas*, the other 80% being in the proportion of 50% having never practised any other combat sport, 15% former boxers (English or French boxing), the rest belonging to other sports (wrestling, athletics, rowing, etc.)." The grading system operating in France at that time was, with practice periods in parentheses: 8th kyu to 4th kyu, white belt with red thread (3 to 6 months); 3rd kyu to 1st kyu, brown belt with red thread (1 to 2 years); 1st Dan (2 to 3 years), 2nd Dan (4 to 7 years), 3rd Dan (5 to 10 years), 4th Dan (10 to 20 years). All black belts were with red thread. 5th Dan was "exceptional." Plee at the time was Technical Director of the Karate Section of the French Federation of Judo and of the European Karate Union. Later of course, in 1967, a date beyond the confines of this project, Plee's, *Karate: Beginner to Black-Belt*, appeared in English, and that too was to become famous.

One would have thought that everything would have been fine at the end of 1958, and that all the effort and hard work put in by Plee and Bell would have strengthened their relationship, but things went badly wrong. Bell was acting as Plee's agent for the book, and problems arose over a cheque of Plee's, from Putnam, that Bell was supposedly having trouble disposing of. Things became really rather unpleasant, not just on this issue, which involved politics, but at a personal level as well, as letters dated March 1959, clearly show. These letters actually make rather depressing, not to say sad reading, with one party being particularly accusative, and nothing really would be gained, other than a bit of sensationalism, from quoting from them. Let us leave it at this moment, and simply say that two honourable gentlemen disagreed. The last piece of correspondence the author has between the two men was a letter Bell wrote on the 3rd June 1959, where he noted that, "I am prepared to

First European Karate Union meeting in Paris under Master Murakami – 1958/ 59. Vernon Bell is seated on Murakami's left.

forget this unpleasantness and continue as before on good business and personal relationships," but Bell never saw or spoke to Plee again.

Side-stepping the above problems, some interesting historical material does materialise from the early 1959 letters. For example, in a hand-written note to Bell dated the 17th February 1959, Plee mentions that, "... Mr. Nam ... has formed his own Federation to receive funds from the Vietnamese Embassy. We are [the author believes the next word is "united"] to exclude it and expulse [expel him?] from France." In the same note Plee also mentioned that, "Mr. Murakami is gone – contract is finished." However, Murakami was to reside in France for many years to come, teaching karate widely in Europe, as was Hoang Nam.

The end of 1958 saw Bell take another grading in the grounds of his parents home in Hornchurch. The BKF grading register for the 28th December 1958 shows that R. Armstrong, H. Rayner, J. Russell and J. Sen were all promoted to 4th kyu; P. Conlon, F. Fox and E. Hughes graded to 5th kyu, and P. Clarke to 6th kyu. Prior to this grading, Bell had failed G. Izzard, on the 4th September 1958, at Hornchurch.

Although Bell had hoped for reconciliation with Plee, the cord had been broken, and things could never be the same again. On the 25th

June 1959, Bell made an important decision and wrote to Master Minoru Mochizuki, President of the Yoseikan. Bell noted: "It gives me great pleasure to write this letter since this is the first direct letter by me on behalf of the BKF to our parent organisation, but I wish this to be the first of a long and pleasant correspondence. Since the rather shaky position at present of the European Karate Union ... the karate movement both in England and Europe is at a cross-roads and there is much interference in this country from unauthorised bodies and judo organizations..." Bell then continued by explaining the difficulties he had encountered with the French Federation. Bell wrote: "Therefore, the BKF Committee and myself have decided that the only way to save the karate movement in this country and to consolidate it, after four years of hard work and sacrifice to establish it ... is for our Federation to have a personal, close and direct liaison with yourself and the Yoseikan. We would like your advice and help on every karate matter, so that the BKF will always take the right step on every karate decision. Firstly, I would like your own official recognition to be recommended in respect of myself (on behalf of the BKF) to be the official Yoseikan representative in this country, and will be grateful for an official letter of authority from you in this respect ... Secondly, I would like official recognition and authority of the Yoseikan for me to grade for the BKF and for the Yoseikan to recognise, accept and register direct all such BKF gradings. Thirdly, for the Yoseikan to issue official grading cards both to myself and BKF members, and any other such documents as may be necessary, especially licences, badges etc."

In the above letter of the 25th June 1959, Bell also mentioned an official Yoseikan Instructional film. This film does indeed exist, but it isn't of Yoseikan karate, but JKA karate, details of which have been given earlier in this book.

Also mentioned is the possibility of setting up a new European Karate Union with Jurgen Seydel of the German Karate Federation. Bell noted that this new union would be, "free from monopoly, prejudice or domination of any one Federation." Bell had had Mochizuki's book, *My System of Aikido*, translated by Ernest Hughes, who readers may recall started training a year earlier, and requested Mochizuki's permission to get this book published in Great Britain, for which Bell would act as agent. Bell noted that he was the agent for Plee's *ABC of Karate-Do*.

Although the author will jump ahead of events slightly, it is least confusing to deal with the limited Bell/Mochizuki correspondence now, as one unit, over some eight months.

The red Yoseikan badge worn by early Shotokan practitioners in Great Britain

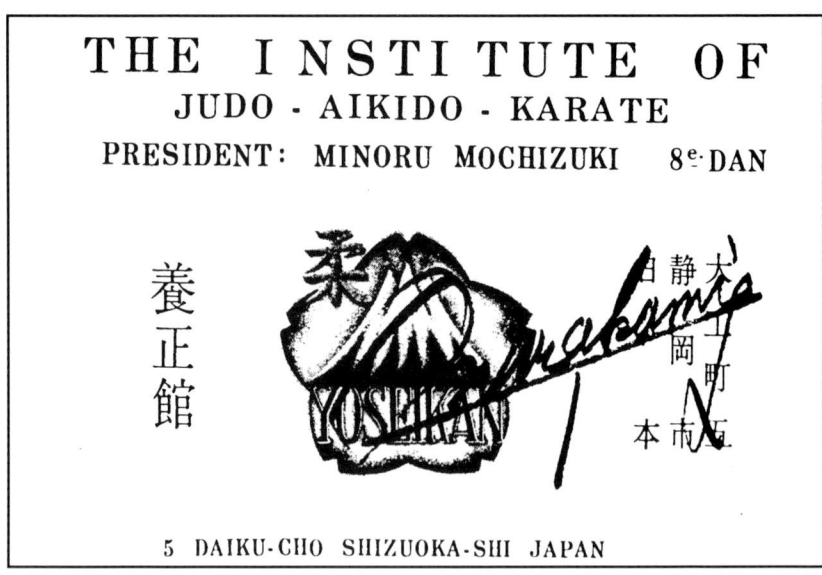

Vernon Bell's Yoseikan licence

柔　道　合　気　道　唐　　手 JUDO·AIKIDO·KARATE		
段　　　級 GRADING	日　時 DATE	教　　師 TEACHER
GOKYU 5 ᵉˑDEGRÉ		
YONKYU 4 ᵉˑDEGRÉ		
SANKYU 3 ᵉˑDEGRÉ		
NIKYU 2 ᵉˑDEGRÉ		
IKKYU 1 ᵉˑDEGRÉ		
SHODAN 1 ᵉˑDAN	1/14/57	村上哲次
NIDAN 2 ᵉˑDAN	19/7/59	村上哲次
SANDAN 3 ᵉˑ DAN		
YONDAN 4 ᵉˑDAN		
GODAN 5 ᵉˑ DAN		

Vernon Bell's Yoseikan licence

Master Minoru Mochizuki replied to Bell's letter on the 27th August 1959. It is a most interesting letter in that Mochizuki had some considerable sympathy, to say the least, with Bell's position. Mochizuki noted: "First of all I agree gladly with your plan that you and your group are going to make the development of karate and aikido hand in hand with Yoseikan. And so, if you recommend somebody's degree (Dan), I will send you his licence." Master Mochizuki also allowed Bell to progress with his book's publication, though he noted a number of mistakes in the French translation, and that he was researching additional points. Mochizuki also recommended that Bell, "must take effort of inviting a nice leaders and professors of karate and aikido,"

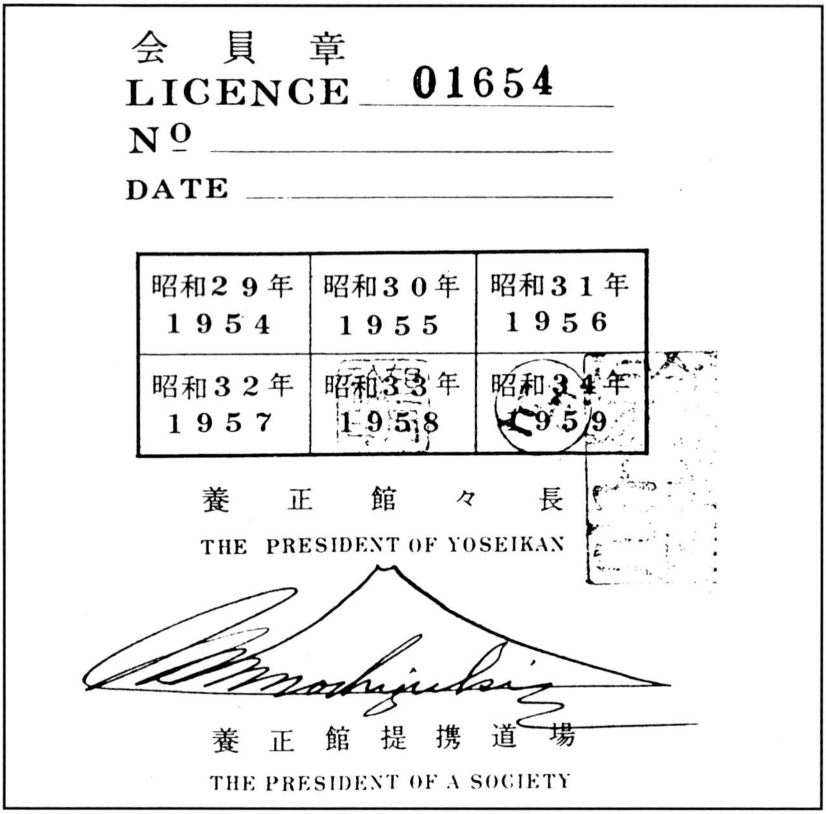

会　員　章
LICENCE　01654
Nº
DATE

昭和２９年 1954	昭和３０年 1955	昭和３１年 1956
昭和３２年 1957	昭和３３年 1958	昭和３４年 1959

養　正　館　々　長
THE PRESIDENT OF YOSEIKAN

養　正　館　提　携　道　場
THE PRESIDENT OF A SOCIETY

Vernon Bell's Yoseikan licence

noting that this had been the downfall of another martial artist known well to Bell. This letter, as in those to follow, finished with Master Mochizuki's 'Mount Fuji' signature in blue ink.

Mochizuki wrote again to Bell on the 20th September 1959, stating considerations about Bell's notion of a new European union, and financial and presentational matters dealing with the aikido book.

Bell replied to Master Mochizuki on the 10th December 1959. Apologising for the delay in replying noting that, "I have seventeen Judo clubs and five hundred pupils spread over an area of fifty miles. Also, I run a karate *dojo* with many pupils, ju-jitsu courses, many displays, gradings, and travel three hundred miles per week to many courses. I also have many Student Teacher Black-Belts to train, and am senior instructor to the County Education Authority, so you see I have much business." Well, much of this may have been so, but the author is

Vernon Bell's Yoseikan 2nd Dan karate certificate signed by Minoru Mochizuki and Tetsuji Murakami – 19th July 1959.

not sure about the "many" karate pupils! Bell continued: "I have noted all your remarks regarding liaison of our British Federation with the Yoseikan, and I confirm that this arrangement is our only concern. Neither I, nor my Federation have business now with Mr. Plee or his French Federation. Instead, we will co-operate and work directly with you and the Yoseikan. I would like you to send me a certificate of Yoseikan for my *Nidan* grade to which I was promoted by the master Murakami when he visited Britain to take our course on the 19th July 1959, at Hornchurch, whence he promoted me from *Shodan* to *Nidan*. He issued me a Yoseikan grading card for this grade and signed it. I enclose a banker's draft for five American Dollars for this diploma which [I would ask you to] please despatch as soon as possible."

Further information was provided in this letter concerning the potential publication of the aikido book, the details of which will not be gone into here for much has been written on the Plee book, and aikido is not the subject of this book. However, Mochizuki's work was not published in this country to the best of the author's knowledge, despite Bell's considerable efforts. Bell mentioned two other interesting points in this letter, which are worthy of note. Firstly, Bell wrote that he had, "recently attended a two day course in London under Mr. Tadashi Abbe

(6th Dan aikido) at the *dojo* of Mr. Kenshiro Abbe. Tadashi has now returned to Paris and Kenshiro has left England to live in Italy for good [This was not how it turned out however, for Abbe actually returned to England for some years]. This is as well, for Kenshiro Abbe has been advertising himself as 8th Dan karate..." Secondly, Bell wrote: "My pupils and I are interested in establishing a British Aikido Society affiliated to the Yoseikan. If you will permit this, will you send me a Charter to authorise its establishment and Certificate of Affiliation to the Yoseikan, and if you think fit, is it possible for you to give me Honorary 1st Dan in aikido so that I may promote aikido in Britain, having some status myself. I have studied your book closely and practice aikido every week with my pupils and have a good knowledge of your techniques in the book."

Mochizuki replied to Bell's letter on the 22nd January 1960. It is a short letter. With regards to the BKF affiliating itself to the Yoseikan, Mochizuki wrote: "Will you consult with instructors of Yoseikan who have been working in Europe such as Mr. Kondo, Mr. Sugiyama and Mr. Murakami." One very nice sentiment that Mochizuki shared with Bell is worth repeating: "I know that you are busy as I. I hope you will do the best. It is necessary to work hard when young." There was no immediate honorary *Shodan* for Bell in aikido.

Bell replied to Master Mochizuki on the 24th February 1960. It is the last letter to have survived between the two men. Bell noted that he was very disappointed that the aikido book he was attempting to get published had been turned down. However, what is interesting about this letter, is the following: "Karate in this country has fallen behind a little for aikido has become very popular and in London the Aikido Kwai has been formed by the London Judo Society under the instruction of Mr. Senta Yamada, 5th Dan aikido, who recently arrived in this country." Bell and four of his pupils had apparently been refused membership (the author will not continue with this, as it has no bearing on the subject of this book). With this letter, Bell sent all the grading cards to Japan to be stamped.

Readers may be interested to know that Bell was attempting to get other books published also. For example, Reikichi Oya's two books, *Karate-do*, which had been published in 1953, and *Karate-no-Naraikata*, first published in 1956. Much correspondence was gone into, and in Bell's case expense for translations, but not one of the book projects ever materialised in English – at least to the author's knowledge. Bell was also thinking of having the *kata* from Gichin Funakoshi's *Karate-do Kyoha*n translated, but that also never materialised.

During this period, an important and influential student in the history of British Shotokan started his karate training – Terry Wingrove. Terence Stanley Victor Wingrove was born on the 8th May 1941, and at the time of his application to the BKF on the 3rd July 1959, he was living in Southgate, London N14. His occupation was an apprentice (trainee designer) working for Cossor Radar and Electronics Limited in Harlow, Essex. He had interests in judo, cacti and chess. He was tall and slender in build and a member of the Walker Judo Club (see below) in Southgate, the Risley Judo Club and the Lynch Judo club, both in Tottenham. He recalled to the author: "I had an early interest in things oriental having seen my first martial arts demonstration, judo, when I was eight or nine. My first judo instructor was Ted Mossom in 1952. I attended the London Oratory School, which was near the Budokwai. I stopped training under Mossom and then started again under Vernon Bell in 1956. I started ju-jitsu under Bell, with Barry Shepherd, in 1956 also. After a while, Vernon Bell started to talk about karate, but you could learn it only on an invitation basis. It wasn't a case that anybody could join on application. You had to be above a certain grade in ju-jitsu or judo. You were vetted. I must say that Vernon had a very good screening process. I must say this. He did turn a lot of people down. People would come along to the *dojo* and he'd say, 'Sorry, I don't think you're suitable. Try judo or ju-jitsu.' He directed them to something that he thought would benefit them. If you were accepted, provisionally, you were invited to a karate demonstration. I first learned ju-jitsu in Vernon's parents' house with Shepherd. We could see these people outside, and by invitation we were allowed to watch a class going on. Vernon was going back and forth to Paris to see Plee; I don't know how many times he went. He'd come back with booklets, things printed by Plee, and we practised on an almost hand to mouth basis – Vernon would learn something, bring it back, and we'd practise it. Vernon said to me that I ought to do karate, and I said that I'd like to do it because I didn't have the build or strength for judo. I couldn't see it down that line and I liked the look of the karate. At that time in the class there were people like Sen, Armstrong, Revill and Rayner. Everyone at that time wore white *gi*, but Vernon came back from France after one trip with a black *gi*, and it was decided that you could wear either a white or black *gi*. In the summer of 1959, I remember, at Maybush Road, half the class would hide in the orchard at the bottom of Bell's parents' garden and the other half would try and get through to the other end without being caught, and we had to use karate techniques. There were also *makiwara* on some of the trees in the garden.

Leonard and Elsie May Bell supported and encouraged their son in his introduction of karate to Great Britain – in the garden of 12, Maybush Rd, Hornchurch (*c.* 1960).

"Vernon Bell was a good teacher and his parents encouraged him in his martial arts. He wore the Yoseikan black and red belt, which was to distinguish a karate Dan grade from a judo Dan grade. Vernon taught us mainly *ippon-kumite* and *sanbon-kumite*. Freestyle was very hit and miss, and there were no definite points. No one ever scored a point. It was attack, then counter-attack. You never saw a series of attacks. You normally saw someone parry and then just punch or kick. It was much more primitive, and had much less movement. There was also a greater emphasis on control, because we wore no boxes or protection. The atmosphere in those early days was competitive, terrifically competitive. When I first started, students would free fight on the lawn of 12, Maybush Road. It was no holds barred, and students would end up in the rose bushes. This animosity went right out of the class and lead to punch-ups out the front [of the house] and all that sort of thing. This was a point that Vernon didn't stamp on, and he should have done. He didn't stamp on it hard enough and actually encouraged it, because he thought it was giving people guts ... [two of the students, in particular, had a feud]. When Murakami came over later, he thought this was normal, and kicked you into the rose bushes. The number of people who went into those roses and got themselves cut to bits ... It was a different attitude and Vernon encouraged hard spirit. Murakami was very keen that you touched the *gi* and that he saw the movement on the *gi*. Later, at brown-belt grade, he said you should have full control, and know exactly what you can do with your fists and feet."

It may be of interest to readers to learn that the author first began his martial arts training with judo in 1960 under Terry Wingrove and Brenda Revill at Wingrove's *dojo* at Walker Primary School, Waterfall Road, Southgate, having been introduced to the art by an ex-paratrooper, Kenneth Cooper. The author remembers this early training very vividly. He would like to state that he considers what he learned then, initially as a child of seven or eight, never to have left him. The atmosphere in that small *dojo* was disciplined and correct. It was first-rate instruction for some eighteen months to two years, and it was partly that early judo that motivated the author to take up karate – the spirit had been directed. Vernon Bell visited the *dojo* many times, and Hiroo Mochizuki also taught judo there, later. The author would go so far as to say that the atmosphere of that judo training, under the auspices of the Amateur Judo Association, during those golden days of martial arts in this country, provided the inspiration for the writing of this book.

Vernon Bell and the BKF members performed many displays at local meetings and outdoor events to further introduce and interest the public in karate at this time. Terry Wingrove recalled: "We did a lot of demos in 1959 and 1960, karate, judo and ju-jitsu. We seemed to be out every weekend. Vernon Bell would say to the audience after our display, 'Ladies and gentleman, we challenge anybody in the audience to pit themselves against one of our boys,' which was a ridiculous thing to say. If you did a demo during the day that was okay, but in the evening, when people had had a few drinks ... It was interesting at times and a few situations happened when people got up. It was like a side-show at a fair, you know, come and wrestle the funny man. We were on a hiding to nothing. We couldn't hit them; we had to apply holds. The worst demo we ever did was at a mental institution. We went up there in the afternoon. We got changed in one tent and the girls got changed in another. We heard these screams, and a couple of the inmates had decided to join the girls and could not be evicted without a little violence, to say the least. This started the afternoon off well, and it was forcibly suggested to Vernon not to offer any challenges. Well, this was like showing a red flag to a bull, and he did it. We had people who were mentally disturbed up, screaming at you and charging. One of the nurses came up and asked us to stop as the inmates would be up all night."

Bell actively sought publicity in the local press, as a letter to the editor of the *Romford Recorder*, dated 17th July 1959, clearly shows. Bell wrote: "I would like to bring to your notice details on the enclosed circular regarding a two day course on Karate-do (Japanese boxing) which our Federation is holding at the above address [12, Maybush Road] this coming weekend, the 18th and 19th July inclusive, under Tetsuji Murakami (3rd Dan of Yoseikan of Japan) the highest ranking teacher of karate outside of Japan [this was not in fact true], and the only Yoseikan delegate in Europe. Should you be interested in covering this course, our Federation would welcome your co-operation and any publicity that you can afford us will be gratefully acknowledged. You are welcome to send your reporter and, if possible, a photographer, at an appointed time conveniently arranged between us. If you are interested would you telephone me between 10.00 and 10.15 a.m. on Saturday 18th or between 1.00 and 1.30 p.m. to fix an appointment. Hoping to have the pleasure of hearing favourably from you tomorrow..."

Readers will recall that Murakami had in fact been in Paris some eighteen months prior to his first visit to Britain. Initially, in 1958, the BKF had been unable to raise sufficient funds for him to come over, and afterwards the master's timetable had become fully booked, so a visit was not possible in any case. Bell, of course, had taken private lessons from Murakami in Paris, and trained under him in a number of classes. Murakami was now acting independently, his associations with Plee apparently having finished.

The earliest training in Britain under Master Murakami was conducted on the lawn tennis court and in the orchard of Bell's parents' bungalow at 12, Maybush Road, which has featured prominently in this book so far. The bungalow was, according to Bell, "A fine, old-fashioned chalet type with four bedrooms, set in large grounds. The orchard consisted of one hundred and eighty-five fruit trees." Bell continued: "There was also a lovely old walnut tree there then, the biggest in eastern Essex. In the orchard, the men used to camp out in tents and practise karate with Murakami during the daytime. They were fighting in and out of the trees. Sometimes Murakami and I would get up early in the morning when all the students were still asleep, and attack them with roundhouse techniques, *mae-geri*, *yoko-geri kekomi*s and all the rest. We'd pull the tents down, try and bring their instincts out. We had some wonderful times.

"Murakami was an expert in rope tying. Even without a rope he could put your feet around a tree and your arms in and out of your legs and you couldn't get up. You were sitting down and your arms and legs

Master Murakami

were entangled and you just could not get up. It's true. Murakami was a fully-fledged carpenter and joiner and lived in Shizuoka. His father was a wine merchant, and as a boy Murakami used to work in his father's store. That's how Murakami came to practise Yoseikan – living in Shizuoka. He was selected by Minoru Mochizuki to represent Yoseikan in Europe ... He came to this country for the BKF from the middle of 1959 to 1964 ... He was fabulous. He was a 3rd Dan and later reached 5th Dan from Egami. He was brilliant as a teacher, the best there was, and as a contest man he was close to brilliance. Although he was a bit of a rough diamond, he was a humble little man – he was first-class ... I'll tell you this, Tetsuji Murakami was the only Japanese I've ever met, judo, karate or otherwise, who wasn't money orientated. He wasn't interested in money at all. When he used to stay with my parents in Hornchurch, he would wash his own shirts and dry them out, and help with clearing the table and the washing up. He'd sleep upstairs in a large bedroom where Abbe had stayed a couple of years before. Murakami would bathe when he got up, and then again in the afternoon. He'd say to me, 'Bell, how many pupils have you got today on the course on the tennis court?' I'd say, 'Twenty to twenty-five, *Sensei*.' He would say, 'Right, I'll take one-third [of the money], you take the rest.' He was the only instructor who ever did that.

"I can see Murakami now, a short, thin man with a gold tooth at the front, a little toothbrush moustache, brush of black hair, swarthy skin, with his little pseudo-Italian suits and nice flowered ties. He was gentle (! – see later), never violent. He never got over the time I beat him in a hand-wrestling contest in Plee's *dojo* in 1958. He never forgave me for that. I'll tell you this little story. When Master Murakami was staying with my parents he would inspect my father's fourteen-hand mare. My father had a trap and could often be seen driving his pony and trap around Hornchurch; in fact he was famous for it. Murakami always fancied a go in this, but he was useless at conducting the horse. One day the horse galloped and I was sitting alongside. I was quite alarmed actually, because I was no hand with a horse either."

Details have survived of Murakami's first course. Training was from 10.30 a.m. to 1.00 p.m. and from 3.00 p.m. to 5.30 p.m. on the Saturday and Sunday, whilst training on the Monday was from 11.00 a.m. to 1.00 p.m. and from 3.00 p.m. to 5.00 p.m. Fees were three guineas per head. A deposit of one pound and ten shillings was payable by 28th June, and the remainder by the 11th July. Alternatively, students could pay the whole fee by the 4th July. Bell wrote on the course circular: "The BKF will be firm in this respect [no monies returnable] for reason that this course has been specially arranged for the benefit and advancement of our practising members, and much effort and negotiation has gone into the effect of arranging this course with Master Murakami and we have guaranteed him his fee of twenty pounds, plus all expenses and living, and it is the duty of each and every member of the BKF to do his utmost to attend this course to ensure success, for failure of this course may prevent a further visit of this high ranking master. Estimate to cover the course from loss has been fixed at between thirty-five and forty pounds, a figure which must be covered by enrolments on this course ... For the sake of the karate movement and for your own interests and advancement, we advise you to take the whole or even part of this unique course [if a student could only attend a part of the course they were still obliged to pay the full amount] under the highest graded and senior instructor of the Yoseikan in Europe. The course will be recognised by Yoseikan and EKU." In the event of wet weather – for it was intended to train in the open air – practice was to be conducted at the St. Mary's *dojo*. The conditions that weekend were in fact dry and sunny.

Although Bell mentioned a weekend course in his letter to the *Romford Recorder*, and the above details also show that three days were planned, it is believed that Murakami's stay in England was actually closer to a week in duration.

Terry Wingrove was at Murakami's first course: "When Murakami arrived, he was a very hard man. Murakami and Hoang Nam were like chalk and cheese. I'll tell you something. When Murakami came over to Europe he called a meeting in Plee's *dojo* of all the European delegates ... Seydel, Malatesti, Cherix, Vernon Bell, plus some French – all black-belts. Murakami lined them up in the *dojo* and decided to show them who was boss – really hurt people. He said, 'I'm the boss, you do what I tell you.' Vernon was the only one who really stood up to him. He had a good knowledge of ju-jitsu, very good at ju-jitsu, and he gave as good as he got. When he came back, Vernon said, 'Things are going to be hard from now on.' The first course that Murakami gave was devastating to say the least. He tore up everything we'd done before and said we'd start again. This was a big thing. We started again. We started with just how to hold the fist, just punching, you know. He was absolutely ruthless with the top grades like Armstrong, Rayner and Manning, he really was. I think he broke their hearts over the next two years. I was only a young kid, so it didn't make any difference, but they were in their twenties and they didn't like it. They kept saying, 'I'll punch him! I'll kick him! I'll shoot him! I'll kill him! – I'm not going to be humiliated like this.' I'll tell you the sort of thing Murakami did. We'd be in

Master Tetsuji Murakami on his first visit to Great Britain, in a group photo with BKF students in the garden of 12, Maybush Rd, Hornchurch – July 1959. Standing to the Master's left is Reg Armstrong, and between them and behind is Terry Wingrove – July 1959.

Mae-geri practise under Master Murakami – 1959

zenkutsu-dachi and he would stand on your back leg. Now that's okay if you know it's going to happen, but if you don't know...! He'd kick the inside of the thigh, which is quite normal, but he'd also kick the kneecap and it caused problems, injuries, and some people gave up. He would

Master Murakami demonstrates *mae-tobi-geri* upon Reg Armstrong – 1959

Master Murakami in the process of demonstrating *yoko-tobi-geri* upon Reg Armstrong – 1959.

act on the principle that feeling is believing. He was very physical, and extremely good technically. He had to have acupuncture on his spine because of rheumatism and other things. He was a truly dedicated *karateka* though, no question about that. On his first course in this country he gave a demonstration on Vernon's [parents'] lawn. We had a stopwatch. He started at *Pinan* 1 and went through to *Pinan* 5. We'd

Master Tetsuji Murakami teaching *mae-geri* – 12, Maybush Rd, Hornchurch (July 1959).

Master Murakami teaching *shuto-uke* in *kokutsu-dachi* – 12, Maybush Rd, Hornchurch (July 1959).

Master Tetsuji Murakami teaching *mae-geri* – 12, Maybush Rd, Hornchurch (July 1959).

Master Murakami teaching *shuto-uke* in *kokutsu-dachi* – 12, Maybush Rd, Hornchurch (July 1959).

never seen *Pinan* 4 and 5. Then he said 'Time me.' We timed him. He went a thousand miles an hour. I can see it now. Bang, bang, bang, bang. Unbelievable. With full focus and *kime*. When I saw this I was greatly impressed, so much so in fact that it pulled me out of my college electronics course. I'd never seen anything like that. It was light years

Master Murakami performs a *mawashi-geri* on brown-belt, Mick Manning, at the St. Mary's *dojo* – *c*. 1959.

away from anything I'd done. I worked for Cossor Electronics, a very famous radar company, and I was very fortunate for my boss was Lord Burghley, the man who won the 1926 Olympic Gold medal for the hurdles. Whenever I needed time off he always gave it to me."

The first proper karate grading under a Japanese, Tetsuji Murakami, ever to be held in Great Britain, was taken on the tennis court at 12, Maybush Road. The BKF grading register shows that on the 17th July 1959, R. Armstrong, H. Rayner and J. Russell, were graded to 3rd kyu. Two days later, J. Trotter graded to 6th kyu and R. Wardle to 5th kyu (having double graded). As noted in Part II, Trotter is a mystery, for he graded successfully on this occasion, having failed in March (see next paragraph), yet in January he was advertised as 3rd kyu at the Scarborough display (this is likely to be a judo grade, for no record exists in the BKF grading register of a J. Trotter before this date). There is additional evidence to show that a M. Sheehan also graded that day to 5th kyu, but his name does not appear in the grading register. However, the most important grading on the 19th July 1959, other than Bell's promotion to 2nd Dan, of course, was that Michael Manning graded to 2nd kyu, and thus became the first man to be promoted to that grade in this country.

Murakami's 1959 Hornchurch grading aside, all remaining gradings that year were held under Vernon Bell at the same location. The BKF grading register shows the following students graded, in order of date: 2.1.59, J. Goss – 6th kyu; 23.3.59, J. Trotter – fail; 1.6.59, P. McEvoy – fail; 18.6.59 – P. Milner – fail; 27.6.59, J. Goss – 5th kyu; 25.8.59, R. Carter – fail; 16.9.59, F. Gille – fail; 1.10.59, G. Dougherty – fail; 23.10.59, S. Gunns – fail; and, 31.10.59, J. Farkas – fail. In 1959, under Bell, nine students graded, all of whom were novices – only one (who was successful twice) passed. It was called keeping the standard up.

The first ever karate Summer Course was held between the 7th and 12th September, 1959, at the Ippon Judo Club, situated in the basement of the Imperial Private Hotel, 9-11, Ramshill Road, South Cliff, Scarborough, Yorkshire. The hotel was some two hundred yards from the sands, spa and bathing pool, and a few minutes from the town. This arrangement had come about owing to the kind offices of Peter Jaconelli, a 3rd Dan *judoka* and instructor at the club, and a Mrs. Turner, proprietor of the Imperial. It was the first of a number of annual summer courses organised by the BKF. A copy of the single page of course details (course details in the years to come had as many as four foolscap pages of single-spaced type), is still in existence. The course was under the direction of Mrs. C.F. Bell (Yes – there *was* a typing error in the original!), though it was hoped that Master Murakami would be in attendance, and negotiations were proceeding with this in mind. The course fee was £5 5s., which included the grading, but not the registering of the grade! The course was limited to twenty students, all of whom were obliged to pay in advance. Training times were 10.00 a.m. to 12.30 p.m., 2.30 p.m. to 5.00 p.m. and 7.00 p.m. to 8.00 p.m., daily, so things were pretty gruelling. Apart from the usual entry requirements to the course – that trainees had to be current licence holders and BKF Associate or Country Members – the course details are interesting because, "Either sex over sixteen and under fifty-five years of age," were invited to attend. Bell and the BKF had therefore lowered their minimum age from eighteen, but it is the only case in the existing BKF literature that states a maximum age. The details also note that, "You need not be a sportsman or experienced in other sports," and that, "You must be fit and healthy and sound of wind." The course was also, therefore, intended for students who would start their karate practice with the course (but such trainees had to join the BKF before commencing their training). Bell had reserved thirty-five vacancies at the hotel for students and their friends and families. Interestingly, spectators were allowed in the *dojo*, space permitting, as long as they were relatives of students on the course.

There does not, however, seem to have been a grading at the end of this course.

Bell recalled that the *dojo* was rather unpleasant: "I remember you had go down some wrought iron stairs to the basement. There were mirrors on the walls, and the walls were peeling. There were pillars in the middle of the room, and there was this smell – of mildew, of damp. There were no windows and the mould was on the floor as well."

The course details also provided information on the black karate *gi*, already mentioned, which Bell and the BKF were selling. A jacket and trousers cost £3 5s. A white belt cost 3s 6d, and a BKF badge, 10s 6d.

The St. Mary's *dojo* in Upminster was going well. Some students' application for membership forms to the BKF and, one imagines, to the St. Mary's *dojo* in particular, and in many cases the required references, from the period 1958-1962 have survived. Information on students will be provided in order of BKF application date, giving age and occupation at the time of application to the BKF, hometown (where possible), and month and year of BKF application. Home town is important here because the author has largely inferred *dojo* affiliation based on students private addresses: Maurice Sheehan, 19, instrument maker from Loughton, (August, 1958); John Goss, 31, sergeant in the Canadian Army, (December, 1958); James Trotter, 18, clerk from Dagenham, (April, 1959) – Bell noted that Trotter was, "one of the best stylists in the BKF"; Robert Wardle, 16, porter from Loughborough Park, London, (April, 1959); Malcolm Harknett, 23, insurance clerk from Shoeburyness, (July, 1959); Donald Sheehan, 19, of unknown occupation, from Loughton, (September, 1959); Ian Hughes, 19, craftsman's mate from Basildon, (October, 1959); George Williamson, 24, presser from Canvey Island, (May, 1960); Kenneth Ghose, 32, of unknown occupation from Herne Hill, (June, 1960); Victor Maxwell, 18 year old shipwright from Ilford, (June, 1960); John Alibone, 32, driver from Billericay, (July, 1960); Raymond Evans, 21, scaffolder from Edmonton, (July, 1960); Terence Evans, 18, lifeguard from London, (July, 1960); Brian Hammond, 19, auditor from Elm Park, (July, 1960); Robert Buckner, 23, labourer from Canvey Island, (August, 1960) – Bell noted that Buckner was, "One of the best stylists in the BKF ... [and] the best pupil of Murakami." Buckner left the BKF in 1961, a 3rd kyu.

Then there was George Stubbings, 34, toolmaker from Basildon, (September, 1960); Ernest Tillett, 28, sheet metal worker from Canvey Island, (September, 1960); Kenneth Goult, 18, clerk from Ilford, (December, 1960); Richard Lamport, 17, engineer (May, 1961); Suzette

Hubbard, 43, guest house proprietor (September, 1961); Douglas Smith, 33, carpenter (March, 1962); Kenneth Joy, 16, apprentice plater (April, 1962); Edward Knight, 33, welder (April, 1962); Michael Hull, 24, metal worker (May, 1962); Thomas Jardine, 35, manager (July, 1962); Anthony Ansell, 23, sales manager (October, 1962). Of unknown date of joining at this time are, Sidney Flateau, 30, a patissier from East Ham, and David Williams, 28, a dictograph inspector from Benfleet.

It was at the end of 1959 that, like Terry Wingrove, another important instructor in the history of British Shotokan began his karate training. James William Neal was born on the 27th November 1937, and applied for membership of the BKF on the 1st November 1959. At the time he was living in Romford, and was a roof tiler by occupation. His employers considered him to be conscientious, trustworthy beyond doubt, and gave notice of his punctuality. Neal was a quiet, sensitive man, reasonably small in height. He had served in the Army for two years, leaving in May 1957. When he joined the BKF he was in good health, with interests in judo and football. He was destined to become the first man to be granted a black belt in Britain under Master Kanazawa (see later).

It is thought that training at the Wheatsheaf pub continued until the early spring of 1961, thereafter it was no longer available and a new *dojo* had to be found. Regrettably, what would have been a potential shrine for Shotokan *karateka*, like the old 12, Maybush Road, has been destroyed. Kenton Street was severely shortened to make way for a concrete monstrosity known as the Brunswick Centre, which was completed in 1972. Prior to this, Kenton Street ran parallel with Marchmont Street to form a T-junction with Bernard Street. Only a small portion of Kenton Street now survives. In yesteryear, both Handel Street and Coram Street bisected Kenton Street. Today, Kenton Street stops at Handel Street. For interested readers wishing to visit the site, directions will now be given.

If one walks the very short distance up Kenton Street from Tavistock Square, crosses over what remains of Handel Street (it has been partially blocked off) and ascends the steps onto the Brunswick Centre, No. 42, the Wheatsheaf, used to stand where there are now shops, on the right-hand side (when looking towards Bernard Street in the distance), before the original bisection with Coram Street, and in line with the surviving buildings on the left hand side of Kenton Street. With a little imagination, and a close look at the surviving buildings in Kenton Street, a fairly accurate picture of what it was all like can be obtained.

Details of a course held at the Wheatsheaf by Master Murakami on Saturday, 1st April 1961, surely is very close to the last training session

Kenton Street, London, WC1, in 1994. Where the road is now blocked off the Wheatsheaf *dojo* used to be.

– if not the last. Training commenced on the first floor at 10.00 a.m. and continued to noon. Afternoon sessions lasted from 1.30 p.m. to 3.30 p.m., and then again from 4.45 p.m. to 6.15 p.m. Training on the Sunday was held at the St. Mary's *dojo*, and included an aikido session from 2.00 p.m. to 4.30 p.m. Course details reveal what was practised on the two-day course: "Preparatory exercises, postures of attack and defence, methods of parrying and counter-attack, methods of walking and turning, attacking stances and changing positions, techniques of hitting with the fist, finger, arm, side of hand, elbow etc., and kicking with the foot and heel etc., combination techniques, 1st, 2nd and 3rd Combat *kata*, free practice, attacks and defences, 1st *Pinan kata*, self-defence, contest, etc." Murakami was being paid £30 for the course plus all expenses, and Bell estimated that between £50 and £55 would be required to break even.

After the Wheatsheaf became unavailable, not far away in the Gray's Inn Road, another pub was chosen on a temporary basis. "The Pindar of Wakefield was a strange *dojo*," Vernon Bell recalled. "The training area was semi-circular, like a half-moon shape, and it had a very solid, concrete, pink coloured artificial floor, and it was so cold. The landlord was quite co-operative, but he didn't want us in there for any length of

The Pindar of Wakefield, now the Water Rats Theatre, as it was in 2001. The BKF *dojo* was on the first floor.

time, and he made that very clear, because other activities were going on. I think the British Horse Society met there. None of the men who moved from the Wheatsheaf to the Pindar of Wakefield liked it at all.

They were very unhappy there and the spirit went out of the club completely. There wasn't a family atmosphere any more and attendances started to drop. We were only able to train one night a week. It was early spring and still cold. It felt like winter. The whole place was freezing, even though it had luxury velvet curtains, nice tables, and so on. There was something about the place. It didn't have any atmosphere for training. We stayed there for about two or three months."

Bell continued: "Then we moved to Abbe's judo school off the Caledonian Road. Abbe had no compunction about us using his *dojo*, which was really nice. I used to take private aikido lessons from Abbe there; one pound ten shillings for half an hour – a lot of money in those days. I remember the three outside concrete steps that led up to a blue, arched double door, upon one door of which was a heavy circular doorknob. It was a large, airy *dojo*, old though, with no changing rooms and no showers. Most of the windows were broken and my students asked me if they could practise in plimsolls or socks. I wouldn't allow it in this *dojo*. I told them that the Japanese did it in bare feet on rocks, under waterfalls and what have you, and if they could do it so could we. I said, 'I don't care if the wind blows up your trouser legs, around your testicles, and comes out of your earholes, mate, we're doing it exactly how it's always been done in Japan, and that's that. If you don't like it you can leave and don't come back, but we're the only karate organisation.' There was plenty of room there all right. An old judo mat laid over the floor, dirty old canvas over it, but I'll tell you this, the atmosphere and spirit was fantastic. There was a bench all the way around the *dojo* and people used to come in, sit down and watch. A lot of people came in to watch, even Abbe used to watch, and O'Tani. Mister Naessens from Belgium came – he became Harada's man. Naessens was in the International Budo Council. We trained there three times a week, if I remember correctly. We stayed at Abbe's *dojo* for about two or three months also, before moving to Marshall Street Baths for a few weeks, but that wasn't suitable either, though I forget the reason why." [Eight years after Bell provided this information, he could not recall having had a *dojo* at Marshall Street Baths, but wanted his earlier recollection recorded for posterity, as, given the nature of human memory and the passage of time, it was likely to be the more accurate].

Terry Wingrove trained in judo at Abbe's *dojo* and practised karate there with the BKF. The old *dojo*, believed to have been in Denmark Grove (No. 5?), N1, a half a mile off the Pentonville Road, no longer exists, having been, along with the surrounding area, demolished to make way for a new housing development. Wingrove recalled: "It had a very low ceiling. If you threw someone you ran the very real risk of whacking their feet against the ceiling, that's how bad it was. It was dank and it smelt. You could smell the sweat in the *dojo* from the night before. The windows were all boarded up. It was a bad *dojo*."

Master Mitsusuke Harada (see later) taught at Abbe's *dojo* from early December, 1963. He recalled, "When I first came to Britain, I taught at Abbe's dirty old basement *dojo* – a church hall about five or six minutes walk from King's Cross station … It was a very cold *dojo* in the winter and quite small. It was also damp, with mildew climbing up the interior walls. There were no showers and no changing rooms. I remember once, when a lady student turned up, we had to wait outside the *dojo* to let her get changed before the men went in and got changed. It was basic. The advantage of this *dojo* however, was its location and the fact that the judo mats were permanently fixed to the floor. The mats were covered with a canvas overlay which protected them" [*Reminiscences by Master Mitsusuke Harada* (Clive Layton, KDS Publishing, 1999, page120)].

Bell continued: "Then we moved again just down the road to the Horseshoe pub in Clerkenwell, which turned out to be a very important *dojo* in the history of British karate. We must have moved there in the autumn of 1961, something like that, and we left in 1964, training twice a week. Instead of the small clubs that we had had at the Wheatsheaf, the Pindar of Wakefield and the Abbe Judo School, the membership increased at the Horseshoe and we blossomed right out. The Horseshoe was a very, very vital *dojo* in the history of British karate. The size of the membership that we later took to the Kentish Town Baths and especially Lyndhurst Hall enabled me to get the Japanese over in 1965."

Terry Wingrove recalled that Vernon Bell took the Horseshoe, "on the quick, because he couldn't get another *dojo*. I remember that. When we first had it, it stank of booze." Further details on these three *dojos* will follow later.

Bell continued: "We used to like pubs, and being a family-type club we liked to socialise, as I've mentioned before. All our chaps would have a drink and knew each other after *dojo* hours. They would go round to one another's homes, train together in their little rooms. We used to encourage them to do this – to increase the spirit. It was never a case of you come to the *dojo*, do what you're told and go home. No, it was never like that. That's what I'd like to say about training then, in the early days. It was a family affair. It wasn't Vernon Bell the big black-belt and they were simply the pupils. No, we were all friends together."

PART IV

For some three years, the BKF had been purely London and Essex based, attracting people from the capital and the surrounding Home Counties. In 1960, a Liverpool *dojo*, though apparently unregistered with the BKF, was started under Frederick Gille, who applied for BKF membership on the 9th September 1959. The thirty-nine-year-old bearded design engineer was, at the time of his application, a 5th kyu in judo of the Napier and English Electric Judo Club, situated on the outskirts of the city. Gille had attended a course at Maybush Road, but had failed his first grading on the 16th September 1959. Gille later resigned from the BKF, but he left an extremely important legacy.

Early members of the 'unofficial' Liverpool Karate Club were essentially fellow judo students of Gille's, to whom he showed what he had learned on the BKF course. Later, pupils, such as Andrew Sherry, from Jack Britain's ju-jitsu club based in Sheil Road, Liverpool, became involved. The very first Liverpool karate *dojo* known to the author, was at the David Lewis Theatre, in Toxteth. This *dojo*'s wooden floor was unsatisfactory however, as students kept getting splinters in their feet, and they only trained there once. Practice then moved to Harold House Jewish Boys Club, Chatham Street, where training continued to early 1963, before the club moved to the YMCA Red Triangle, based at 126, Everton Road. In the 8th December 1961 edition of the *Liverpool Daily Post*, under the heading, "They Call it Karate," and subtitled, "Sport That's the Last Word in Self-Defence," an unknown reporter, believed to be James Feather, wrote about the "recently formed North-West Branch of the British Karate Association." The reporter was game enough to try a little karate for himself and aimed a punch at George Galletly's head. The reporter wrote: "The punch had hardly started when a wrist as hard as a crowbar flashed up from nowhere and parried my blow." The article is accompanied by a photograph of Fred Gille performing *gedan-barai* in *zenkutsu-dachi*, with Vernon Bell performing a *shihon-nukite* to Gille's face. Gille is dressed in a white *gi*, Bell in a black *gi*. The clipping was sent to Bell by James Feather of the *Liverpool Daily Post*, who noted that the evening of the 17th December 1961, "was a most interesting occasion." The first BKF club affiliation

THE BRITISH KARATÉ FEDERATION

Chief Technical Adviser/Coach/Grader
Master Tetsugi Murakami (3 Dan Yoseikan)

Chairman & National Coach
Vernon C. F. Bell, F.S.J.M. (2 Dan Yoseikan)

Established 1957 by official charter under the auspices of YOSEIKAN Japan
Affiliated to; Japan Karate Association. International Karate Federation
and European Karate Federation.

Affiliation Certificate

This is to Certify that the official .... L.......... branch of this

Federation has been duly Certified in the name of:

Frederick. M. Gille.A.M.I.E.D.

with Headquarters at 161,Hunts Cross Ave.Woolton. Liverpool.

The appointed Area Officer of the Federation for the area s of Lancashire

is Mr. F.M.Gille of The above address

(Signed) *Vernon C. F. Bell*, F.R.C. Ps.D.

Sept

National Coach & Technical Director

V. C. F. BELL, (Nidan)
12, Maybush Rd. Hornchurch, Essex.

Cert.No. C 1961

Date Issued 1:3:62.
176~

This Certificate at all times remains the property of B.K.F.

The Liverpool *dojo*'s first Affiliation Certificate to the BKF – September, 1961

certificate was issued in the name of Fred Gille on the 1st March 1962.

Over seventy-four BKF membership application forms have survived from the BKF Liverpool *dojo* to 1965. The considerable BKF literature still in existence with regard to the Liverpool *dojo* is almost entirely administrative, and of little interest.

The author will now present the BKF application for membership data on the said Liverpool students. Names will be presented

Vernon Bell performs a *jodan-shihon-nukite* upon Fred Gille at Harold House Boys' Club, Liverpool – December, 1961.

alphabetically followed by pupils' ages and occupations at the time of BKF application, and the date of BKF application will be given in brackets. A number of the following individuals would become particularly famous in Shotokan circles for various reasons: John Ashton, 21, civil servant, (13.10.63); Terence Astley, 31, storekeeper, (15.6.61); Clifford Bagshaw, 18, apprentice machinist, (19.1.63); Terence Barry, 27, sales engineer, (8.10.61); Geoffrey Bell, 16, salesman, (6.2.65); Norman Bell, 16, apprentice rubber technologist, (25.4.63); George Bingham, 34, sales engineer, (21.8.61); Ian Bleasdale, 18, clerk, (26.6.65); Leslie Bleasdale, 40, signalman, (10.7.65); Keith Bloomfield, 21, glass cutter, (23.9.62); Alan Burleigh, 13, schoolboy, (30.3.64); Clifford Butler, 35, electrician, (26.7.61); Anthony Casey, 18, electrical engineer, (30.6.63); Edward Casey, 26, security officer, (3.1.65); Kenneth Caulfield, 24, insurance agent, (14.1.61); Joseph Chialton, 16, painter,

BKF Liverpool *dojo* – 1961. To Fred Gille's (sitting, centre) right is Jimmy Neal. Among those who were to become well known in Shotokan were Terry Astley (3rd from left, front row), Andy Sherry (2nd from right, front row), and Kenneth Caulfield (1st right, front row). Charles Naylor is 3rd left, back row.

Jimmy Neal flanked by Vernon Bell and Fred Gille at the Liverpool *dojo* – 1961

(15.3.62); William Chiverton, 33, sales representative, (23.5.63); Francis Cope, 27, toolmaker, (—.3.62); Alan Dewar, 27, shop manager, (22.10.61); Gerald Dicker, 28, electrical engineer, (20.9.61); Leonard

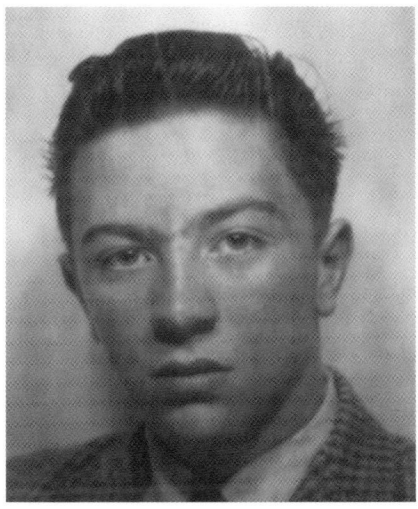

The photograph that Terry O'Neill submitted with his BKF application form when aged sixteen. O'Neill was to become one of the finest *karateka* this country has ever produced.

Doft, 19, mechanic, (19.5.63); John Donoghue, 17, mechanic, (12.8.61); Melvyn Duggan, 22, design engineer, (9.9.65); Robert Eccles, 24, trainee industrial chemist, 13.12.65); Raymond Edwards, 18, trainee auto setter, (6.12.64); David Elliott, 19, student, (12.1.63); Gerald Frodsham, 18, apprentice bricklayer, (9.10.61); Harry Frost, 20, clerk, (13.7.62); George Galletly, 29, sales contractor, (29.9.61); John Galletly, 15, schoolboy, (4.3.62); Frederick Gillmore, 26, driver, (7.1.63); Joseph Grant, 26, metal polisher, (19.12.64); Thomas Greenhalgh, 18, apprentice plumber, (15.9.63); Brian Hesford, 20, service worker, (8.9.63); Hollis Inniss, 30, teletype operator, (15.3.63); William Jones, 30, hospital orderly, (28.9.65); Hilary Jordan, 35, medical photographer, (5.2.64); Barry Juxon, 28, teacher, (1.6.61); Thomas Kilty, 22, labourer, (3.10.63); Gordon Marguerie, 26, driver, (14.7.63); Edward Marply, 19, trainee civil engineer, (28.4.63); Kenneth May, 25, contracts engineer, (8.10.61); Kenneth McCaldon, 19, apprentice plumber, (24.6.61); Shaun McConnell, 17, student, (2.4.62); Peter Meir, 25, sales engineer, (6.9.61); Stanley More, 16, student, (5.4.62); Brian Morris, 28, fireman, (22.3.65); Kenneth Murphy, 17, apprentice joiner, (14.9.63); Charles Naylor, 28, sales engineer, (31.8.61); John Newman, 19, apprentice engineer, (22.9.63); Terence O'Neill, 16, schoolboy, (21.5.63); James Pape, 40, sales manager, (30.6.63); John Pape, 16,

Members of a course held at the Upminster *dojo* that was well attended by Liverpool BKF branch members – early 1962. From left to right, kneeling: unknown, unknown, T. Astley, A. Sherry, unknown, E. Hughes. From left to right, standing: unknown, unknown, C. Naylor, unknown, A. Smith, E. Ainsworth, R. Woolfall, A. Ruddock, A. Dewar, J. Love.

office boy, (—.—.63); John Parkinson, 38, security officer, (26.5.65); Charles Penrose, 33, schoolmaster, (23.6.63); Kenneth Rimmer, 18, apprentice baker, (4.12.64); John Sharkey, 19, rent collector, (3.5.65); Peter Sharkey, 15, schoolboy, (28.3.65); Andrew Sherry, 17, painter, (9.6.61); Brian Simon, 16, apprentice joiner, (13.1.63); Kevin Skinner, 26, representative, (29.4.62); Paul Sloan, 17, unknown occupation, (16.8.61); Hugh (Alan) Smith, 24, greengrocer, (22.10.61); Roy Stephens, 19, apprentice plumber, (21.3.62); William Strefford, 20, fitter, (9.9.63); Edward Travis, 24, unknown occupation, (26.9.61); Francis Vernon, 33, boilermaker, (21.5.63); Michael Walls, 20, labourer, (29.6.61); William Whitehead, 18, decorator, (18.3.62); Thomas Wignall, 36, steel erector, (14.7.61); Frederick Williams, 25, arc welder, (25.9.61); William Williams, 18, apprentice toolmaker, (14.9.63); James Wilson, 31, manager, (21.9.61); Richard Woolfall, 18, apprentice plumber, (25.3.62); Roy Yarwood, 20, apprentice joiner, (15.9.63). Additionally, the names of the following Liverpool BKF students appear as members in correspondence only: K. Brown, S. Coy, P. Cunningham, E. Delaney, G. Green, D. Hardman, M. Keay, M. Mathieson, R. McCorrie, D. McGovern, T. McNally, E. O'Neill, G. Sherlock.

Master Murakami performs a *mawashi-geri* on 3rd kyu, Reg Armstrong, at the St. Mary's *dojo*, Upminster – 1960.

In the first half of 1960, Bell conducted only three individual gradings, all at Hornchurch. Michael Manning was promoted to 1st kyu on the 1st February 1960, and in so doing gained a place in the history books as the first BKF member to have reached that grade. Bell, in a letter to Minoru Mochizuki, dated the 24th February 1960, had recommended Manning for promotion. Bell wrote: "He is in-charge of beginners' classes and was graded to 2nd kyu by Mr. Murakami on the 18th July, 1959. He has been doing karate for four years regularly every week, and has good execution of all five *ippon* and *sanbon kata* and first three *Pinan kata*. He can defeat six lower kyu grades in succession in *Shiai*, and his technique is very good." An A. R. Martin and a J. Lydon, who attempted 6th kyu on the 13th and 14th April 1960, respectively, both failed.

On the 17th July 1960, Bell appears to have held a grading at the St. Mary's *dojo* following a weekend course. The BKF grading register shows that the following novices were promoted to 6th kyu that day: J. Alibone, B. Hammond and E. Harris.

The 2nd Annual Summer Course of the BKF was held in Scarborough, Yorkshire, commencing Sunday, 14th August to Thursday, 25th August 1960. Master Murakami was instructing for the whole of the course with Vernon Bell assisting. The course venue was, once

BRITISH KARATE' FEDERATION
(KARATE' CLUB OF GREAT BRITAIN)
(Affiliated YOSEIKAN, JAPAN)

announce

2ND ANNUAL SUMMER COURSE
of

KARATE'-DO

(the most deadly, effective, scientific system of JAPANESE BOXING with NAKED HANDS and FEET)

under the

MASTER TETSUGI MURAKAMI
(3rd. DAN Master Grade of YOSEIKAN)
Highest graded & greatest exponent of this Art outside of JAPAN

assisted by

VERNON C. F. BELL (2nd DAN of YOSEIKAN)
(National Coach of B/K/F)

at Dojo of IPPON JUDO CLUB
IMPERIAL PRIVATE HOTEL
9/11, Ramshill Drive, South Cliff, SCARBOROUGH, Yorks.

14th-26th AUGUST 1960   FEE £5/5/0

(Course open to any person, either sex, over 15 years, previous experience unnecessary). Limited number only so apply NOW to avoid disappointment. Course details, circular, B/K/F leaflet on receipt of 2'6d P.O. and S.A.E. to :- V. C. F. BELL, 137, Hillview Avenue, HORNCHURCH, Essex.

ACE PRINTING CO.

The BKF 2nd Annual Summer Course poster – 1960

again, the Ippon Judo Club *dojo*, situated at the Imperial Private Hotel, Scarborough. The cost of training for the ten-day course, which included the grading, was five guineas. Seven days' training, without the grading, was three pounds and fifteen shillings. All fees were payable in advance. Course registration took place in the *dojo* at 9.00 a.m. on Sunday the

14th August, and daily karate training times under Murakami were, 10.00 a.m. to 11.30 a.m., and 11.45 a.m. to 12.45 p.m. In the afternoon, between 4.00 and 5.00 p.m., Vernon Bell took, "free practice and tuition for ladies and beginners." Between 7.00 p.m. and 8.00 p.m. each evening, aikido was taught by Master Murakami, who claimed a 3rd Dan in aikido at this time. Master Murakami was being well paid for this course, receiving £50 plus all living expenses, and it was estimated that between £70 and £80 had to be obtained from enrolments to cover the course's costs. Hotel accommodation (with Bell) came to £32 12s; incidental expenses for Murakami were £5. It is interesting to note that the BKF spent £8 3s. 2d on publicity and advertising, and £4 7s. 6d on printing posters and duplicating leaflets. Murakami's return airfare came to £8 12s. Full board accommodation could be had at the hotel at a cost of between 18s 6d. and £1 4s., a night. Each student had to book his own accommodation directly with the hotel.

It would appear, from the course details, that Bell and the BKF had relaxed their membership rules a little for, "Any person, either male or female, over the age of sixteen years, whether with or without any knowledge of karate, may enrol on the course." The details contain the following sales pitch: "No experience or special ability in any other sport is necessary to be able to learn karate, which is a completely different and unusual form of sport unlike any other, and any average person of normal intelligence, [and] reasonable physical fitness can benefit from its training. It is easy to learn [and] it requires no special aptitude or ability. Karate is of special benefit to women because it is graceful, smooth and agile, and has harmonious movements. There is no risk of injury whatsoever if one practises seriously. Age is of no account in becoming efficient in this art, neither is size or weight. It is the finest form of self-defence known, as well as being one of the finest systems of physical culture, moral training and self-discipline, ... [which] most other sports lack. It is said that once you have tried karate, all other sports are tame in comparison and you never leave it." This description was evident in subsequent course literature. The details finish with, "Here is your opportunity to learn a fascinating art under the highest ranking master outside of Japan," which, of course, was not true, but who knows what Bell had been told? The membership fee to the BKF in 1960 was one guinea.

Terry Wingrove attended this course and described it as one of the very best that Murakami ever gave. Wingrove recalled: "This was when Bob Buckner had just won the football pools the week before. He had a brand new Vauxhall. He spent money and we all had a wonderful time."

Master Murakami attacks Bob Buckner with *mae-geri* at the 1960 Summer School in Scarborough.

Wingrove remembered a number of funny asides associated with that course.

"Vernon wouldn't let us go up to Scarborough on our own for some reason, so we all met at the Upminster *dojo*. Vernon's idea, and I swear this is the absolute truth, was to get a map of England, and draw a line using a ruler from Upminster to Scarborough. Now, the Wash is there, and he drove all the way north at thirty-five miles an hour. It took thirteen and a half hours to get from Upminster to Scarborough. This almost caused a riot. This almost caused a fight in Lincolnshire. We drove up through Essex, Suffolk and Norfolk until we came to the Wash. 'Where's the bridge?' Vernon said. I replied, 'There is no —— bridge over the Wash, even I know that.' So, we had to go all the way round. Murakami was going potty. All those back roads. Eventually we got there and Jaconelli was waiting for us. He owned restaurants, hotels and so on, and eventually became Lord Mayor of Scarborough. He was immensely rich and he gave all the people on the course a gold sovereign. He was a little Italian man,

BKF Summer School – Scarborough, 1960

Master Murakami attacks Bob Buckner with *yoko-tobi-geri* at the 1960 Summer School in Scarborough.

a lovely man. Jaconelli said, 'Where have you been Vernon, where have you been?' and Vernon said to us, 'Don't you say a word!'

"It was late, and Bell went upstairs with Murakami. 'I don't want any noise, all rooms are allocated,' Vernon said. I was with Maxwell, Buckner and two others – five of us in one room. I told the others I'd had enough of Vernon and I'd have him in a couple of days.

"In the evening we'd go dancing. Vernon had brought his dancing shoes and would go to the ballroom. When he was dancing with a girl, we'd go up to her and say, 'Excuse my father, you know, mental. He's just come out of a lunatic asylum. He's got disgusting habits.' Vernon would say, 'What are you saying? What are you saying?' By the end of the evening no one would dance with him and he couldn't understand why.

"On the third day we kept knocking on his door at night and asking, 'Mr. Bell, what time does the course start in the morning, only I'm not quite sure?' You could hear Vernon call out, 'You leave me alone! Wingrove, I know it's you!' We had a chamber pot, and I asked everybody to contribute, and everybody had a pee into this great big chamber pot. I took the light bulbs out from the lights in the corridor outside Vernon's room and put this pot outside Vernon's door. We started again, 'Mr. Bell! Mr. Bell!' Vernon Bell was shouting from inside his room, 'I'm going to get you! Right! That's it!' He came straight out of the door and put his foot in the pot. The pot sprang up and the contents went all over him. He didn't know what it was and thought that it was water. It was too dark. He came downstairs. I was in the wardrobe hiding. Maxwell was in bed, fast asleep. Vernon came in through the door and then twigged what was over him and shouted, 'You dirty bastard Wingrove!' He got hold of Maxwell and went bang! Bang! Maxwell was all groggy. I was still in the wardrobe. 'You dirty swine Wingrove!' Vernon shouted. The next morning, he said that he didn't want any more of this, 'It's a disgusting, dirty thing,' and he looked at me. I told Murakami and he couldn't stop laughing. Vernon's attitude, his way of doing things was so ... dogmatic wasn't the word. And thirteen and a half hours to Scarborough!"

A list of successful students who graded during the Scarborough course, under Murakami, is available. On the 20th August 1960, E. Shaw and A. Tranter both from Stoke, Staffordshire, graded to 5th kyu. On the 23rd August 1960, the following graded to 5th kyu: R. Buckner from Benfleet, Essex; P. Butler from Sunderland, Durham; C. Cabot, from North London; F. Kidd from Middlesbrough, Yorkshire; T. Laverick from Sunderland, Durham; V. Maxwell, from Ilford, Essex; R. Salmon,

BKF Summer School – Scarborough, 1960

from Southend, Essex; and, T. Wingrove, from North London. No one appears to have graded beyond that. C. Cabot is not mentioned in the BKF grading register. The grading register also shows that a C. Celsi and an E. Stoke graded to 5th kyu, but no other details of these individuals have survived.

Vernon Bell had wanted to advertise the 1960 karate Summer School in the form of a 'box' advertisement in *Judo* magazine, and had written to the Advertisements Manager at 91, Wellesley Road, Croydon, Surrey, on the 14th June 1960, to this effect, noting that the course would be, "under the master, Tetsuji Murakami, 3rd Dan of the Yoseikan." The reply to this letter, dated the 15th June 1960, by A.R. Menzies of Judo Limited, was to have an enormous effect upon Bell and subsequently would completely change the course of Shotokan history in Great Britain. Menzies' letter noted: "Regarding your karate association, we are given to understand that the only official organisation in Japan is the Japan Karate Association, which was founded by Funakoshi Gichin, and is recognised by the Japanese Ministry of Education. As there are so many spurious organisations in the world purporting to be official representatives of accepted Japanese Associations dealing in the various martial arts of Japan, you will understand our need, as publishers with a world-wide circulation, for careful scrutiny of all proposed advertisers.

Consequently, perhaps you would be good enough to supply us with details of your judo and karate grades, and the names of the associations issuing them."

This reply troubled Bell deeply, and he set about trying to understand who exactly was "official" in that far off land. Bell, as we know, had heard of the JKA, but enquiries to Plee had apparently gone unanswered. Bell wrote to Master Minoru Mochizuki, head of the Yoseikan, directly, on the 19th July 1960. Bell requested that his Yoseikan *Nidan* diploma, which had been conferred upon him one year earlier by Murakami, be sent. Bell also sent a banker's draft for $5 to pay for it. However, the bulk of this letter concerned his new-found problem. Bell wrote: "I would like your advice on a second and most important matter. Recently, I wrote to the British Judo Association magazine (Judo Limited) requesting permission to put an advertisement in their magazine regarding our Summer Course under Mr. Murakami. [A] Copy of my letter to them [is] herewith [enclosed]. In reply, they state that our British Karate Federation is more or less not recognised, and further state that they understand the only official organisation in Japan is the Japan Karate Association, founded by Master Funakoshi, and is recognised by the Japanese Ministry of Education. (A copy of their letter is enclosed – please study closely). Let me have your advice on (a) is what the B.J.A. say quite true? (b) Is the Japan Karate Association the true authentic body for karate in Japan? (c) Was it founded by the Master Funakoshi? For I have always been led to believe that he founded the Yoseikan. (d) What is the relationship between the Yoseikan and the Japan Karate Association? Does it recognise the Yoseikan? (e) Are grades conferred by the Yoseikan recognised by the Japan Karate Association?

"Will you please consider all these points carefully in the order I have stated, letting me have your opinion and advice, and also the procedure we should adopt towards this B.J.A. decision, for unless our British Karate Federation has a definite policy towards this line adopted by the British Judo Association, then the whole of British karate and the name of the Yoseikan will suffer irreparable harm in Britain just when, after five years of hard work, we are beginning to be known and karate is now being accepted up and down the country and everyone knows of it and the BKF. A leading British newspaper, the *Daily Mirror*, in a letter to an enquirer, who is a pupil of mine, stated that they regarded me as the only responsible and qualified man in this country to teach karate. I have already mentioned this to Mr. Murakami, with whom I will discuss it in full in August on our

Summer Course. Meanwhile, he has advised me to seek your counsel immediately, and this I am doing, since I have no one else to advise me in this country, and I appeal to your great experience and knowledge on these matters to give me this advice. All karate men in this country regard the Yoseikan and yourself as the only authentic karate body in Japan."

Bell received a reply to this letter, dated the 8th September 1960, from the General Manager of the Japan Karate Association, Masatomo Takagi. It was the first communication from the JKA Bell had received. The JKA headquarters were then based at No.13, 1-Chome Yotsuya, Shinjuku-ku, Tokyo. Takagi's letter, uncorrected, read, in part: "We have your letter with many thanks. We regret that we did not write you until this date. Yesterday I met Mr. Mochizuki and heard about you. We, as Japan Karate Association, we wish to take care the matter when we have report from Mr. Murakami. Please ask him to report to us soonest possible."

Murakami never did report to the JKA as later correspondence shows. There were no further letters between Bell and the JKA until 1963. These are extremely important and are studied, in depth, in *Volume II* of this work.

In the intervening period between receiving the letter by Menzies and writing to Master Mochizuki, Bell had acquired a new karate book by Nishiyama and Brown, published by Tuttle. The day on which Bell wrote directly to Master Mochizuki, he also wrote to Master Hidetaka Nishiyama at the JKA. It was a case of a double attack, in order that some resemblance to the truth might manifest itself. Bell wrote: "I have recently purchased a book called, *Karate – The Art of 'Empty-Hand' Fighting*, written by yourself and Mr. Richard Brown, which is now on general sale in this country. I have found this book of immense interest and value, both to myself and my members.

"I am founder of karate in this country and the present leader, as well as being the only Japanese trained, qualified black-belt in Britain. I run karate under the name of the British Karate Federation and as you can see we are affiliated to the Yoseikan, which I have always been led to believe was the only official governing body of karate in Japan. However, since obtaining your book I realise that yours is an official body of repute, and authentic, and I understand from the British Judo Association that yours is the official governing body in Japan for karate, and also that your organization is recognised by the Japanese Ministry of Education. These facts impress me greatly and I would like to know if I am correct in thinking them. Accordingly, I would like to apply for individual membership of your Association and would also like to affiliate the British Karate Federation to the Japan [Karate] Association in order to register our grades and to be recognised by you. I am prepared to pay any monies due for these things and to complete any necessary enrolment and affiliation procedures.

"I was taught karate by Mr. Plee (3rd Dan of the French Karate Federation), also by the Masters Hiroo Mochizuki (2nd Dan) and Tetsuji Murakami (3rd Dan), over the last five years. I was graded 1st Dan by Mr. Plee on the 1st April 1957, and [*Nidan*] by Mr. Murakami in England on the 9th July 1959. Both grades are registered with the Yoseikan. I would like to know if your association is prepared to accept, recognise and register my two grades. If so, I would like to receive the official diploma of *Nidan* of your organization as well as an official Affiliation Certificate for my Federation from the Japan [Karate] Association. Any costs we are prepared to pay. Furthermore, I am prepared to act as your official representative in this country for your organization if you would so wish. I am a full-time professional Judo coach (3rd Dan) by Kenshiro Abbe and teach in fifteen clubs under the Ministry of Education. I am enclosing some leaflets of our Association regarding the origin of karate in Britain, our Yoseikan status, etc. for your guidance. I will be very pleased to hear from you on these matters as soon as possible and will accept your decision as final, but I look forward to your recognition and to a long and pleasant association."

Any reply Bell may have received to the above letter has been lost, though all seems to have gone quiet for a number of years.

Another course, following on from the second BKF Summer School, was held from the 26th to 31st August 1960, and was based at Hornchurch. The following people were graded by Master Murakami: 6th kyu – C. Alibone from Billericay, Essex, and E. Harris from Raleigh, Essex; 5th kyu – R. Richardson from Brentwood; 4th kyu – J. Neal from Romford and J. Wijesundera from North London; 1st kyu – M. Manning from Grays, Essex. Presumably, Manning had his grading officially ratified by Murakami. C. Alibone and E. Harris are not mentioned in the BKF grading register, but an R. Martin, of whom nothing else is known, other than that he failed his 6th kyu four months previously, was double graded to 5th kyu – perseverance paid.

Six letters survive from Murakami to Vernon Bell. All are handwritten in English by one of the master's French students, though Murakami signs all. Details of these letters will be given as appropriate, the last being in 1963. The first of these letters however, was written on the 18th November 1960, concerning a planned December course. It

Master Murakami concluding training at the Upminster *dojo* – 1960. Directly behind Murakami is Jimmy Neal, and to their left, Terry Wingrove.

reads: "I am very pleased to know that you are in better health now. As for your 2nd Dan diploma, I am sending it to you and I hope you will receive it with my letter. I agree with you upon all that is said in your letter [all but one letter from Bell to Murakami, in 1963, is lost]. My fee is as before: 30 N [old French Francs] an hour of course."

The above December course had been pre-empted by the second letter from Murakami to Bell that still survives. Dated the 5th December 1960, the letter confirms Murakami's time of arrival for the course. However, this letter also contains some extremely important information, the truth of which was later to be disputed. Murakami wrote: "Please, the next time when you have something to ask for to the Japanese Federation, warn me first and don't write directly to Japan. I was sent to Europe to be their representative and must be aware of all things concerning karate." Bell took this statement as truthful, after all, it was from the Master, and left it like that for the next three years.

Master Murakami visited England one more time in 1960 then, holding a four-day, seventeen-hour course, between the 16th and 19th of December at Hornchurch. No further details are available on this visit other than who graded and some financial figures. Gradings were held on the 16th and 18th December, and the following students passed: 6th kyu – M. Dinsdale, K. Goult, K. Mansfield, S. Morgan, J. Shepherd,

An early group photo from the St. Mary's *dojo*, Upminster – 1960. From left to right, kneeling: C. Alibone, J. Neal, M. Manning, R. Richardson, unknown; standing, left to right: J. Wijesundera, unknown, unknown, V. Bell, T. Wingrove, R. Harris, Master Murakami, unknown, J. Weisner.

Training at the St. Mary's *dojo*, Upminster – 1960. From left to right: unknown, C. Alibone, T. Wingrove, Master Murakami, B. Hammond, P. Richardson, J. Williamson (obscured), R. Harris (obscured), J. Wijesundera, J. Neal, R. Buckner.

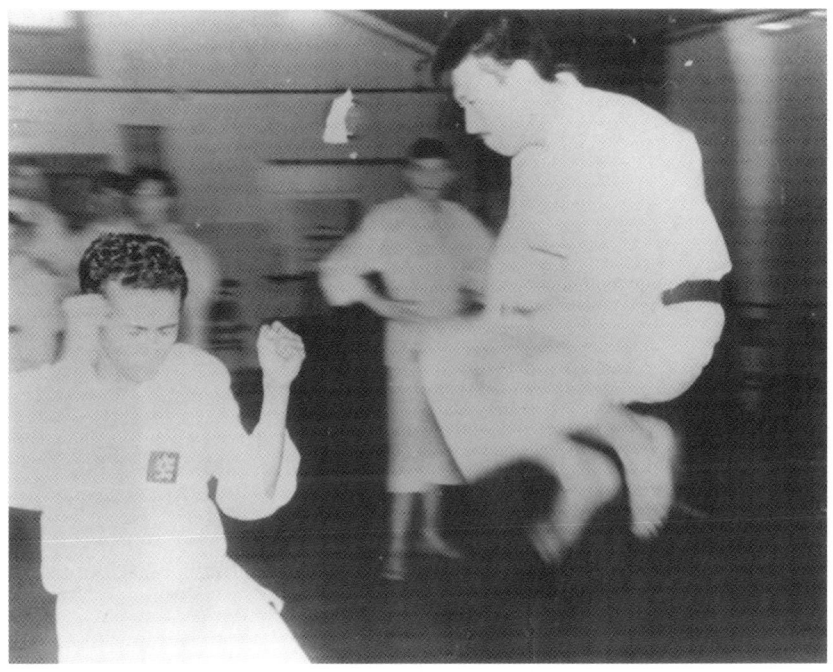

Wijesundera receiving the Murakami treatment – Upminster *dojo*, 1960

Training at the St. Mary's *dojo*, Upminster – 1960. From left to right: T. Wingrove, unknown, unknown, P. Richardson, C. Alibone, Master Murakami, J. Williamson, B. Hammond, J. Neal, R. Harris.

Terry Wingrove, Master Murakami, Jimmy Neal and Bob Buckner – Upminster, 1960/61.

G. Stubbings, E. Tillett, D. Williams; 4th kyu – R. Buckner, V. Maxwell, J. Neal, K. Richardson, T. Wingrove; 3rd kyu – J. Wijesundera. Jimmy Neal was registered as having passed 4th kyu in August with Wijesundera. Either the previous entry for Neal was in error, or he failed his 3rd kyu in December, the latter being the more likely. It appears from the BKF grading register that all those attempting 6th kyu failed under Bell on the 16th and they re-took the grading under Murakami on the 18th, and all were successful. Bell had previously failed Stubbings and Tillett on the 11th and 22nd September 1960, and Shepherd on the 15th October 1960, at Hornchurch. On the 23rd October 1960, an F. Soall failed his 6th kyu.

Over one hundred BKF kyu gradings have so far been recorded in this book, covering a period of some three years and eight months. These gradings have been taken chiefly from the BKF grading register and other miscellaneous (mostly back-up) sources. The distribution of BKF grades gleaned from BKF grading register entries and other sources are as follows: 1957 – 21 gradings; 1958 – 22 gradings; 1959 – 16 gradings; and, 1960 – 44 gradings. In the next calendar year, there were a further ninety-six recorded gradings. We can infer from this almost doubling of previous gradings, that karate was beginning to become properly established. Individuals were continuing to train, and the art was

A group shot of members of the St. Mary's *dojo*, Upminster – 1960/61. Sitting, left to right: Bob Buckner, J. Wijesundera, Master Murakami, Jimmy Neal, Terry Wingrove.

Group shot at the St. Mary's *dojo*, Upminster - 1962. Members sitting, left to right: Brian Hammond, Ken Goult, B. Sheppard, Master Murakami, D. Williams, Jimmy Neal.

attracting new members. In the years to follow, 1962 saw well over one hundred people grade, as did 1963. Some eighty people graded in 1964, but this was a deliberate holdback policy, for reasons that will be made clear later. The year 1965 saw an enormous expansion, with over two hundred and twenty-five recorded grades being awarded. It is possible however, that the true number for 1965 exceeds that figure, as not all gradings may have been recorded. In 1966, BKF records become incomplete as not all grading results appear to have been submitted to Bell for recording. All known details about the gradings from 1961 to mid 1966, when this book ends, will be provided.

Murakami was paid £29 2s. for his teaching on the December, 1960, course. His hotel accommodation was £8 4s. 6d; the rent on the two halls booked was £6 4s; incidental expenses for Murakami for entertainment, meals out etc., came to £3 1s. 1d; and his airfare, by Skyways, was £8 10s.

The Wednesday, 21st December 1960, edition of *The Romford Times*, carried a report of a visit to Romford from Paris by thirty-three-year-old Master Murakami. Under the heading, "These Men Can Kill – But Promise They Won't," the unknown reporter starts his piece by saying: "Twenty men were training in deadly earnest in Romford at the weekend – training to kill. They were being taught karate, the art of Japanese boxing – and before they started they had to promise never to use it outside the course. Because one blow from a trained karate man can kill." Pupils on the course watched as the, "wiry ... seven-stone master twisted limbs and body at will, [and] moved with the speed of a cougar." Murakami was wrongly described as, "the only man outside Japan who is allowed to teach this art." It may interest readers to know that Murakami's visit cost the BKF £50 for seventeen hours' tuition. The Romford course attracted some thirty-five BKF members. Vernon Bell was quoted in *The Romford Times* as saying, "We usually get the studious type, the person who has never done any other sport ... and there are NO teddy-boys or rough-necks in this bunch." Two photographs accompanied this report. The first, by David Gossling, is one of the finest pictures of Murakami ever taken. He is shown performing a *yoko-tobi-geri* some five feet in the air. The second picture shows Master Murakami performing a groin-height *mawashi-geri* on a nineteen-year-old Terry Wingrove.

The year 1960 is of interest also, in the history of British karate, because Terry Wingrove trained at three *dojos* in Paris. He recalled: "I used to train with Murakami in France. I used to go from Lydd by plane to Beauvais, and then catch a bus. It was a shuttle service and was famous because it only cost £7 return. By this time Murakami spoke a

Master Murakami in the process of delivering a right *yoko-tobi-geri* upon Victor Maxwell. Lawns Social Club, Romford – December 1960.

little French, and I could also. It wasn't quite as bad as pointing and saying, 'You, me, cup of tea.' I remember that Murakami used to tell us that it would take eight years of hard practice to reach *Shodan*, and that 5th Dan was the highest grade awarded. He was the hardest person I ever graded with. I failed my brown-belt [3rd to 1st kyu] grades eight times. I'm proud to say that. The training in Plee's *dojo* was excellent.

Plee was a very nice man. I first went there as a white-belt, threw my arms and legs about, no problem. Put a white belt on and you can't go wrong – I've learned that!"

The third *dojo* that Wingrove visited was not quite so accommodating – Jim Alcheik's *dojo* in the Avenue Parmentier, Paris. Readers may recall that Alcheik had actually trained at the Yoseikan in the early 1950s and was teaching karate and aikido. Wingrove recalled: "I trained with Jim Alcheik, though his real name was Jean Alcheik. He was the greatest martial artist ever, and I mean ever, to come out of Europe. He came back from the Yoseikan a 4th Dan in aikido, [a 2nd Dan in karate, a 2nd Dan in kendo, and a 3rd Dan in judo], and believe me he was good. His *dojo* was the hardest I've ever seen, including anything I've ever seen in Japan or Okinawa [Terry Wingrove subsequently lived in Japan for some twenty years]. Vernon wouldn't train there. I went to see Alcheik, like a naive and stupid kid, just nineteen years old. His *dojo* was amazing, real state of the art. He was teaching real fighting karate as a martial art. In this class you beat the hell out of each other. Eventually one person would fall to the ground injured, or seriously injured. The first time I went to that *dojo*, the very first time, I walked in and they said, 'Who are you?' There were three minders on the door. I said that I was from England, and they said that Mr. Alcheik was expecting me. I walked in and I'll never forget what greeted me. There was this man, aged about thirty-five to forty, with a bald head, a brown-belt, and a young lad about eighteen who was wearing a white belt. I'll never forget what happened. They were doing freestyle and the white-belt turned to walk out. The brown-belt scooped him into the air, both legs, and he landed on his head, splitting his head wide open. The brown-belt didn't even look at him as they dragged him off. The blood was all over the floor. That was my introduction to Alcheik's *dojo*. Anyway, Alcheik asked me if I wanted to train and I said that I did. I realised within the first ten minutes you had to hit someone – the usual rubbish, I'm stronger than you. I didn't have a good knowledge of karate at the time, but I had a good knowledge of ju-jitsu. I had put on a white belt and I was against this other brown-belt. It was hard. He cut my face and I got angry. I threw him on the floor and broke his arm with a lock. I never had any problems in that *dojo* after that. It was a serious *dojo*, about twenty-five to thirty students, of which only four or five were white, the rest were Algerian and from the other Magreb countries."

Alcheik was assassinated on the 29th January 1962. He was killed in an explosion along with eighteen others. There are numerous stories, but it appears to have been connected, somehow, with an independence movement concerning a North African country.

It was around this time (the exact date is unknown, but either 1960 or 1961) that Bell instigated the, "1st Senior Grades Special Two Year Coaching Course," a course approved by Master Murakami. The course was designed to, amongst other things, train instructors for the future to brown and black-belt level, so that the BKF could progress. Designed for those of at least eighteen years of age and holding a minimum grade of 4th kyu, the course curriculum was comprised of: "Anatomy, physiology, nervous system, pressure points, nerve points, eight methods of revival and restoration of life processes, death blows, first three *ippon kata*, first and second *kata* of *sanbon*, first five *kata* of *Heian*, first three *kata* of *kumide*, first and second *kata* of *koshiki*. All techniques of fist, palm, fingers, wrist, elbow, forearm, shoulder, head, knee, shin, foot, sole, heel and toes. First three *kata* of self-defence, first two combat *kata*, first *kata* of *Ju-No* (education), fifteen combination techniques, twenty-five attacks and counter-attacks with hands and arms, twenty attacks and counter-attacks of foot. Karate techniques for street fighting, fifteen karate techniques against a boxer, fifteen karate techniques against a wrestler, demonstration *kata* for display, and the scientific study of other systems of Chinese boxing, kempo, yawara, ju-jitsu, etc. [A] complete history of karate, contests, and refereeing procedures. The curriculum will also cover class discipline and coaching, personal instruction, class organisation, course procedure, organisation, opening and running clubs, management of clubs and branches, teaching techniques, grading procedure and organisation; [also] how to grade. All matters of theory and practice befitting what a *Shodan* should know, and be, as an instructor."

At the end of the two years, the student would receive either a 1st kyu or *Shodan* certificate. For those who graduated with a 1st kyu, Bell wrote: "The student can progress upon a further special curriculum course in preparation for examination to 1st Dan of Yoseikan – time 9-12 months. This course includes teaching procedures and techniques; opening, operating and managing a karate *dojo*; grading examinations; higher systems of *kutsu*; advanced anatomy and nervous system, etc.; methods of selecting pupils, training schedules, etc.; Karate-do as a system of physical culture and education for men, women and children, etc.; karate and the law."

The price of the course was £2 2s. a month, payable three months in advance. Conditions for the course were strict. It seems as though Terry Wingrove and Jimmy Neal were the only two students to complete the course.

Master Murakami with Alan Ruddock – early 1960's

On the 1st January 1961, Bell graded Alan Ruddock to 6th kyu after a weekend course at 12, Maybush Road. Ruddock was shortly to found the Irish Karate-Do Federation, based in Dublin, and, later, would travel to Japan, but became disillusioned with karate in Tokyo, and changed to aikido, studying under Morihei Ueshiba.

Bell was still plugging away at the demonstrations, both indoor and outdoor. On Tuesday, 28th February 1961, for example, a demonstration

Master Murakami and Terry Wingrove sparring at the Upminster *dojo* – 1961/62.

was given to the Hornchurch Division of the Young Conservatives. A letter from a Miss A. Kerr, the Honorary Secretary, makes it clear the display of judo and Japanese boxing went very well. She noted, "I think most of the members realised the advantage of knowing a few of the more simple throws and it was great fun being given the opportunity to actually try some on your patient and willing pupils."

An example of an outdoor demonstration given at the time was for the Horticultural Society Summer Show, held in the grounds of the ABRAC Works, Blackhorse Lane, Walthamstow, on Saturday, 22nd July 1961. Bell and his students, on this occasion, gave a forty-minute display of judo, ju-jitsu and karate.

Master Murakami held his next grading at the Upminster *dojo* on the 2nd April 1961, following a weekend course. The BKF grading register shows the following people successfully graded: 6th kyu – J. Alibone; 5th kyu – K. Goult, B. Hammond, E. Harris, S. Morgan, A. Ruddock, J. Shepherd, E. Tillett, D. Williams; 3rd kyu – R. Buckner, T. Wingrove.

Around this time, the exact date is unknown, Martin Stott, in Manchester, was advertising karate. Terry Wingrove recalled: "He went to Paris and came back and put an advert in the paper. Vernon went and chased him – typical Vernon. The man, Stott, was all right, but it all fizzled out." [In his letter to Bell dated the 21st May, 1961, Stott had noted that: "I have managed to persuade Master Tam-Mytho to come to London to teach a stage of karate from the 8th to the 24th September, with your help of course. During the first week we will give exhibitions in London which, if possible, will include a programme on television and in the second week he will teach a stage of karate." Presumably, nothing came of this venture].

Wingrove continued: "Kenshiro Abbe was also trying to get a karate man into Britain. Finally he got someone from Belgium, an ex-pupil of Alcheik's, and he taught one or two courses. I think this man's name was Stassart, but I'm not sure. But Vernon was the number one man, no question about it."

The BKF then, was running happily in Essex and London and training in Liverpool had just begun. Over the next few years, karate began to spread more widely throughout Britain. One of the men responsible for this was Gordon Thompson, whose interest and initiative allowed for the growth of Shotokan karate in the north-east of England. He completed the application form for BKF membership on the 25th January 1961, aged thirty years, and his form shows that at the time of joining his interests lay in mountaineering, opera, judo (he had graded to 2nd kyu) and electronics.

Gordon Thompson recalled: "In the army I had been stationed in Egypt and, as is always the case when you are on active service, boredom is one of the chief problems. So I became a member of the boxing team. I was never good enough to represent the battalion, but I was always considered good enough to give those that did represent the battalion a good work out. In other words, I was a chopping block." Thompson left the army in 1953.

The Railway Institute, an organisation for railway personnel, had a large gymnasium, in Queen Street, York, near the station where Thompson worked as a coach-builder for the railway, and a judo section was being formed (there were various "sections" – boxing, gymnastics, tennis, weight-lifting, and so on). Thompson, who had had enough of boxing, continued: "In those days there was not a lot to do after work. The country was only just recovering after the Second World War, and there were virtually no clubs for young men to go to, so the new judo section soon had sufficient members to get off to a good start ... Well, after a couple of years or so the word 'karate' cropped up. I asked our instructor, Jim Piggot, 1st Dan, what karate was. At this time judo was the only martial art that had been heard of in England, and the British Judo Association to which we belonged was a very strong organisation.

The photograph that Gordon Thompson submitted with his BKF application form – 1961.

Black-belts ... were nearly as rare as hen's teeth, so their opinions were held in great respect. Well, Jim started going on about karate. He said that a bunch of morons in Japan were busy mutilating their fists so that they could smash boards and the like. They were of low intelligence and would not be allowed near a judo mat, etc. This invective occurred not just this once, but every time anything to do with martial arts other than judo was mentioned, and not just by Jim Piggot, but also by any other senior grade who came to the club. After a while I thought, 'They protesteth too much' ... Then somewhere I saw advertised the famous book, *Karate: The Art of 'Empty-hand' Fighting*, by Nishiyama and Brown. Anyway ... being an awkward sort of so and so, I sent away for it and brought it down to the judo club. Well, you would have thought I was taking bacon to Jerusalem, and I was told to take it away and never bring it again! I found the book fascinating, and John Clark and I tried to work at some of the things that were in it. I can see now that we had no chance of learning anything of value, but nevertheless we found it very interesting. Then one day we had a visitor to the club who knew a little bit about karate, although he did not practice it himself. He told me to write to Mr. Vernon Bell at 137, Perryman's Farm Road, Ilford, Essex, who was running the only club in England. As you can guess, I did so that very night.

"I got a strange letter back, pages and pages of it. I was informed that he was the father and founder of the only club in Great Britain, the British Karate Federation (BKF), and that he was the only qualified black-belt in the country etc. He said I could join the organisation if I wished, and he would sponsor me and get a seconder. Apparently you had to be proposed and seconded at a meeting of his organisation. Included in the envelope were two duplicated foolscap sheets ... that caused me the utmost astonishment. I had never seen anything like them in my life and I haven't since ... One of them was an application form for membership of the BKF ... [the other] an 'Oath of Allegiance!' The promises we had to make! ... We also had to go to our doctor and undergo a medical. The questions were on the application form and had to be answered by the doctor who signed a declaration that the answers were correct. I did it, but I couldn't look my doctor in the eye for months afterwards – I felt a right nit. Finally, we had to sign both forms over a sixpenny stamp ... and have them witnessed by two persons of standing in the community – Ye Gods!

"With tongue firmly stuck in my cheek, I filled out both forms and sent them off. I was accepted, in fact I never knew of anyone who was not accepted, and in the same envelope I was informed that ... [a course] ... was going to be held at St. Osyth, near Clacton, with Mr. Murakami as the instructor. I was invited to attend, and an application form was included in the envelope. [The one-week course was from 5th-12th of August 1961] ... It was held in a holiday camp and we used the central hall during the time the bar was not open. I went there on my motorbike. I had a souped-up Norton Dominator at the time..."

The Summer School became important not only because of

Thompson's attendance, and what was to follow from that, but also for the attendance of Edward Ainsworth, a twenty-six-year-old cabinet-maker from Saltcoats, Ayrshire. Ainsworth was a *Shodan judoka* and ran two judo clubs at the time of joining the BKF on the 13th July 1961. In a letter to Ainsworth dated the 27th June 1961, Bell noted the following, which might seem extraordinary today, but these were pioneering days: "I urge you to make every effort to attend [the course] in your own interests. Contrary to the opinion of your friends, the BKF has no official representatives nor trained instructors in Scotland, therefore, if you make the effort to attend and come on this long journey and study under Mr. Murakami and myself for one week, you will pass out as a 5th kyu. If you do this we can appoint you as our official Area Representative for Scotland and grant you a charter to establish a Karate Section..."

Ainsworth did attend the course and set up a *dojo* in Auchen Larvie, between Saltcoats and Stevenston, Ayrshire. It proved to be a small *dojo*, and only ten BKF membership forms have survived. These will be mentioned now, as no more will be made of the Ayrshire *dojo* in this book. As usual, the ages, occupations at the time of BKF membership, and date of application for membership will be given: Patrick Bannerman, 18, apprentice sheet metal worker (13.5.63); Joseph Bell, 25, process worker (21.10.61); Hugh Hackett, 20, engineer (23.12.62); James Kelso, 21, foreman (7.5.63); John Malley, 40, processman (24.1.62); Edward McGowan, 27, labourer (24.4.63); John McLean, 17, student (16.11.62); James Mitchell, 25, assistant company secretary (18.1.62); Robert Park, 19, apprentice electrician (16.10.61); James Shaw, 25, hairdresser (13.10.63).

Thompson continued with regard to the St. Osyth course: "Anyway, I met some of the BKF members outside the hall and some of them seemed as new as I was. I think there were about twenty of us, but I am not too sure about this. After I had been there a few minutes, and, being the only northerner there, I was keeping quiet and wondering what the hell was going to happen, when a bloke rolled up on a lightweight motorbike with a large sticker on the windscreen reading, 'Sexpert.' This turned out to be Terry Wingrove, one of the senior members of the BKF, and a brown-belt ... Eventually, Mr. Bell turned up with Mr. Murakami and, after a little milling about looking for the key and getting the okay, we went into the hall."

In fact, Terry Wingrove had had a narrow escape on his journey to St. Osyth. Wingrove recalled: "Mr. Bell in his usual inimitable style said, 'Everybody follow me,' and we all had to go in a convoy. It was pouring with rain. Vernon had this new Thames van and he never drove more than thirty-five miles an hour. We had more rows over this than anything else. Anyway, he was driving along the road with Murakami next to him. I was behind him on my Triumph Tiger Cub, goggles on and with a passenger. It was absolutely pouring with rain. Vernon went round a corner, missed it, and went straight over into a ditch in these appalling conditions. I couldn't see because the rain was so bad, and I just followed him. I went down into the ditch, and over the roof of his new car. I took off over the hedge. As we landed, we went over. The bike fell on top of me and the hot exhaust burned into my leg – look, you can still see the scar. I was lying in this muddy field, and it was just pouring with rain. Suddenly, I felt the pain of the hot exhaust pipe, and I went Ahhhhh! as it burned into me. I threw the bike off me and it landed on Kenny's [Goult] legs. So to this day we've both got burn marks on our legs. Vernon was going, 'Will you come out of there. Look what you've done to my car.' It's funny now, but it wasn't so funny then."

Gordon Thompson continued: "Mr. Murakami was a small, dark man, and smoked like a chimney. He was a nice chap with, as I found out later, quite a sense of humour. The training seemed quite hard to me, but it was not nearly as hard as some of the sessions I had later on in my karate career. He was the first high graded *karateka* I met, and I was tremendously impressed ... whatever organisation he came from or represented, he was a great fellow and *karateka* ... We trained twice a day for two hours a time, and started off with very basic techniques. We were in long lines and went through the basic techniques standing on the spot. They were broken down into three or more actions, and I remember Mr. Murakami going round the whole class again and again correcting each and every person there. The senior grades were given harder training, of course, and we moved on during the week, but, as was to be expected, as a beginner, I did not understand half of what was happening. I just got on with what I had been told to do, and worked as hard as I could. Mr. Bell did not train, in fact only once did I ever see him in a karate *gi* and that was in his own *dojo* in London. Mr. Murakami did not speak English, but French. Terry Wingrove and Mr. Bell spoke French and did the interpretation when necessary, which was not at all often. I thoroughly enjoyed the course ... Unfortunately, I had to go home before the course ended – the money ran out [having just returned from three weeks climbing in Austria] ... I was camping in a field and living as cheaply as I could, but on the last day but one I was out of cash, out of grub, and had only just enough petrol to get home.

Master Murakami performs a *mae-tobi-geri* upon brown-belt, Jimmy Neal, at the 1961 Summer School at St. Osyth. Gordon Thompson, from York, is believed to be obscured by Murakami.

"I only had a few words with Mr. Bell, as he always arrived late, bringing Mr. Murakami with him, and also dragging him away the minute the training was over. I thought nothing of this at the time, but later on we all found out why this was so ... Anyway, on my last day at the St. Osyth course, I went up to him and apologised for having to leave early and asked him to convey my apologies to Mr. Murakami who was standing next to him. There followed a short conversation in French, and then Mr. Bell turned to me and said that "the old fellow" thought that I was doing quite well, and as I could not get to the grading, which was being held on the last day of the course, he would give me my first grading anyway. That's how I got my yellow-belt. In those days there were only six kyu grades and the first gave you the right to wear a yellow belt. He was as good as his word, and early in the New Year I got my grading card with my grade on it. It was dated 4th August 1961..." (the date being an administrative error, since the course was from the 5th to the 12th August, as has already been noted). Gradings for students on that summer school were either on the 12th August or on the 14th August, following a further two-day course. Thompson's 6th kyu grading date is recorded in the BKF grading register as the 24th August 1961.

It is of interest to note here that, in a reply letter, dated 16th June, 1961, to Martin Stott, mentioned earlier, who at the time was training with Tam-Mytho, at the Centre Français de Karaté, based at 221, Bd Raspail, Paris 14e [Stott notes that his instructor was a 3rd Dan in karate, 2nd Dan in aikido and 1st Dan in kendo], Bell provides the minimum time lapse between gradings in the BKF. Bell wrote: "Mr. Murakami, as the only expert in Europe, clearly states that in Yoseikan karate an average man working three times a week with two hours hard practice each time can obtain his promotions in the following times: Beginner to 6th kyu – 2 months, 6th kyu to 5th kyu – 3 months, 5th kyu to 4th kyu – 4 months, 4th kyu to 3rd kyu – 6 months, 3rd kyu to 2nd kyu – 6 months, 2nd kyu to 1st kyu – 9 months, 1st kyu to 1st Dan – 18 months." It would therefore take a minimum of four years' hard practice – some one thousand two hundred and fifty hours, to reach *Shodan*. Bell also noted that the time limit between Dan grades was: "From 1st Dan to 2nd Dan is 2 years, from 2nd to 3rd Dan from 3 to 5 years ... [and that at that time] ... there are only eight 2nd Dans in Europe all conferred by Mr. Murakami." Bell was one of these eight *karateka* of course. Bell also noted: "Mr. Murakami is the only person eligible and qualified to grade in Europe for the JKA and Yoseikan..." As has been previously mentioned, this notion was to be disputed later on, as we shall see, but Bell believed it to be true at the time.

Seaview Holiday Lido, situated some eight miles from Colchester on the B1069 and four miles from Clacton, was actually two miles from the village of St. Osyth, along Beach Road, a third-class concrete road. Accommodation for instructors and students alike was in caravans. The camp was large and licensed, holding several hundred four-berth caravans of good quality. Each caravan had electric light, calor gas, blankets, crockery and cutlery. One had to bring one's own bed linen. All caravans were to be booked individually by students at a cost of approximately seven or eight guineas a week, irrespective of the number of occupants – as long as it did not exceed four. Meals could be obtained from the camp's restaurant and cafeteria. It was not, however, necessary to stay at the camp in order to attend the karate course, as was the case with Gordon Thompson, though the vast majority of students did.

In an interesting statement, which Bell wrote on the course details intended for club secretaries, he noted: "This course has been specially arranged for the benefit and advancement of all persons and members,

Master Murakami about to deliver a right *yoko-tobi-geri* upon brown-belt, Terry Wingrove, at the 1961 Summer School at St. Osyth. Douglas Pettman, from Lincoln, is first left, and Edward Ainsworth, from Scotland, second left.

and much effort and negotiations have gone into the effort of arranging this course with Master Murakami, and we have guaranteed him his fee which is rather high, plus his expenses and living, and it is the duty of each and every member of the BKF to do his utmost to attend this course to ensure success, for failure of this course may prevent a further visit of this high ranking master. Estimate to cover course from loss has been fixed at over eighty pounds, a figure which must be covered by enrolments on this course. Any losses will be borne from BKF funds. This course will not be cancelled even though only a few people enrol." This statement had been on the details of previous annual courses as we have seen, and remained so for some years to come. Membership to the BKF was still one guinea, plus ten shillings for a licence.

The course at St. Osyth, described, incorrectly, in course details as the fourth annual summer school of the BKF – it was actually the third – had been a great success. Training had been held in the main hall of the Entertainments Pavilion of the holiday camp. Bell had prepared

A class practising at the 1961 Summer School at St. Osyth. Master Murakami is paired up with Terry Wingrove at the far end of the line.

four pages of information on the course, which he distributed to all BKF members. Course application forms and other literature were obtainable upon sending a two-shilling postal order to Bell. Regarding the *dojo*, Bell wrote: "The pavilion has a highly polished marley-tiled floor, coloured lighting, stage, bar, changing facilities, children's playroom and a dance floor. It is situated in the centre of the camp and very accessible."

Details of the course are as follows. At 5.15 p.m., on the date of arrival, students registered with Bell in the *dojo*. Fees, payable in advance, were seven guineas or the full seven-day course, which included the grading. Training times were between 11.00 a.m. and 1.30 p.m. and 6.00 p.m. and 7.30 p.m., with a grading on the last Saturday commencing between 3.00 p.m. and 3.30 p.m. Those successful in their grading had to pay an additional two shillings and sixpence for registration of grade! Training was split so that Vernon Bell took the complete beginners for the first few days, whilst Master Murakami took those with experience and those who had previously graded. In the last two or three days, all students trained with Master Murakami. The "Course Curriculum" was as follows: "Preparatory exercises, toughening exercises and procedures, postures of attack and defence, methods of parrying and counter-attack, methods of walking and turning, attacking stances and changing positions, techniques of hitting with the fist, fingers, arm, side of hand, elbow etc., and kicking with the foot and heel, etc. Combination techniques, 1st, 2nd and 3rd combat *kata*, attacks and defences, 1st *Pinan kata*, self-defence, contest, conventional *kumite* (free practice) *ippon kumite*." The course details noted that, "All of this course will be devoted to pure Yoseikan karate, with a little self-defence instruction by the National Coach separately for those interested."

We are fortunate that some facts and figures survive with regard to this summer school, for one weekend course and an aikido course, that appear on two sheets. The summer school raised £95 11s; the weekend course, £35 14s, and the aikido course £14 5s. BKF enrolments came to £3 7s, licence fees to £3 and grading registration fees to £1 15s. The selling of badges raised £1 7s. 6d. The total BKF intake for the period 5th to 14th August 1961, came to £154 19s. 6d. The outgoings were: Murakami's teaching fees – £97 18s, Murakami's return airfare – £9 10s, Murakami's hotel bills for Romford and Clacton – £12 1s. 6d, Bell's hotel in Clacton – £7 17s. 6d, and, Murakami and Bell's petrol, general and incidental expenses etc. – £32 9s. 11d. On the 11th August there had been an accident at the Clubhouse at the holiday camp, and V. Bell and a D. Young are named. The damage came to £11 12s. The total debits to £171 8s. There were some additional outgoings including *dojo* rent, printing, duplicating and so on, and things are not as clear as they might be. However, the courses for that period appear to have run at a definite loss.

The St. Osyth course was reported on page 13 of the *East Essex Gazette* on the 18th August 1961, in the "Sport Spotlight" column. Under the heading, "Karate Master Had The Crowd Spellbound," the unknown reporter noted that the venue had been suggested by a former employee of the centre, David Williams, who was a student of the BKF, and that when asked, the camp proprietor, Terry O'Dell, had readily agreed. The opening paragraph, in bold type, noted that, "Hundreds of caravanners watched spellbound as Master Tetsuji Murakami, highest ranking legitimate karate exponent outside Japan and an ex-Japanese champion, put members of the British Federation through their paces. For that privilege they had travelled from all parts of Great Britain and Ireland and combined attendance at this fourth summer course with an annual holiday." A very brief karate biography of Vernon Bell was given, as were the usual benefits of karate training, such as it being suitable for women and that age was no barrier (one member, the reporter noted, was over fifty and an exclamation mark was placed after this statement). The perceptive reporter noted that, "Once it [karate] has been tried, all other sports seem tame in comparison." The course was, as previously noted, divided into two parts, with Vernon Bell teaching the beginners and the "strict and exacting" Master Murakami, the more advanced. What is particularly revealing in this account of events however, is contained in the last paragraph: "Mr. Murakami proved that he could relax in a charming manner in his leisure moments. Mixing freely with the caravanners and Federation members, he challenged them to darts and table tennis at both of which he showed he was no novice; similarly, he quickly mastered the intricacies of a high-powered motorcycle. In short, he proved a VIP who went down in a big way and Terry O'Dell was most impressed by his oriental visitor." A good photograph of Master Murakami performing "the jumping scissors kick" (actually *mae-tobi-geri*) upon a student performing *gedan-barai* in front-stance was also included.

Whether Master Murakami actually mastered the intricacies of a high-powered motorcycle is debatable, and makes for an amusing story. Vernon Bell remembered: "My old friend Terry Wingrove was a brown-belt at the time. He arrived at St. Osyth on his motorbike. Master Murakami had the caravan next to me and he was game for anything – disco dancing, darts, anything. He was a versatile little Japanese. A lovely little man I thought he was in those days. Wingrove said, '*Sensei*, you drive motorbike?' and Murakami said, 'No! Me not drive motorbike,' in his pidgin French and English. Wingrove said, 'You have go. Sit on saddle and I'll start engine.' So Murakami sat on the bike. It was started up, put in first gear, and Murakami went straight through the side of a caravan and fell off the motorbike. Wingrove just stood there looking at his bike and all the other pupils just laughed their heads off. Murakami just got up, dusted down his little pseudo-Italian suit and said, 'O.....h, Wingrove!' Murakami laughed at the joke. He could laugh at himself. He died too young."

The following students successfully graded at the end of the course (or as has already been noted, two days later): 6th kyu – R. Barker, S. Dalton, D. Flateau, B. Juxon, R. Lamport, G. McLeod; 5th kyu – E. Ainsworth and D. Pettman (both of whom passed 6th kyu as well – so they double-graded); 4th kyu – C. Cabot, K. Goult, B. Hammond, A. Ruddock, J. Shepherd, D. Williams.

"When I got home," Thompson recalled, "I went to the judo club as usual and told them all about my experiences. I got a mixed reception. The higher the grade the person was, the more they condemned my actions, and they all lined up to bash me. Well at least they tried to. Mr. Piggott did so with the greatest of ease, but the others did not find it so easy. However, some of the junior grades expressed an interest, and after the judo session was over, I would show them some of the things I had learned. It met with the great disapproval of the higher grades of course, but there was nothing they could do about it. I suppose you could say that our little gathering was the first karate club in the area. Well, we carried on like this for a few months and a couple of chaps turned up looking for the karate club. They were Tony Aydon and Patrick O'Donovan, who became, and still are, very good friends of mine, although they no longer practise. I had to tell them the situation, and they joined the judo club purely for the karate instruction I gave at the end ... We wanted to start a proper karate club, but in York there was absolutely no place where we could train. The judo club was unavailable ... then one day, one chap ... came up to me and told me he had arranged for us to train at the Irish National League Working Men's Club twice a week. It was not an ideal arrangement, but it was a start. We had to join the working-men's club of course, but that was no trouble, as we were all working lads. It prevented any juniors joining, but that was no trouble at the time, as the idea of karate was that it was something for adults and not children. In fact, karate was completely unknown to the public – they thought it was a place in India. Anyway, we got started and held a meeting in the Black Swan in Peasholm Green to formulate the way we wanted the club to be run. I wanted to get started on the right foot and drew up a constitution. We elected the usual club officials, chairman, treasurer and secretary, and never regretted taking the trouble. Among the bumph Mr. Bell had sent me in his first letter was a long sheet of instructions on how to start a karate club. We had, according to this, to go to the police, get their permission, fill in a couple of forms ... John Clark undertook to see the police and make enquiries as it all seemed very strange. He came back playing hell. The police had looked at him as if he was mad, and told him that if he wanted to start a club then all he had to do was go ahead ... [Apparently, Vernon Bell's recommendations were based on the experiences of a certain French karate organisation, and Bell was being cautious, which was to his credit] ... Well, we got started and registered ourselves with Mr. Bell as the North-East Branch of the British Karate Federation. After about six months the club took off, and we had as many members as we could cope with."

On the 24th September 1961, Bell travelled to Liverpool and conducted a training session and grading. The BKF grading register reveals that the following people passed: 6th kyu – T. Astley, G. Bingham, C. Butler, K. Caulfield, G. Dicken, J. Donaghue, K. McCaldon,

Douglas Pettman (front row, far left) at the St. Mary's *dojo*, Upminster - 1961. Other members of the group are, from left to right, sitting: R. Armstrong, Master Murakami, J. Wijesundera, B. Hammond; standing, left to right: unknown, unknown, S. Dalton, D. Flateau, R. Lamport.

Instructor training for BKF Area Representatives (and others) at the Upminster *dojo* – 1962. From left to right: D. Williams, B. Shepperd, K. Goult, G. Thompson, J. Neal, E. Ainsworth, Master Murakami, unknown, T. Wingrove, A. Ruddock, M. Smith, D. Pettman.

Members of the BKF Lincoln *dojo* at RAF Scampton – 1961. From left to right, back row: unknown, Thomas Smith; middle row: unknown, Victor Wingvist, Brian Henn, Arthur Logan, Douglas Pettman, unknown; front row: George Fletcher-Baker, Bernard Purbrick, Oliver Coffey, Kwet Sam Ng Man Kwong.

P. Meir, A. Sherry, P. Sloan, M. Walls, T. Wignall, F. Williams, J. Wilson; 5th kyu – F. Gille, B. Juxon, C. Naylor (Gille and Naylor passed 6th kyu as well); 4th kyu – B. Patsby (or perhaps "Patshy" – Bell's writing is not clear). Patsby appears to have passed 6th kyu and 5th kyu as well. Nothing else is known of this gentleman.

Bell returned to Liverpool in December 1961, and conducted a grading on the 16th. The BKF grading register reveals that the following people passed: 6th kyu – T. Barry, A. Dewar, G. Galletly, K. May, H. A. (Alan) Smith, E. Travis; 5th kyu – F. Williams.

Another BKF club that was established on the 20th September 1961 was based at RAF Scampton in Lincolnshire. Training was held at the base's gymnasium on Mondays and Wednesdays between 7.00 and 9.00 p.m. It appears that BKF affiliation was short-lived however. Little is known about this *dojo*, other than the thirteen membership application forms that have survived. Douglas Pettman, 33, an electrician, became the BKF Area Officer, completing his BKF application forms on the 20th May 1961. Pettman had attended the August Summer School, and had been promoted to 5th kyu. The students at the club, for whom details are available, were all serving in the RAF. Their names, ages, and date of application form completion are as follows: Gerald Archer, 17, (6.11.61); Michael Beazer, 24, (11.12.61); Francis Carroll, 23, (12.10.61); Oliver Coffey, 19, (19.10.61); George Fletcher-Baker, 33, (22.10.61); Brian Henn, 20, (18.10.61); Kwet Ng Man Kwong, 29, (3.10.61); Arthur Logan, 23, (24.10.61); Gerald Nixon, 27, (26.9.61); Bernard Purbrick, 31, (5.10.61); Thomas Smith, 25, (17.11.61); and, Victor Wingvist, 23, (14.9.61). In correspondence, the names Ashton, Farrell, Gibbons and Knight are also mentioned.

Vernon Bell conducted the Scampton *dojo's* first karate grading on the 29th October 1961. The BKF grading register reveals that the following people passed: 6th kyu – O. Coffey, B. Henn, K. Kwong, A. Logan, G. Nixon, B. Purbrick, V. Wingvist; 5th kyu – R. Barker; 4th kyu – D. Pettman. The second and last grading at the club was held under Bell on the 14th February 1962, when G. Archer, M. Beazer and G. Fletcher-Baker became 6th kyus, and K. Kwong and V. Wingvist, 5th kyus.

PART V

It was late in 1961, November to be precise, that Vernon Bell started to teach members of the United States Air Force at their base just off the Watford Road, Denham, Buckinghamshire. Bell had in fact given a historically very early thirty minute demonstration to the American Airforce on Sunday the 4th August 1957, at Reading. In a letter to Plee, dated the 10th August 1957, Bell wrote: "It was well attended and very successful. In the audience were several Americans who had studied karate in Japan and they were very impressed with our display and thought it very good, and some of them wished to visit me and the BKF to receive a weekend course, and I hope this turns out to be successful." With regards to the Denham Base however, Bell corresponded with a Lieutenant Kenny, and the club, which had some fifteen members, had its last training session between 11.45 a.m. and 1.30 p.m. on Saturday, 31st March 1962. Bell was paid twenty-five shillings per hour – he was thus paid £15.00 a month with £3.00 travelling expenses. Payment was made by cheque and sanctioned by Major E.R. Sipes for the USAF.

Records still exist to show that the following USAF personnel based at Denham trained with Bell at that time: William Bailey, Stanley Cowan, Andrew Davis, Edward Daniels, Manuel Echeverna, Edward Flint, Francis Kiernan, Arthur Malia, Bruce Norris, Gerald Persons, (?) Smith, Gerald Sullivan and Millard Thornton. Norris was the fourteen-year-old son of an Air Force colonel at the base. Cowan and Thornton had, according to their application forms for BKF membership, seen karate demonstrations when based in Japan. The average age of the students of the Denham *dojo*, which was located in the base's film studio, was twenty-four and a half years, with a range between (an exceptional) fourteen and thirty-one.

Master Murakami conducted an eight-hour practice session at the USAF base in early to mid December 1961, but did not take a grading. He did, however, grade at the St. Mary's *dojo* on the 10th December, and the following people were promoted: 5th kyu – B. Henn, S. Dalton; 4th kyu – E. Harris, A. Malia; 3rd kyu – J. Shepherd.

On the 31st December 1961, Bell took the grading at Denham. The BKF grading register shows that the following people successfully graded that day: 6th kyu – F. Alonso, S. Cowan, E. Daniels, M. Echeverna, R. Norman, G. Persons, G. Sullivan; 5th kyu – B. Norris. On the 27th January 1962, E. Flint and F. Kieron graded to 6th kyu, and on the 13th February 1962, M. Thornton was likewise graded by Bell.

Master Murakami conducted a course and grading at Denham on the 24th March 1962, a week before the club's closure. The following Denham members were promoted: 6th kyu – J. Winichx (BKF grading register entry is unclear); 5th kyu – F. Alonso, E. Daniels, M. Echeverna, R. Norman, B. Norris, G. Sullivan, M. Thornton. On the same day, St. Mary's *dojo* members, A. Love and J. Chisholm were graded to 6th kyu, and J. Neal and T. Wingrove to 2nd kyu.

John Chisholm was to become an influential figure in Shotokan karate, and features later in this work. He completed his application forms for BKF membership on the 9th December 1961, aged twenty-six, when working as a rigger at the Elstree film studios. He had had previous martial arts experience in judo, having studied at the Bomber Judo Club, Queen Elizabeth Road, Southampton, and had attained 5th kyu grade.

The outstanding member at Denham was Arthur Malia. He reached 2nd kyu before returning to America. Malia was twenty-two when he started training with Bell and had actually studied and graded in Mo-Dok-Kwan (Dang-Su-Do) in Seoul, South Korea, in the late Fifties. Bell and Malia corresponded, and in a letter to Malia on the 14th November 1963, Bell noted that because Malia, "did a great deal to raise the standard of karate training both in the USAF and the BKF ... you [Malia] are now being made an honorary life member of the BKF, and it gives me great pleasure to do this." Malia had trained for two years and Bell appointed him a Junior Instructor and asked him to accept the official appointment of BKF representative to the USA. What is of interest regarding Bell's letter are the following quotes relating to Japan Karate Association recognition (see later). He wrote to Malia: "Because I know your ability so well, and since you hold Mr. Murakami's grades, and since the BKF is now directly affiliated to the JKA and has been recognised as the only official organisation for Britain ... [Malia was given the freedom to] instruct at your base and wherever else you may travel, and since Murakami is a Dan grade of JKA you will be teaching the official system of Japanese karate." Bell noted that he was re-grading Malia and that, "I am grading you under my new grade of *Shodan* of JKA. Furthermore, please study the copies of the two enclosed letters which will prove our new status..." With this new-found status, Bell advised Malia to, "contact immediately the official JKA organisation

Master Murakami leads a class at the USAF base, Denham – 1961/62

Master Murakami leads a class at the USAF base, Denham – 1961/62

Master Murakami leads a class at the USAF base, Denham – 1961/62

Master Murakami instructing at the Denham *dojo*, Buckinghamshire – 1961/
62. Terry Wingrove is to be seen extreme left.

Vernon Bell at the USAF base at Denham – 1962. Left to right, standing: Thomas McAndrew, Arthur Malia, Edward Daniels, Vernon Bell, Eric Roberts, Carl Ulich, Bruce Norris, Laurence Monski; kneeling: Millard Thornton, Richard Norman.

for America – The All American Karate Federation, Los Angeles, California – and introduce yourself as our representative."

Other members of the Denham *dojo* corresponded with Bell from America also. Stanley Cowan, for example, wrote to Bell after having returned hurriedly after notification that his nine-year-old daughter was seriously ill. Cowan wrote: "I am sure going to miss those Saturday morning workouts with you. I sure did enjoy them very much..." When Colonel Norris returned to the States, taking his family with him, Bell wrote to Masters T. Okazaki and T. Sugiura at The Karate Association of Philadelphia, 6135 North 18th Street, Philadelphia, Pennsylvania, providing a reference for Bruce Norris and requesting that the keen young man be permitted to train with them. Bell in fact received a Christmas card signed by Okazaki and Sugiura that year.

The closing of the Denham *dojo* came as a great disappointment to Bell. In a letter to Calvin Robinson (see below), Bell noted that he had been informed by telephone by Lieutenant Kenny that the karate section was to close on the 20th March. Bell wrote to Robinson: "The USA can no longer pay a civilian instructor which has come as a surprise to me for we have [had] a very flourishing karate section here every week since November. All the men are very disappointed for it has been sprung upon us, but I think some opposition has been put up, in a roundabout way, by certain judo black-belts who are on the base who have never shown any interest in karate..."

When the Denham Air Force *dojo* closed, Vernon Bell, with Art Malia's help, was able to continue the following month, using the base's gymnasium, but on a private and independent basis, with members paying the usual BKF monthly fees (though there is some evidence to suggest that Bell was re-hired by the USAF). The first training, on this basis, was held on Saturday, 21st April 1962. In a reply to an unknown airman interested in participating, Bell wrote, on the 17th April, that the following rules would apply: "Class times 11 a.m. to 1 p.m. in the gymnasium and lateness will not be expected. The class will be limited to ten members maximum, each of whom will pay ten shillings per week for their two-hour class one month in advance from the 21st of April to the 19th May, being two pounds which will be due payment on arrival this Saturday, for which a subscription card will be issued to each member for all the payments. No part payments will be accepted and no fees for individual classes will be allowed. Once having paid for this one-month's karate class in advance, the pupil will be saved a vacancy each week in this class until such time as he makes a further arrangement with his tutor. If he does not attend one week, no fees are returned and irregular attendance will not be tolerated, so the answer is for you to decide that if you wish to receive your karate in the future and have regular instruction, then, you must abide by these class regulations, and once having accepted them, abide by our decisions, for as a private *dojo* each member has a definite duty to the others and himself to attend punctually and regularly each week without interruption and pay his way, for this is the only way the class can function and exist." The Denham *dojo* class committee (as Bell termed it) who assisted Bell with the classes, was made up of Messrs. Malia, Thornton and Daniels.

Master Murakami visited the Denham *dojo* on Saturday, 9th June 1962, holding a course and grading between 2.30 and 7.30 p.m., having come immediately from a morning session from High Wycombe (see below). The grading in the afternoon was for USAF members only. Details for this course still exist. Interestingly, the BKF course details claim that, "Mr. Murakami has recently been appointed Official European Representative of the Japan Karate Association, who thoroughly recognise this course." The two-day course (the Sunday training was held at Upminster) cost £3 or £3 10s including grading.

The following people graded: 6th kyu – R. Jones, C. Ulrich; 5th kyu – J. Winichx (BKF grading register entry is unclear); 4th kyu – B. Norris; 3rd kyu – A. Malia. On the 7th July 1962, Bell graded M. Echeverna to 4th kyu.

Karate training at St. Mary's on the 10th June 1962, was from 10.30 a.m. to 12.30 p.m. and then from 2.00 p.m. to 4.00 p.m. There was grading syllabus tuition from 5.00 p.m. to 6.00 p.m., and then a grading between 6.30 p.m. and 7.30 p.m.

Terry Wingrove assisted Master Murakami on the Denham base and recalled: "Murakami didn't like Americans because he thought they were weak. He'd go out of his way to knock black people down and anyone else he thought was inferior. I suppose he was still fighting the Second World War. Murakami was the sort of person who took either an immediate liking or disliking to someone, and you could see it straight away. His technique was very sharp and very powerful. He had disproportionate hands for the size of his arms; great big fists. He did *makiwara* and had hands like a manual worker, which he was, or which he had been. He taught us how to use the *makiwara*. Murakami particularly liked to kick cocky people out of the class and knock them down to size. That was his forte. He would have no hesitation in humiliating you in front of anybody.

"At one of the courses at Denham – I was partnering Murakami as usual for a demonstration – Murakami said that I should attack. At the time he was looking at the class and talking to them. I went straight in and hit him on the side of the head, by the eye. It came up like I don't know what, and I thought, 'Oh God!' He didn't say a word, and just carried on, and I knew I had it coming. I just knew. I said, 'I'm sorry *Sensei*,' and he said, 'That's all right, that's all right.' About ten minutes later it was time for the next demo and that was it. Bang! Knocked out. He hit me on the stomach here, just here, just as I was about to exhale. If he wanted to knock you out on the face, he'd hit you on the tic douloureux [trigeminal nerve]. Murakami was an expert at that. I believe that it is the most painful point on the entire body. Murakami would knock you out as though you were a yo-yo. You don't see that in a class now. I think the worst I had was when Murakami knocked me out five separate times in one day. I suppose he knocked me out over twenty times in all.

"Now you can be objective about it, compare apples and pears, but in those days we didn't know what was what. When a man waved his fist in the air you didn't know how effective it was, so Murakami would say, 'Give me your best man,' and bang, you'd go down. Murakami

Master Tetsuji Murakami and Terry Wingrove demonstrate *ippon-kumite* at Denham USAF base – 1961/62.

would say, 'This is how it works,' because there was no other way to show it. Subsequently, everybody knew it worked and he didn't have to show that technique again. I was a fortunate guinea pig because I kept coming around, some people weren't so fortunate and he did hurt some people badly. Mick Manning [who readers may recall was the first person to be graded to both 2nd and 1st kyu in Great Britain], for example, had his leg broken with a *fumikomi* by Murakami, and he never came back to karate which was a great shame. It was a case of, 'I've told you before,' and bang, [Manning apparently did not have his back leg straight in *zenkutsu-dachi*] – that was in 1962, I think. Murakami would slap students quite hard around the face, and we wouldn't see them again. I saw him do that on numerous occasions. Vernon can verify that. If you were with someone who you thought you'd give an easy time to, you know, when he parried you moved your arm to help him, or if you didn't carry the punch through with power and determination, Murakami would definitely come round and slap you on the face or kick you up the pants. Murakami knocked out Jimmy Neal. You never knew it was going to happen. Bang, and the next minute you were on the floor."

Unfortunately, things came to an unpleasant and abrupt ending at the Denham *dojo*. In a letter to Lieutenant Kenny, dated the 18th July

Master Tetsuji Murakami has just countered Terry Wingrove during *ippon-kumite* at Denham USAF base – 1961/62.

1962, Bell wrote: "I wish to complain very strongly regarding the manner of the conditions to which I have been subjected in the termination of the karate class at Denham, which I regard as entirely unsatisfactory and completely unbusiness-like and which I feel most resentful." It had been decided that the base would close and Bell had not been informed in writing that he would lose his *dojo* which he thought only correct and proper, and sought remuneration as he considered one month's notice and payment to be in order. Bell did receive some money (whether Denham paid is unclear), for back payment for ten weeks' tuition at the Third Air Force USAF Base in Ruislip, which had commenced on the 28th April. The letter confirming payment came from Robert H. Baker,

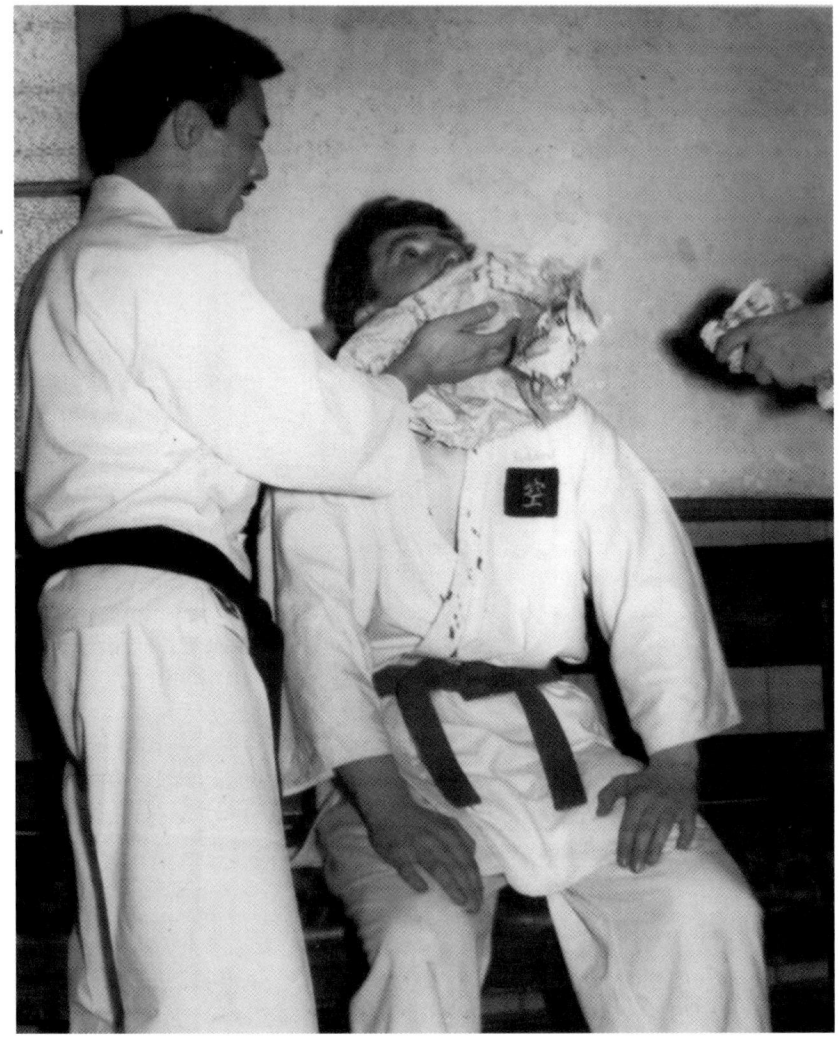

Murakami administering aid to an Irish *karateka* with a nose bleed (*c.*1962)

Chief of Special Services, who noted the apology for the "tardiness of this payment," but also noted that, "Your work with our people has always been of the highest caliber and we express appreciation for the fine courses you ran for us."

When the Air Force-paid Denham *dojo* closed, Art Malia, who was then the BKF Area Officer for Buckinghamshire and a member of the BKF General Committee, also managed to arrange for another USAF base, in Daws Hill Road, on the Amersham Road, High Wycombe, some fifteen miles away, to cater for karate training. Practice started there in April 1962, and continued until November that same year. Vernon Bell recalled the novel location for the demonstration that he and BKF members gave to potential students. "Being a missile base the demonstration was held underground. That of course was very unusual, but I also remember giving an earlier demo' on the back of a moving lorry during the Three Towns Carnival [Romford, Dagenham and Ilford]."

Training at the 3929th Air Base Squadron (Strategic Air Command) seems, from the remaining correspondence, to have been fraught with problems for Bell, mostly involving USAF bureaucracy, and a certain apathy on the part of some students. Training was held on Saturday mornings, mostly between 10.30 and 12.30. Though there were fifteen members, attendance at classes was poor. The average age of participants, who came from all over the States, from California to Florida to New York (as they had done at the Denham base), was twenty-two. The highest rank of a licence holder was a Captain John Owens Jnr. from Massachusetts, who was thirty-three years of age. The youngest student was seventeen-year-old Erik Roberts. The other thirteen members were: Rufus Adams, Richard Allori, Francis Alonso, Richard Baumgartner, Alphonso Fields, Frank Fusco, Roger Jones, Albert Kuhner, Lawrence Manski, Thomas McAndrew, Richard Norman, Carl Ulrich and Bobby Joe Wood. Master Murakami trained there on Saturday, 9th June, from 10.30 a.m. to 1.00 p.m. at a rate of three guineas an hour.

Vernon Bell conducted a grading at High Wycombe on the 22nd July 1962. The BKF grading register shows the following students were promoted to 6th kyu: R. Allori, J. Carter, F. Fusco, E. Grant, A. Kuhner and T. McAndrew. Murakami held a grading on the 11th August 1962, and E. Grant and A. Kuhner gained their 5th kyus. On the 29th September 1962, the last High Wycombe grading took place under Bell, when J. Owens was promoted to 6th kyu, R. Allori and F. Fusco to 5th kyu.

Murakami's intended visit to the base on the 3rd November was cancelled in a letter to Bell from Captain William Amos, and the same Captain Amos drew matters to a close when he wrote to Bell that, "Due to the lack of participation in the weekly karate class at High Wycombe Air Station, we wish to cancel all classes as of 10th November 1962." Bell was not to teach for the USAF again.

The third of Master Murakami's letters features at this time. He wrote to Bell from Paris on the 25th October 1962: "When coming back from London, Mr. Kikukawa told me you should like me to come to London on the 2nd November. Such a thing is quite possible for me; so, I shall fly by Air France 852 and arrive to the London Air Terminal at 1400-1430. As I have a course at my club on Monday, I must be back to Paris on the 5th November."

Kikukawa was a university student and a *judoka* of note (he may have been short-listed or selected for the Japanese Olympic team in 1964). Terry Wingrove recalled: "When Vernon Bell found out that Kikukawa was a Shotokan *Shodan* he grabbed him straight away. Kikukawa took some lessons to selected students of the BKF at 12, Maybush Road, but he wasn't here for long, only a couple of weeks."

A short, historically interesting and friendly correspondence grew up between Calvin H. Robinson (mentioned above) and Vernon Bell. Robinson was a *Shodan* in Shorin-ryu karate, who instructed at the 2137th Command Squadron (AACS), Spangdahlem Air base, Spangdahlem/Eifel, Germany. Robinson, a black Staff Sergeant of the 49th Tactical Fighter Wing, had trained in Fukuoka, Japan, for three years and had taught karate since 1957. According to an unknown newspaper article entitled, "Spang NCO Has Wicked 'Open Hand,'" Robinson received his black belt in August 1956, after two years training from the Sho-Lin-Lyn [Shorin-ryu] Karate School in Kasugabara. In another article, again from an unknown newspaper entitled, "Karate Teacher Here 'Exposes' Black-Belts," Robinson and a student seem to have pursued, and had contests with, two suspect claimants to the black-belt rank in Baumholder and Bad Kreuznach, Germany. Anyway, Robinson wrote to Bell on the 10th January 1962, expressing a desire to visit Bell's school to "observe, exhibit and exchange our views on the subject of karate." Bell replied on the 26th January 1962, noting that Robinson's request, "is not normally done and is quite a new venture and one which I have not experienced in my five years of karate." Bell agreed to the meeting, and suggested two options. Either to train at the Denham Base on Saturday between 11 a.m. and 2 p.m., or at the British Legion Hall, Upminster, on Sunday between 11 a.m. and 3.30 p.m. Bell considered the former to be the best option on the 24th March, 1962, when Murakami was taking a course and then they could train at Upminster on the 25th. He noted that the two-day course, with twelve hours training, would cost three pounds per student. Bell noted that the course was open only to BKF members, and Robinson and his students would have to become Associated Members at 17s 6d, with an additional fee of 15s per annum, payable to Master Murakami. In this letter, Bell requested further information about Robinson's grades and experience.

A return letter was received by Bell on the 8th February 1962, and noted the personal and karate career information stated above. Robinson wrote that he was a member of the Shorin-ryu Karate Clubs, Kyoshin-Kai Japan Karate Association, and a coach to the German Karate Association. Robinson invited Bell to contact Jurgen Seydel for a reference. Robinson also proposed that, "I think a karate contest would be in order." Bell replied on the 21st February, obviously impressed by Robinson's lineage, and invited him to become an Honorary Associate Member of the BKF, and sent him a Yoseikan/BKF badge. On the question of the contest Bell wrote: "The idea of a karate contest appeals to me and I suggest a two team *shiai* between your kyu grades and my own under JKA Official Rules on the day of Mr. Murakami's course on the 24th March 1962, at the US Airforce Base, Denham, as a highlight to this course. The match will be referee'd by Mr. Murakami, and you and I will act as judges, and any contestant who excels himself will be re-graded and registered with the EKF. Since Mr. Murakami does not approve of all-out black-belt contests, and does not condone them, then this must be a kyu match." In a handsome gesture, Bell also wrote, "I can arrange for you to have a friendly *jiyu-ippon kumite* with Mr. Murakami himself during this course and you will be invited to attend this course without charge to yourself as an observer, but I must arrange with Mr. Murakami for you to be a participant for two days, and he decides whether you should pay or not, but your pupils must pay a nominal charge for their tuition under the statutes of the EFK." Bell had by this time written to Lieutenant Kenny noting that Robinson might attend the Murakami course and asking permission for him to be able to do this, whether accommodation could be provided, and for a competition to take place. Bell wrote to Kenny stating, "My Federation is treating him (Robinson) as a VIP in the karate world and as such I wish to arrange everything properly..."

Another interesting point about this letter (of the 21st February 1962) was contained in the last paragraph: "Finally, may I have your permission for Airman Alonso and myself to take official photographs in your gym after the class each Saturday without restriction for the purpose of preparing an official book on karate which I am preparing and for which he [Alonso] has been engaged as photographer by proper arrangement." The book, written by Bell, and intended as the official handbook of the BKF was completed but, regrettably, never published. Entitled, *The Manual of Karate-Do*, it had a foreword by Henri Plee and contained the following chapters: The British Karate Federation, The History of Karate, What is Karate, Organisation of Karate, Karate Training, The Postures and Body Mechanism, The Table of Karate-Do Techniques –

Classifications, The *Kata*, *Kumite*, Karate Self-defence, and, Important Notes for all Karateists.

Robinson replied on the 26th February that, "It is with great pleasure and monumental gratitude that I accept Honorary Membership in the British Karate Federation. I assure you that I will wear with pride the official badge of the BKF on my *keikogi*."

On the 23rd March 1962, Robinson wrote to Bell noting: "It is with deep regret that I inform you that due to military commitments, the Shorin-ryu Karate Club will not be able to participate in planned activities on the 24th March 1962, in England." Despite further correspondence the planned contest never materialised.

There is another story concerning a particular member of the American Armed Forces based in Germany that will no doubt be of interest to readers. As has been noted before, Terry Wingrove would regularly visit Murakami's *dojo* in Paris. "I slept on a mat in the *dojo* and lived on bread and wine," Wingrove recalled. "One evening Murakami said to me that I mustn't go out and that he needed me. The *dojo* was locked up and about seven o'clock the door opened and in walked Murakami and two security men. A few seconds later another man walked in and I recognised him immediately – Elvis Presley. Presley came to train with Murakami on Friday nights, and no one else ever knew this. I was the dummy, the stooge. I was told to keep my mouth shut, which I did. It's come out now in books, something like, 'Elvis trained in secret with a Japanese.' Well he did, and that was with Murakami. Presley would spend a weekend in Paris on leave from Germany. He probably trained with Murakami about eight to ten times. It was basic self-defence, *ippon-kumite*, that's all. I thought Elvis was a very nice man, very humble, and he thought that the sun shone out of Murakami. He had wonderful form; a good student. Murakami never graded him. He came to learn, to study, for a period of two to three months, on and off. Elvis Presley became a student of Ed Parker in America. I later met Elvis again in Las Vegas."

Presley had actually had his first karate lesson on the 6th December 1959, at his home in Bad Nauheim, and trained twice a week, three hours on each occasion, under Jurgen Seydel. Presley was apparently most interested in his training, and would practice daily and made astonishing progress. In the unexceptional 1964 film, *Roustabout*, we see three seconds of Elvis in action. Outside a club he disposes of two opponents and a third doesn't try his luck stating, "No! No! That's karate!" It's hardly classic stuff, but it was no doubt influential at the time to the teen set.

Members of the BKF Liverpool *dojo* – 1962. Left to right, standing: Richard Woolfall, Alan Dewar, Paul Sloane, Michael Walls, Kenneth Caulfield, unknown, Andy Sherry, Alan Smith, unknown, Master Murakami, Joe Chialton, Roy Stephens, Terry Astley, Wiliam Whitehead, unknown, unknown, unknown, unknown, unknown, Frank Cope, unknown, unknown; squatting: Charles Naylor, George Galletly, Fred Gille, James Wilson.

Master Murakami held a course and grading in Liverpool on the 25th March 1962. The BKF register shows that the following people were promoted: 6th kyu – J. Chialton, F. Cope, J. Galletly, R. Stephens, W. Whitehead, R. Woodfall; 5th kyu – K. Caulfield, A. Dewar, J. Donoghue, G. Galletly, K. McCaldon, A. Sherry, P. Sloan, A. Smith; 4th kyu – F. Gille and C. Naylor.

In a tribute to Master Murakami, Terry O'Neill and Graham Noble (*Fighting Arts International*, No.43) quoted Andy Sherry on Murakami's first visit to the Liverpool Karate Club and a subsequent incident: "On the very first training session, he [Murakami *Sensei*] came in to the *dojo* and shook everyone's hand ... then he proceeded to 'batter' us all. He'd give us commands in French – he didn't speak any English – and then when we didn't obey him he would begin hitting us, slapping our faces and kicking us in the stomach ... he had everyone terrified! I remember one incident on a course in Liverpool where one of the students – he was a solicitor – ran out of the *dojo* during the middle of the class, after Murakami had kicked him in the leg for doing something incorrectly, shouting back at him, 'Right, that's it ... I'm going to sue you for this.' But despite his strict attitude, his karate was really sharp and impressive. He was very wiry and moved liked greased lightning ...

I'm sure he was one of the fastest Japanese *sensei* I have ever seen."

On the 13th May 1962, Bell returned to Liverpool and the following people graded: 6th kyu – S. Coy, S. McConnell, K. Skinner; 5th kyu – T. Astley, F. Cope, J. Chialton, J. Galletly; 4th kyu – K. Caulfield, A. Dewar, G. Galletly, C. Naylor, A. Smith. Interestingly, of those attempting 5th kyu and above, only Caulfield passed outright, all eight others were given honorary (temporary) grades. Honorary grades had been given before under the BKF, the earliest recorded being 2nd April 1961, when R. Buckner and T. Wingrove received honorary 3rd kyus from Murakami at Upminster. (Prior to that on the 28th June 1958, the BKF grading register reveals the letter "c" after "New Grade" for R. Armstrong, P. Conlon, H. Rayner, J. Russell and J. Sen. This could mean "conditional" but then it could equally mean "credit." All passed their next grading directly). To the 13th May 1962, in over five years, only eight honorary grades were recorded. The author has not made specific reference to these to date, for there is little point, and will continue in this vein to 1964 up to 4th kyu. From 3rd kyu onwards the letter "H" will be inserted after the grade if the award is recorded as honorary. On the 11th June 1962, Liverpool members, R. Stephens and R. Woolfall passed their 5th kyu grade under Murakami at the North-East Yorkshire branch grading.

Vernon Bell was very busy indeed spreading the word of karate and the BKF. This is best revealed in a letter he wrote to J. Gargin, a 2nd Dan of the British Amateur Judo Federation, and their General Secretary. Bell knew Gargin well, as both belonged to The Society of Judo Masters. Gargin was Chairman of the society and Vernon Bell was on the Committee and represented the National Judo Association. The correspondence between the two which is of particular relevance here, concerned the organisation of a karate demonstration that Bell and members of the BKF were to give at the Top Floor Gymnasium of the Kensington Institute, Wornington Road, North Kensington, on Wednesday, 21st March 1962, at 8.00 p.m., and the subsequent request for a karate *dojo* to be sited there (a judo *dojo* had flourished for some years). Admission to the display was free and was, "to be presented exactly as a general Karate-do class is held and instructed for all grades..." It was thus an unusual deviation from the BKF's normal routine. The exhibition included, "preliminary class exercises, basic postures, stances, methods of parrying, attacks and defences, walking and turning movements, techniques of hand, arm and foot, two *kata* of *Heian*, free practice, contests, combat *kata*." The programme noted that,

Vernon Bell and Master Murakami with members of the Irish Karate-Do Federation. Alan Ruddock is furthest right.

"The purpose of the display is to educate the audience as to the true nature of Karate-do as a competitive sport, physical education and recreational activity, comparative with other sports to develop fitness, health and mental/physical co-ordination, etc."

The demonstration was a great success, and a small report appeared in the *Kensington News* on the 6th April 1962. It was noted in the piece that, "An enthusiastic audience" watched the display, and that, "After... [the] introductory speech, the twenty members of the display team gave a very thorough and convincing demonstration of the various movements and exercises of karate. It was the first time that karate had been shown in Kensington, and proceedings ended with Vernon Bell answering the audiences numerous questions. A *dojo* was subsequently sited at the Institute, but the evening classes lasted only a few months.

Bell noted in his letter to Gargin dated the 16th March 1962: "I am rushed off my feet with a flood of work regarding my forthcoming display, Mr. Murakami's course next weekend, gradings and judo displays, and I am engaged for twenty-four hours of the day to the middle of April and have not even had time to read a newspaper or eat regularly ... due mainly to the increased interest in karate all over the country, which has caught me rather unprepared, and as it is so involved I have to do everything myself ..."

Fred Kidd had attended the first and second BKF Summer Courses at Scarborough, and had built up a small following in Middlesbrough. One of his very early students was Walter Seaton, who joined the BKF on the 6th February 1962, though he had trained with Kidd since 1959. Seaton recalled: "After Fred had been to the first Scarborough course and told me about it, we practised and talked about karate all the time." Walter Seaton, searching for a fitness regime to replace the training undertaken during National Service, began karate when aged twenty-three, and soon came under the influence of Master Murakami whilst training in the North-East of England. Seaton explained his introduction to karate, his first encounter with Murakami, and his opinion of this great "*karateka* of the old school," so: "I knew of a boxing gymnasium in Middlesbrough and decided to make a visit. On entering the gym I was stopped dead in my tracks because instead of the expected boxing gloves and shorts, a couple of people were punching and kicking fresh air and were dressed in what looked like white pyjamas. This was my first view and impression of what turned out to be Shotokan karate. I realised there and then that the work rate was sufficient to fill my needs and decided to get involved in this most unusual art. That decision was to have a profound effect on the rest of my life. I discovered that the art being practised was a form of Shotokan karate called Yoseikan, and that a Japanese instructor called Tetsuji Murakami, who lived in Paris, would make visits to the club to give high-grade instruction and conduct grading examinations. Mister Murakami was at that time a 3rd Dan, and as I got to know more about the art of Shotokan karate and the grading system, someone with the rank of 3rd Dan seemed almost god-like. Visits by Mr. Murakami happened at least once a year and were organised by the British Karate Federation, the General Secretary and Chief Instructor being Vernon Bell from Hornchurch in Essex. Vernon was himself a 1st Dan [actually 2nd Dan] and, to the best of knowledge was the only karate black-belt in the country at the time. As the weeks went by, I found the training got more and more interesting, and a number of other people joined the club, which was known as the Middlesbrough

Karate Club [and later as the Budokan]. The club organiser was Fred Kidd, who was involved with boxing and judo. One day Fred announced that the much feared and talked about Tetsuji Murakami was coming to England and would visit the club. My first sighting of Mr. Murakami was, to say the least, a bit of a disappointment. I had been expecting a man as big as his reputation and when this small but dapper Oriental entered the *dojo* smoking a full strength Capstan cigarette, the image I had built up in my head was completely shattered. This man was far too small to live up to his reputation. Within half an hour I had the shock of my life.

"That first session started as I expected, the warm-up exercises were hard but good. When the actual technique training started I found myself witnessing a power from this small man that was shaking the whole building. The *dojo* itself was the first floor of an old church building, and a coffin maker occupied the ground floor. It had a very high ceiling and the only access was via a wooden staircase outside the building. The only facilities were electric lights and an old ascot heater, which provided a single shower of sorts. There were no toilet facilities, but we kept a bucket for emergencies, and even Murakami had to use it on odd occasions. The wooden floor was basically quite good for training on, but nail heads needed to be knocked down on a regular basis and there were a number of holes in the floor which in winter months blew cold air into the *dojo* ... and we could see the coffin maker working through the holes in the floor. Many a time I thought we would need his services sooner rather than later. I still remember thinking what the hell had I got myself into. At one end of the *dojo* there was a permanent judo mat and a small office/changing facility about ten by eight feet, heated by a single bar electric fire. There was no heating in the *dojo* itself (not that we needed heaters once training started). As well as the usual boxing equipment such as punch balls, punch bags (these were used more for kicking than punching), mirrors, skipping ropes and Indian clubs, we had three standing *makiwara* and one fitted to a wall. Sometimes, when we used the wall-mounted *makiwara*, plaster fell down from the heavily plastered ceiling. We also had a rope and pulley for stretching stiff legs back into their normal state. Once, when I was using the wall-mounted *makiwara*, a doctor of medicine was visiting the *dojo*, and remarked that he could hardly believe the human body could take such a pounding without serious injury.

"Then came the discipline and the physical aspects of Mr. Murakami's training methods. I really did believe that I had already experienced the

Master Murakami, cigarette in mouth, washing his feet before/after a lesson (*c.* 1962).

limits of physical endurance and overbearing discipline during my service with the 1st Battalion of the Green Howards – how wrong I was! No sergeant-major I met ever imposed such discipline, as did Mr.

The Murakami *gi* badge

Murakami. The only thing we were allowed to do without his express command was breathe.

"After the first session under this incredible man, I found myself in a complete daze for days after. Sleep was impossible that first night. My mind was continually going over the things I had seen. The punches and kicks just would not leave my mind. It was more than a mental image – the feeling was still in my body. It was some days later before it dawned on me that Mr. Murakami had spoken virtually no English during his instruction. It was all done with demonstrations and the kicking of our legs, when stances were not up to the Murakami standard. Over thirty years later I still get a pain in my left rib area where he once kicked me, and I often wonder if it is still the result of the psychological shock of fighting that man.

"The training itself consisted of *kihon, renrakuwaza* [techniques practised in combination], *ippon-kumite, Taikyokyu kata, Heian kata* and free fighting ... After the shock, and more important the incredible value of that first training session under Mr. Murakami, whenever he came back to England I would travel to the other *dojo* which at that time were at the Red Triangle in Liverpool and at Vernon Bell's club in

Hornchurch. Nothing stopped me from visiting these *dojo* for that valuable training. Where Mr. Murakami was teaching, I went.

"There was no pre-arranged grading syllabus. We were told at the time of the examination what was wanted ... I remember on one occasion when Andy Sherry failed his 3rd kyu examination. At that time I was promoted to 5th kyu at my third attempt. It was not due to lack of practice – it was Murakami's standards. He was a perfectionist, and he wanted everyone who trained to be the same. Many students trained only once, and you never saw them again.

"As time went by Mr. Murakami managed to grasp enough English to allow some verbal communication. On one occasion, when I travelled by train with him to Liverpool, we were comparing life in the British Army with life in the Japanese Army, and he told me that he fought in World War Two and that he specialised in silent killing of soldiers on guard duty using only his hand and a knife.

"Murakami was one of the few *karateka* that I have seen who could make the ultimate karate fist. He really could hold his fingers so that the tips fitted solidly into the bottom finger joints, so making the most solid fist possible. I kept trying for years to achieve such a fist but never could make my fingers and joints supple enough. Whilst everything Murakami did was of an outstanding nature, his jumping kicks were quite incredible and his jumping side-kick was such that it had to be seen to be appreciated, and anyone seeing it was smitten, forever trying to emulate it. The only comparison I can make regarding his speed, agility and power would be to liken him to a tiger. Even when you made what may normally be considered a successful defence against a pre-arranged attack, your whole body would vibrate and shake down to the feet because of the sheer speed and power of the attack. On one course, a green-belt had a full beard set (quite unusual among younger people in those days), and I remember seeing out of the corner of my eye Murakami taking hold of the green-belt's beard and giving him a good slap across the face with his other hand. I was not aware of what this poor unfortunate had done, I just remember thinking, 'Good for him,' meaning I was glad it wasn't me.

"Green-belt was 6th kyu [Yellow-belt has also been noted], which was the lowest grade Murakami would award. Still on gradings, I remember the first time I failed my 5th kyu under Murakami. I practised the syllabus every day before training for the next six months and when the time came to take the re-test the syllabus was different – those were the days!

Master Tetsuji Murakami

"One of the most vivid non-training memories I have of Murakami was when, after training, a group of us went to the local Chinese restaurant to eat, and when the waiter had carefully laid out the table, Murakami seemed to adopt a hostile attitude and asked him to take all the cutlery and plates away and change them because he had spotted a finger mark on something. I thought at the time it was some sort of Japanese-Chinese racial problem, but many years later when I was in Japan, I discovered just how particular the Japanese can be when it comes to cleanliness and personal hygiene. Anyway, after the meal, conversation got around to a summer course that Murakami had held in Scarborough before I started training. It seems that Murakami and some of the more senior students had been training outdoors and on the way back stopped to watch some open air boxing or wrestling, and one of the contestants could see that Murakami was a black-belt and challenged him to a fight in the ring. Apparently, after politely refusing a couple of times, Murakami asked if he could be allowed to perform a *kata* in the ring. After the performance the challenger insisted on giving Murakami an apology and a handshake, and that must have been the time when someone coined the phrase 'lucky devil.'"

Walter Seaton believes that Master Murakami's appearance on the ITN News (though ITN have no record of this – perhaps it was a live performance?) was the real start of large numbers of people in Great Britain taking up karate.

Gordon Thompson tells of another incident concerning Murakami that also occurred in a Chinese restaurant. "Mr. Murakami was a Japanese man of the old school. He did not like the Chinese ... [at Chinese restaurants] I am told that he always sat bolt upright, swivelling his eyes watching the waiters as they walked by. Well, one day, one of them was a bit flustered or something and made the mistake of reaching across the table directly in front of Mr. Murakami. He grinned, and brought his forearm down across the reaching arm in a crushing block. I am not sure of the sequel, and anyway you will appreciate that the whole story is second or third-hand, so I can not guarantee it, but it has the ring of truth about it."

The York club was running of course, and Gordon Thompson, John Clark, and others would make the fifty-mile journey to Middlesbrough to train with Master Murakami on the occasions he was teaching there. Later, in 1965, a club would open in Sunderland, and another in Hymers College School in Hull. As Gordon Thompson recalled, "There were three of us with motor bikes in the club at the time, and so six of us went up to Middlesbrough. Remember in those days car ownership was very rare, the roads were uncrowded and you could go miles without meeting a car. We graded a couple of times at Middlesbrough..."

As regards day-to-day training at the Middlesbrough *dojo*, Walter Seaton recalled that: "On reflection, in that *dojo* in those days, nothing could be classed as normal. However, all training sessions commenced with a good exercise workout consisting of flexibility, strength and stamina exercises. [A normal class had about ten students, but the ranks swelled to twenty or so when Murakami visited]. The training itself always started with basic technique practice, then usually some partner work or *kata* training, and in any case always ended with a free-fighting session, sometimes two or three opponents against one. The free-fighting itself was a peculiar mixture of Murakami's freestyle, boxing, and one kick or punch should finish an opponent. A strange mixture it may have seemed, but it was definitely effective. As a matter of interest, the "one technique should be enough attitude" was the basis for karate competition fighting in the early days. In an effort to come up to the fitness standard set by Murakami, myself and some of the other members used to do a twice weekly pre-training run through the streets of Middlesbrough in our karate *gi* and bare feet. But no matter how hard we tried, we never seemed to achieve the state of fitness that would both satisfy Murakami and get us through one of his sessions without severe muscular stiffness for days afterwards. On reflection, local people must have thought we were mad – maybe we were. However, we knew Murakami would be back and we always had to prepare for the occasion."

So impressed was Walter Seaton with Murakami that after his instructor stopped coming to England for the BKF in 1964, Walter changed his style to Wado-ryu so that he could once again have close contact with Japanese instructors. Nevertheless, Walter Seaton acknowledges that Murakami's methods and standards still have an effect on his karate life, despite the passing of over thirty years. In fact, Walter Seaton did not give up his Shotokan karate immediately, but continued "practising both styles for about three years, by which time I realised that I could only do one style successfully." Walter Seaton received his JKA *Shodan* on the 5th May 1968.

An early trainee under Walter Seaton and Fred Kidd at the Middlesbrough *dojo* was Pauline Bindra (née Laville), who was to become the first female JKA Shotokan black-belt in Britain. The exact date she started training has, unfortunately, been lost, but she was (for what it is worth) ungraded in March 1964. Pauline had been training in judo for four years at the prestigious Middlesbrough Judo Club founded by Fred Kidd and Syd Carr (and four others), which had some two hundred and fifty members at that time, a quarter of the membership being women (being one of the largest clubs in England), and had reached blue-belt. She had been advised against taking an interest in karate.

Pauline recalled: "The judo instructors kept saying this is really bad stuff, you shouldn't do it, it's just started in this country, it's evil, and all this rubbish. So, we went down there to have a go at Walter [for sending them letters about karate practice] and we saw it and we liked it. A few of us went." Pauline Bindra used to train at the *dojo*, which she recalled had a very dark wooden floor which often gave rise to splinters in the feet, "two or three nights a week. I only ever saw about six people [at a lesson]. There were three girls, but they dropped out ... I remember going up and down in these funny stances, and thinking what the hell am I doing this for? Walter Seaton was such a kind, considerate instructor. So calm, so much patience. I couldn't believe that anybody would have such patience with us stupid women ... I think we all have Walter Seaton to thank for bringing women into karate as early as he did, because if he hadn't had the foresight to do it, nobody would have bothered ... I remember there were punch-bags hanging up and men hitting them. I thought, 'I'll never be able to hit like that.' I said, 'How do you expect me to do that?' and Walter Seaton said, 'Don't worry, you don't have to do it.' Walter Seaton was a brown-belt, and Fred Kidd was a brown-belt. I was totally confused, but I liked it."

At the end of 1963, Pauline Bindra travelled south with her sister, Louise, in the hope of finding work. They lived at a hostel in Gower Street, London. In Middlesbrough, Pauline had been a trainee nurse, "But I didn't like it ... they didn't give me time off to do karate," she recalled. "Luckily I learned typing at school. It was where you got your fingers rapped with a ruler if you looked at the keys. So I passed my RSA exams at school, and I got a typing job in London. The wages were fantastic compared to what they were in the north of England." Pauline Bindra features more prominently later in this work.

Some application forms for membership to the BKF, surnames A to H, have survived for the Middlesbrough *dojo*. Information will be presented in the usual way: Matthew Appleton, 29, welder, (15.9.63); George Bell, 25, gas burner, (13.2.62); John Bender, 24, joiner, (17.9.63); Karaly Baver, 24, slinger, (10.7.62); Denise Bedford, 16, coil winder, (27.12.63) – one of the first women to hold a BKF licence; David Benson, 20, apprentice blacksmith, (5.12.62); David Bentley, 18, draughtsman, (4.8.64); Arthur Blair, 17, apprentice fitter, (11.4.63); Leslie Chambers, 18, fitter, (31.12.63); Dennis Crawford, 16, instrument artificer, (7.2.64); Lawrence Crinnion, 18, apprentice fitter, (8.4.63); Ronald Day, 20,

Master Murakami teaching at Lawns Social Club, Romford – 1962

electrician, (6.4.64); John Feldman, 15, apprentice fitter, (8.1.63); Michael Fish, 22, labourer, (15.9.63); Michael Furlonge, 16, warehouse boy, (-.8.63); Malcolm Gee, 19, apprentice fitter, (30.7.64); Vincent Gollogly, 17, student, (15.7.63); John Gough, 18, chemist, (16.5.62); Norman Green, 19, apprentice plater, (8.4.64); Charles Haslett, 33, process worker, (18.2.64); Geoffrey Heywood, 20, operator, (3.6.62); Francis Higgins, 17, apprentice draughtsman, (4.4.62); Kevin Horkan, 18, apprentice fitter, (14.3.62); Jeffrey Hudson, 17, instrument artificer, (29.4.62).

The year 1962 saw more gradings than any other under Bell and Murakami, with some one hundred and forty being undertaken. A number of these have already been mentioned, the remainder will be given now.

On the 10th June 1962, Murakami, at the St. Mary's *dojo*, graded A. Love to 5th kyu, and K. Goult and D. Williams to 3rd kyu. On the 16th of July, J. Chisholm was graded to 5th kyu.

Members of the BKF Liverpool *dojo* – mid to late 1962. Left to right, standing: All unknown, except back row, extreme left, Jack Green (of Blackpool). On Master Murakami's immediate left is Terry Astley. Frank Cope is standing between and immediately behind Murakami and Astley. Michael Walls is the last but one on the right, arms folded. Front line, kneeling, left to right: Joe Chialton (immediately in front of Paul Sloane), Andy Sherry, Roy Stephens, William Whitehead, George Galletly, Alan Smith, Alan Dewar, Richard Woolfall.

BKF Liverpool *dojo* – 1962. Master Murakami corrects Richard Woolfall. In the foreground, with beard, is Alan Smith.

Master Murakami defends against an *oi-zuki* from Terry Astley. Next to Astley is Alan Smith, and Richard Woolfall is furthest back and to the left – Liverpool, 1962.

Master Murakami attacks Alan Smith – BKF Liverpool *dojo*, 1962. From left to right, Andy Sherry, Alan Dewar and George Galletly, look on, amusingly.

Master Murakami visited the North Yorkshire *dojo* on the 11th June, 1962, and the following people were promoted to 6th kyu: G. Bell, D. Benson, F. Higgins, K. Holan, J. Hudson, W. Seaton, E. Summer; 4th kyu – F. Kidd.

Bell would sometimes grade individuals separately at St. Mary's. There are three incidences of this in 1962. On the 16th July, London member, K. Bodimeade was graded to 6th kyu. On the 5th August, Upminster member, E. Knight was graded to 6th kyu. On the 3rd December, Upminster member, L. Dacosla was graded to 5th kyu.

On the 8th July 1962, Bell held a grading in Liverpool. The following were promoted (readers will recall that some students held temporary grades previously): 6th kyu – S. Coy, G. Frodsham, S. McConnell, P. Meir, S. Moore, K. Skinner; 5th kyu – T. Astley, C. Butler, F. Cope, J. Galletly, M. Walls, K. Whitehead; 4th kyu – A. Sherry.

The Grange Farm Centre was the site for the Summer School under Master Murakami in 1962. The following students graded on the 17th August that year: Liverpool *dojo* – 4th kyu – T. Astley, A. Dewar, A. Smith, R. Stephens, R. Woolfall; 3rd kyu – C. Naylor, A Sherry; Upminster *dojo* – 4th kyu – J. Chisholm, A. Love. From Scotland, E. Ainsworth was graded to 4th kyu. Also in attendance were members of the Dublin *dojo*, who also graded, but the history of Irish Shotokan is not the subject of this book and details will not be gone into.

On the 20th August 1962, Liverpool members S. Moore and J. Chialton were graded to 5th kyu under Murakami, and G. Galletly and K. McCaldon, 4th kyu. The following day, at the North Yorkshire Branch, K. Bauer, J. Clark, J. Gough and J. Sparkes were graded to 6th kyu, whilst F. Higgins, W. Seaton and G. Thompson were promoted to 5th kyu.

The final gradings of 1962 show that North Yorkshire members, G. Heywood and J. Sparkes were graded to 5th kyu by Murakami; F. Higgins and W. Seaton, to 4th kyu, and F. Kidd to 3rd kyu, on the 3rd November. The following day, in Liverpool, K. Bloomfield and H. Frost were promoted to 6th kyu by Murakami; J. Chialton, F. Cope, J. Donoghue, R. Stephens and R. Woolfall, to 4th kyu. On the 5th November 1962, B. Williamson and K. Bauer were graded to 6th kyu and 5th kyu, respectively.

Also in 1962, a BKF *dojo* was opened in Leicester under Robert Johnson, a thirty-year-old engineer, who applied for BKF membership on the 4th July 1962, and subsequently became, for a limited time, BKF area officer. Johnson had been in the military police and had apparently trained in various martial arts in India, Ceylon and Singapore. The *dojo* was small in numbers and was a member of the BKF for only a very short time. Only eight membership forms have survived, and this may well be all of them: Richard Boddy, 18, stereotyper, (25.9.62); Barrie Litchfield, 18, engineer, (25.7.62); Robert Page, 32, Royal Navy, (27.7.62); Russell Pyne, 16, compositor, (6.9.62); David Richardson, 21, carpenter, (9.8.62); Trevor Richardson, 27, factory worker, (16.8.62); Kenneth Smith, 28, salesman, (30.9.62); Kenneth Wilkins, 18, butcher, (25.7.62).

A considerable amount of BKF correspondence has survived for the Leicester *dojo*, most of it administrative and lengthy – one of Bell's letters, for example, is eleven pages of single-spaced A4! Some of the correspondence is acrimonious.

During 1963, Bell received letters, and a challenge, from a man living in New Zealand. The correspondence between Bell and this (here un-named) gentleman is some of the unintentionally funniest material the author has ever read. The impression given is that neither really wanted to fight, but honour dictated that neither was going to back down. Two humorous quotes will have to suffice. Bell, in a previous letter had mentioned hypnosis, and the un-named writer noted: "In reference to your hypnosis methods, do you think that a Gung Fu-ist is going to let you gaze into his eyes while you put him into a trance? It is more likely that the Gung-fu man would be focusing his own eyes upon a certain part of your body and readying his fist for [wait for it] the terrible Canton Corkscrew blow, which I can assure you can burst your spleen apart with the minimum of effort. I would not cast a blind eye to these facts for if you do it may be possible that you cast a blind eye literally, and it could be your own ... In China I have seen men with their bare hands pluck bricks from solid walls. Their fists can be thrust through with the same effort, or may I say concentration of Chi. The Chinese know of at least one hundred and thirty nerve spots on the human body for killing. This excludes the methods of maiming, ripping and cutting. The latter method I find very effective. You have offered me two or three of your methods, I return you five, for when I meet you in the near future I shall don the black uniform I am fully qualified to wear, the dress of the Chinese Ripping School. I think white would suit you well. The Chinese regard this colour as for death or mourning."

Bell wrote, in an earlier letter: "I think this is all just big talk and I have no hesitation saying that since you invite me to test not [out?] my systems of the JKA against the so-called Indian and Chinese secret knowledge you have gained in the Orient [I will]. Personally, I do not care what system you use nor what knowledge you have, for I will take you at any time whenever it is arranged and convenient, but since this is a challenge and you have issued it, then you know where my *dojo* is in London – then if you care to visit it by appointment – then you will be quite entertained there. However, [wait for it] if you refrain from using your death touches, then I will not have to use my extensive knowledge of killer ju-jitsu nor my advanced judo techniques, and my own all-out hand to hand death methods of karate *wawara* or *awrologh* [whatever they may be] that are in my possession, nor will I have to use my extensive knowledge of advanced hypnosis and mind infiltration that I could use all in one, besides my seven years of study and practise of the finest and greatest tuition under the Japanese masters Murakami and Mochizuki." It's great stuff, but on to more serious matters.

The London *dojo*, now based at the Horseshoe pub, was beginning to attract more widespread recognition and subsequently more members. Earlier, Michael Collard (see below) had written to a Philip Wright of the *Daily Mirror* newspaper on the 3rd March 1960, requesting information as to where he could learn karate. Philip Wright wrote: "I believe the only person in England who has the necessary qualifications to teach karate ... is V.C.F Bell." So, Bell's hard work was beginning to pay off.

Application forms to the BKF survive from the following members who trained at one or more of the London *dojos* at this time – the Wheatsheaf, Pindar of Wakefield, Abbe Judo School, Marshall Street Baths and the Horseshoe pub between 1959 and 1962. It is possible that some of these members trained solely at the St. Mary's *dojo*. Members applying to study karate with the BKF were not required to state which *dojo* they intended training at. Classification of *dojo* members for this book has been based upon time of application and/or home address, as has been mentioned before.

Details will be given in the usual manner: Kenneth Baily, 26, TV control operator (28.9.59); Laurie Barnett, 36, taxi driver (11.11.62); Lester Burnett, 40, decorator (7.7.60); Cecil Cabot, 54, scientist (-.-.60); Alan Chuntz, 35, driver (11.11.62); Michael Collard, 18, decorator (21.3.60); Richard Dowd, 32, window cleaner (10.10.61); David Edge, 25, clerk (22.3.62); Raymond Evans, 21, scaffolder (3.7.60); Terence Evans, 18, lifeguard (3.7.60); Michael Galleitch, 17, draughtsman (30.10.62); Kenneth Ghose, 32, occupation unknown (29.7.60); Derek Hadfield, 29, private investigator (16.6.62); John Howard, 18, occupation unknown (21.4.62); Michael Jackson, 26, taxi driver (20.11.62); Anthony Lacey, 18, engineer (15.10.61); Richard Lamport, 17, engineer (14.5.61); Cedric Lawrence, 36, taxi driver (25.11.62); Robin Martin, 17, clerk (13.4.60); Brian McKay, 20, printer (17.1.62); James Moore, 32, civil servant (21.6.62); Stephen Morgan, 20, toolmaker (18.12.60); Muthiahpillai Rajasekeran, 22, student (25.2.62); Douglas Smith, 33, carpenter (7.3.62); Hugh Smith, 24, student (27.5.60); Frederick Soall, 17, watercolour manufacturer (20.10.60). An E. Stoker had a BKF licence issued on the 1st July 1960, but nothing else is known of this individual.

Within a space of less than two months, the BKF St. Mary's and London *dojos* attracted two very important members who were later to become influential BKF instructors. Firstly, on the 4th January 1963, Robert Williams completed his BKF application form for membership. A twenty-two-year-old grocer, running his own business, Rob Williams, as he was known, became interested in karate after reading Nishiyama and Brown's book already alluded to. Williams was to become a BKF instructor, and (it is believed) the second student to successfully undertake a black-belt grading under Master Hirokazu Kanazawa in Britain (see later). Williams is featured later in this work.

Secondly, on the 21st February 1963, the great, late and lamented Edward Whitcher, who was to become highly respected in British Shotokan karate, completed his application form for membership to the BKF. Records show that Eddie, who worked in commercial art and lived in Dagenham, had interests in classical music, chess, aeromodelling and motorcycling. Eddie had practised judo for two years at the Campbell Youth Centre, Arden Crescent, Dagenham, reaching green-belt, but a motorbike accident had caused injury to the nerves and muscles in his left shoulder. He suffered great pain when he was thrown on that side in the *dojo*, and grappling was far from easy. He sought to carry on in the martial arts, despite the shoulder muscle atrophying, and karate seemed to offer what he wanted.

Eddie Whitcher recalled his introduction to karate, when aged twenty-one, at Vernon Bell's Upminster *dojo* one Sunday morning, in issue No.1 of the English Shotokan Karate Association's (internal) magazine, *ESKA News* (1980). The reporter was Rod Butler. Eddie recalled: "In my first lesson I was left standing in the corner of the *dojo* in *zenkutsu-dachi* (front stance) for twenty minutes. The person teaching me didn't even have a karate *gi*. When he noticed me standing in the corner he said, 'Oh! You can change to the other side now,' and left me there for another twenty minutes. I was very disillusioned, but decided to persevere for a certain length of time. This was my basic training."

These early training sessions would commence with a five-mile run, followed by two-and-a-half-hours' practice. Brown-belt, Jimmy Neal, was Eddie's usual teacher, and he could generate real enthusiasm and

B R I T I S H   K A R A T E'   F E D E R A T I O N.
(affiliated to E.K.F., J.K.A., Yoseikan)

National Coach & Chairman.		Chief Technical Adviser.
V. C. F. BELL	Application for Membership	TETSUGI MURAKAMI
3 Dan Judo	as	3 Dan Karate-Do
2 Dan Ju-Jitsu	Full/Country/Associate/Member.	3 Dan Aiki-Do
2 Dan Karate-Do		2 Dan Kendo.
1 Dan Aiki-Do.	No..........	

I, (Surname).....W.H.I.T.C.H.E.R.........(Christian Names).E.D.W.A.R.D..A.R.T.H.U.R... hereby wish to make application for membership of the above organisation and submit my personal particulars hereunder, for the perusal of the aforesaid Federation. I confirm that all these particulars are correct and true in every respect, and I agree, if accepted as a member of this Branch to obey and abide by its Rules and Regulations, to uphold its Constitution, to conduct myself in a correct manner at all times (both in and out of the Branch's premises) and to further uphold the ideals and principals of the science of Karate as laid down by the B.K.F. and by the Yoseikan by my personal example and co-operation at all times.

Signed...E. A. Whitcher...............

Witnessed...R. Ranjatram....

1. Surname... W.H.I.T.C.H.E.R...........Christian Names..E.D.W.A.R.D..A.R.T.H.U.R....
2. Permanent address...57,..HITHERFIELD.RD...DAGENHAM, ESSEX......
3. Telephone No. (if any)...............3a. Married/Single.....S.I.N.G.L.E.......
4. Age....21.YEARS.........4a. Date of Birth....21.-.10.-.41.........
5. If under 18 years of age, have you your parents permission to join........
6. Hobbies/Interests...MOTORCYCLING,., AEROMODELLING, CLASSICAL MUSIC, CHESS......
7. Occupation...COMMERCIAL ART........
8. Service in H.M. Forces - a. period...............b. Service...........
   Rank.............Date of demobilisation................
9. Condition of Health....GOOD.............9a. Examiner..DR.HUNTER......
10. Date of last medical..OCTOBER.1959......10a. Place of Exam..DAGENHAM...
11. Have you any Heart/Lung trouble...NO......Details...............
12. Have you High/Low blood pressure......NORMAL.....................
13. Do you suffer from any organic, mental or physical disabilities or weaknesses.
    ....NO.........
14. State names and addresses of present Clubs or Societies which you belong to...
    ...CAMPBELL..YOUTH.CENTRE, ARDEN.CRESCENT,..DAGENHAM, ESSEX
15. Outdoor/Indoor sports played....JUDO...........
16. Names/addresses of previous Karate Clubs...............
17. Have you had previous Karate instruction....NO.........a. by whom........ ...
    ....Place.............
18. Karate Belts held...............a. grade.........b. date of grading......
    ....c. Examiner...............d. Any further
    details of Karate experience...............
19. Where did you hear of this organisation.....THROUGH..JUDO.ASSOCIATION...
20. How and by whom were you introduced....BY..INQUIRING..THROUGH.MR.FOLEY...
21. State type of instruction desired - Private lessons.NO...Class Instruction YES
    Complete study of Karate..NO......(Answer Yes or No to above)
22. State precisely why you wish to learn Karate....TO..IMPROVE.REFLEXES.....
23. State how you became interested in Karate and what decided you that a Course of
    training would benefit you. AFTER.SEEING.MAGAZINE.ADVERTS,...FITNESS........
    In what way.....AS..AN.AID.TO.JUDO...............

Continued....

Edward Whitcher's application form to join the BKF

- 2 -

24. Having reached a standard in Karate, to what purpose do you intend using your knowledge...... SELF..DEFENCE...

25. How do you think you can further the science of Karate and in what way....... .........HAVE..NO..IDEAS..AT..PRESENT..

26. Is your interest in this Branch and Karate as a whole -

   (a) Theoretical   (b) Practical   (c)Philosophical   (d) Cultural

   (e) Scientific   (f) Curiosity   (g)Knowledge   (h) Sport

   ....THEORETICAL.+.SCIENTIFIC...

27. For how long do you intend participating in Karate..AS.LONG.AS.I.AM.INTERESTED.

28. Approx. days and time available for tuition..4.HRS...FRIDAY.+.SUNDAY.......

29. Do you intend/~~desire~~ to take Gradings in Karate.....YES..................

30. How far in your studies do you intend to go..NO..IDEA..AT..PRESENT.........

31. Do you intend helping the Branch outside instruction hours.....NO...........

   If so how....................

32. State briefly what your conception of Karate is..HAND.+.FOOT..COMBAT......

33. Name/Address of your Sponsor in joining this Branch - ....

   ...John..Fuly........40.Kent..Rd..Dagenham..Essex...............

34. Name/address of Seconder in joining.....NIL..............................

   ....

35. I..E..WHITCHER........agree to abide by my answers to the above details, and if for any reason I desire to resign my Membership I will do so in writing, stating my reasons, and giving at least one month's notice to the Branch Authorities.

36. I..E..WHITCHER.....pledge myself at all times to keep and honour my written ~~Agreements with the B.K.F. and by my integrity to keep all verbal~~ and promised arrangements with this Branch forsoever as long as I am a Member.

37. I am fully aware and acquainted with the Constitution, Principles and Objects of the B.K.F. and with the full knowledge of them I desire to become a member. I declare that at all times during my Membership I will to the best of my ability fulfill my obligations as outlined in the Constitution.

   Signature...E.A.Whitcher.............Date...24-2-63.................

   Sponsor/Witness..John Fuly..2nd Witness..7.S.Fhil.............

   [ARF '66 sent 14/12/05

   RECEIVED WITH THANKS.

   £......s......d.

   per pro BRITISH KARATE FEDERATION.
       (Karate Club of Great Britain).

   V. C. F. ~~BELL (3rd DAN)~~
   Chairman/Organiser
   of British Karate Federation.
   137, Hillview Avenue,
   Phone. Hornchurch 42580.
   Essex.

   M/A/R sent..25/3/63..............

   G/C sent....14/3/63.....No........

   LIC. issued..25/3/63. (No.304)...

   E.K.F. Lic.Fee paid............

   Full/~~Country/Ass~~ Member granted..25/3/63
       No.383.....

   "   "   "   " transferred........

   Period............

   Application..25/3/63.post.
   ~~Refused~~........Accepted..21/3/63
   Interviewed..........Time........
   Enrolled..25/3/63............
   A.F.Completed..21/3/63.........
   Fee paid..25/3/63.Amount.£3-14-..
   Resigned.........Cause..........
   Dismissed..........Cause..........

   3n.Case fer auspt pa £3-18/- 25/3/63 Commenced 31/3/63
   ART £2-2-0 pa 3/2/64 (567) Finished Sur 164 gar.
                                          A/R sent nnn 1964
                                          LRF sent 18/17/64 ARF Pd 16/2/65.

BRITISH KARATE FEDERATION.

(affiliated to J.K.A., E.K.F., & YOSEIKAN)

Private and Class Pupil's Declaration and Oath of

Allegiance

I . EDWARD . . ARTHUR . WHITCHER residing at . . 52 . . . .

. . HITHERFIELD . . RD . . . DAGENHAM, . ESSEX . . . .

having been accepted as a Student Teacher/Private Pupil of the B.K.F. to study the science of Karate and kindred subjects fully realise, accept and swear on oath to abide by, and promise to fulfil the following conditions governing the Course(s) I shall be taught:-

1. To practice, participate and study all methods, tricks, movements at my own risk, and to hold no one responsible but Myself for any injury sustained, even if it should result in my death.

2. Never to abuse, misuse or publicise any of the knowledge I shall be taught as long as I live.

3. Never to use my knowledge of Karate etc., however trivial it may be to the detriment, disadvantage or humiliation of a fellow human-being, as long as I live.

4. Never to disclose, repeat, show or practice any method, trick or movement I am taught to any person living, but to keep all my knowledge gained to myself, realising it as a secret, deadly and dangerous art, and I learn it only to protect my own life and family, as long as I live.

5. To use my knowledge only if, and when, my body or life is in danger, or if my family is in danger, or to assist any unfortunate person attacked by hooligans, drunkards, etc., or if I see any woman being assaulted and their personage is in danger. Only then, will I use my knowledge of Karate, or any infirm, aged or young person being attacked, and to use only sufficient knowledge to render incapable the attack commensorate with the force of the attack.

6. Never to appear in public to demonstrate, exhibit or teach, coach or instruct any of the knowledge I am taught of Jujitsu, Karate or its kindred branches to any person(s) classes, bodies, etc., until I am fully qualified to do so, and then only with the written permission of my Tutor and or/my parent Society, Federation or Association, as long as I live.

7. Never to bring dishonour, discredit, abuse or bad repute on my Tutor, Society, my art of Karate, or on the science I am taught, by any bad conduct, loose behaviour, scandal, blasphemy, lies, drunkenness or in fact by any dishonourable word, deed or action on my part, as long as I live.

8. To promise to always **respect**, honour and closely guard and protect all the secret and deadly **knowledge** I shall be taught, as long as I live.

9. To promise to keep all my knowledge from the profane, violent, politically minded, agressive and abusive elements of mankind at all times, as long as I live.

10. To uphold the name, honour, prestige and secret knowledge of my art, my Tutor, my Society and my Federation by my own decent, moral chivalrous, gallant and highest ideals of behaviour and example, as long as I live.

11. To respect the living, honour the dead, to respect and protect the name, honour and personage of womanhood, and children at all times, as long as I live.

12. To protect the weak, the infirm, the aged, the fearful and the lowliest at all times from agressive, violent and abusive elements and circumstances, as long as I live.

Continued........

Edward Whitcher's Declaration and Oath of Allegiance

- 2 -

13. To realise that any deviation, violation, infringement, breakage or abuse of any of my foregoing declarations, will result in full disciplinary action, compensation and retribution by the law of the land, by the Federation, by the Society and by my Tutor to the fullest extent possible.

14. To accept as final, absolute and fullproof any and all decisions by my tutor, Society or Federation on any matter governing the art of Karate and kindred sciences, as long as I live.

15. To realise that all the foregoing conditions, promises and declarations are binding and in force over my personage during my studentship, after graduation, after membership has ceased, in fact, as long as I live.

Pupil's Signature.....*E. A. Whitney*...........

Date...*10-3-63*..

1st Witness.*C. R. Raynham*

Address.*57 HITHERFIELD RD - DAGENHAM, ESSEX*

2nd Witness...*A Brent*

Address....*5A Hitherfield Rd Dag-Essex*

Tutor...................................

Address...................................

B.K.F. Secretary/Official...............

Address...

National Coach
  & Chairman
V. C. F. BELL.
3 Dan Judo
2 Dan Ju-Jitsu
2 Dan Karate-Do
1 Dan Aiki-Do

V.C.F. BELL. (3rd DAN)
  Chairman/Organiser
of BRITISH KARATE FEDN.
137, Hillview Avenue,
Phone Hornchurch 4252
  Essex.

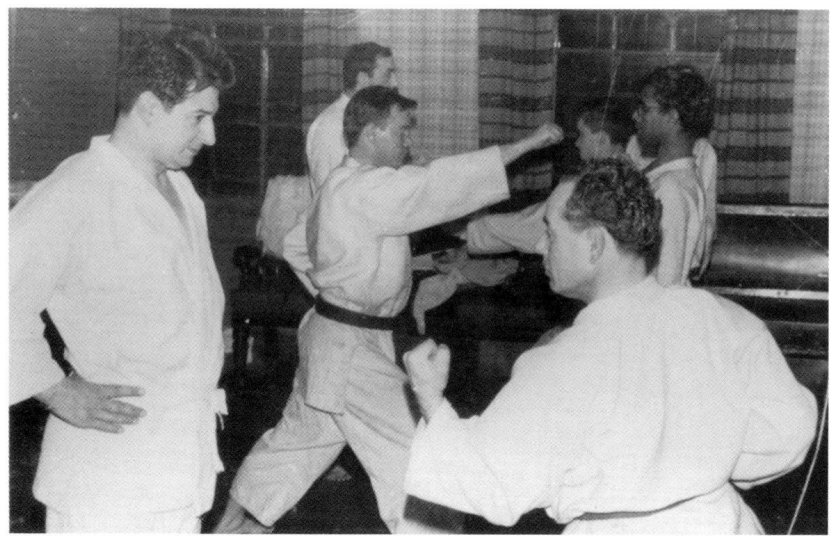

Training at the St. Mary's *dojo*, Upminster – 1962/63

good spirit in the class. There was a lot of stamina work and many repetitions of a few basic techniques. These sessions stretched Eddie's dedication to the limit, but he persisted, and later became the first Englishman to successfully take the black-belt grading under Master Hirokazu Kanazawa (see later).

The number of gradings diminished in 1963. There were four gradings at the St. Mary's *dojo* as follows. The first was held under Murakami on the 2nd February 1963, when L. Barnett, G. Bryans, A. Chuntz and L. Glinnen passed 6th kyu; J. Chisholm passed 4th kyu and A. Love, 3rd kyu.

The second grading, also under Murakami, was held on the 16th April 1963. The results were as follows: 6th kyu – J. Bounds, N. De Silva; 5th kyu – L. Barnett, G. Bryans, L. Glinnen, R. Mills; 4th kyu – A. Chuntz. The third grading was taken by Bell, on the 25th June 1963. It is important because Edward Whitcher and Robert Williams passed their 6th kyu, as did H. Peters and N. Pressman. The fourth grading was taken by Murakami on the 8th November 1963. The results were as follows: 6th kyu – B. Harper; 5th kyu – N. De Silva, L. Gunner, R. Merrick, N. Pressman and G. Stephenson. Vernon Bell also held an individual grading for Art Malia on the 1st November 1963, and Malia was promoted to 2nd kyu.

Murakami held two gradings at the Liverpool *dojo* in 1963. The first was on the 3rd February, when the following people were promoted:

5th kyu – K. Bloomfield, H. Frost, E. Travis; 4th kyu – J. Galletly, K. McCaldon, S. Moore, P. Sloan, M. Walls, W. Whitehead. The second grading was held on the 9th November, with the following results: 6th kyu – L. Doft, F. Gillmore, P. Harley; 5th kyu – D. Elliott, T. O'Neill, J. Taylor; 3rd kyu – J. Robinson. This second grading is particularly interesting for three reasons. It was the first grading for Terry O'Neill, later to become famous not only as winner of a number of national *kata* and *kumite* competitions, and an international competitor for many years, but also as editor and publisher of *Terry O'Neill's Fighting Arts International* magazine. Secondly, T. O'Neill graded from novice to temporary 5th kyu in one go – a rare event in those days; and, thirdly, because an R. Bell graded to 8th kyu – the first time an extended kyu system seems to have been employed.

On the 7th April 1963, Master Murakami made a visit to the newly formed Blackpool *dojo* (see later). The BKF grading register shows that the following students all graded to 6th kyu: W. Ellewood, J. Green, E. Hutchinson, D. Milligan, A. Stewart and J. Taylor. On the 30th June, 1963, Bell visited the Blackpool *dojo* and W. Ellewood, J. Green, E. Hutchinson, A. Stewart graded to 5th kyu, and Liverpool members D. Elliott, S. McConnell and F. Cope graded to 6th kyu, 5th kyu and 4th kyu, respectively.

There were also two gradings held at the Middlesbrough *dojo* under Master Murakami. The first was held on the 14th and 15th April 1963. The following students were promoted: 6th kyu – K. Sharp, J. Sharpe; 5th kyu – D. Benson, S. Kidd, E. Summer; 4th kyu – F. Higgins.

Murakami returned on the 4th August and the successful students were as follows: 6th kyu – E. Pelter; 5th kyu – K. Sharp, J. Sharpe; 4th kyu – K. Bauer, G. Heywood, S. Kidd.

Gordon Thompson recalled the BKF Summer School at Chigwell in late July and early August 1963: "Mr. Murakami was the instructor and on this course I learned a lot about Mr. Bell and his methods. The training was great and I learned another *kata*. We always started late, always – once nearly an hour late ... Mr. Bell kept Murakami on a tight lead ... The training time was supposed to be two hours each session with two sessions each day. Mister Murakami still seemed quite a character. The second session was late in the evening, scheduled to finish at nine o'clock I think, and I am certain that he learned that the pubs closed early, about ten o'clock I think, and after the first day or two he would keep the training session going as long as he could. There were no alcoholic sales on the camp, which suggested that it was something other than a holiday camp ... The result was a mad scramble after the final bow to get changed and out to the pub across the main road outside the camp. John Clark and I had an advantage. We had gone on my motorbike and after the first day I parked it outside the training hall and could jump on it and ride through the camp while others had to run. Cars were not allowed on the road we used, perhaps bikes weren't either, but I was never stopped. The hall we used was more like a dance hall than a gymnasium, but considering the times it was as good as could be expected. Sports centres had only just been thought of and I think that the first of these was only just being built.

"We slept in two-tiered bunks in Nissen huts that were some way from the hall. One day, after the morning training session, we saw Mr. Bell looking all over the place. 'Had we seen Mr. Murakami?' 'No', we said, truthfully, but when we got to our hut there he was lying on one of the bunks smoking his head off. We looked at him, surprised, and he peered around the door, dodged back and lay on the bunk again. 'He's keeping out of Belly's way,' one of the London members told us. (Vernon Bell had a number of nicknames including, 'Bluebell,' 'Tinkerbell' and 'Dumbbell'). This started a train of thought that led me to many conclusions. We had a few laughs with him in the hut and he made it very plain that he was a bit fed up with being dragged off immediately after training sessions. When he had finished his cigarettes, two of them I think, he got up with a sigh, said, 'Mr. Bell,' and went out. A very illuminating encounter."

Regarding Murakami's apparent addiction to cigarettes, Gordon Thompson tells an interesting tale: "Murakami had a number of scars on his body which we saw when he took off his jacket to show how the muscles should be tensed. Some of the London members told us that he had inflicted them on himself with a cigarette. 'Why?' we asked. Apparently, Murakami suffered from rheumatism and he had burned out the pain centres. That was what we were told, and I am afraid you will have to make up your own mind about the truth of this."

Gordon Thompson relates a story as to how someone taught Murakami to swear. "As a result of this, one day Mr. Murakami went into a hotel foyer looked around and said, 'F...ing hell,' in a loud voice, convinced that he was behaving impeccably. He got his own back in the *dojo* however. He was quite a case and liked a bit of fun, so one day during the break, yes, believe it or not, we had a ten-minute break in the middle of the training session, which I think was mainly so that Mr. Murakami could have a smoke, he challenged —— [the individual who had taught him the unfortunate word] to a little game where they got on their hands and knees at each end of a form and pushed against it with

Master Tetsuji Murakami, cigarette in hand, at the Grange Farm Centre – 1963

their heads trying to push each other back. Murakami cheated and used his very hard fists against the form ... [and —— received] a nice headache."

Michael Randall (see shortly) also recalled how certain London *karateka* used to teach Murakami to swear in English. "Of course, the

Japanese don't swear as such. If they want to call you something rude they call you a pig or a dog or something. To be called an idiot in Japanese is really something, you know, you'd have a fight over that. It's the most disgusting thing. No one is an idiot in Japan. If you're called an idiot that's fighting talk, because a pig might have some intelligence but an idiot hasn't got any. If you're called an idiot then that's your lot ... and Murakami would practise swearing to see if he could get it right, completely unaware of what it meant."

Randall remembers attending the Grange Farm Centre in Chigwell, Essex, the following year (1964), and recalled the then thirty-seven-year-old Murakami very well. A particularly impressive feat that Murakami could do, Randall recalled, was to stand facing a wall, about eighteen inches away, and lift his knee up to his chest so his foot just touched the wall and continued to extend the lower leg so that his foot was raised above his head resting on the wall in an axe-kick fashion – an impressive demonstration of flexibility.

Another most interesting story that Thompson remembered concerning Murakami (it may have been at the Middlesbrough *dojo*, or later at Chigwell) was: "One day a member brought in a book by Oyama to show him. I forget the name of it, but it was the first one produced. Murakami took one look at the pictures of him knocking the horns off the baby bull and threw it in the air. When it landed he jumped on it a couple of times, looked at the astonished owner, pulled out his wallet and asked, 'How much?'"

But back to the Grange Farm course of 1963! The 6th [actually 5th] Annual Summer Course was held between Saturday, 27th July, until Saturday 3rd August 1963, with training in the Main Hall of the centre, which was situated in the High Street, Chigwell. Grange Farm became famous for housing a number of early karate courses, including those of Master Harada. It was officially opened on the 12th July 1951, the year of the Festival of Britain, by the then HRH Princess Elizabeth, with Sir Winston Churchill also in attendance. It was a large complex of one hundred and seven acres, with views across the Roding Valley to Epping Forest, and catered for many sports and campers. In the timber dormitories there was space for up to four hundred people. There was, of course, ample space for people who wished to camp. Unlike previous BKF Summer Courses, where the student had to book his or her own accommodation, at Grange Farm it was a block booking and students applied to the BKF. The reservation fee was £4 15s per student. This fee included three meals daily, bunk bed and camp facilities.

Murakami grading record for the morning session of the 2nd August 1963, at Grange Farm.

The format of the course details sent out by Bell was much the same as for previous years. On this occasion it was estimated that £120 would be needed by enrolments to cover the cost of the venture. Students were to register in the *dojo* on the evening of the 27th July 1963, at 7.00 p.m., and the first training session followed from 7.30 p.m. to 9.30 p.m. Daily karate training under Master Murakami was between 11.00 a.m. and 1.30 p.m. and between 7.30 p.m. and 9.30 p.m. Vernon Bell held a free practice and tuition for beginners between 4.00 p.m. and 5.00 p.m. daily. The course grading followed on the 3rd August 1963, beginning at 10.30 a.m. Prices seemed to have gone up considerably. The cost of training was seven guineas either for the morning or afternoon sessions, but not both. If a student wished to train both in the morning and evening, the cost was twelve guineas. The cost of the grading was an additional five shillings. It is interesting to note that by 1963, the minimum age for karate training in the BKF was reduced to fifteen, though this could, as we have seen, be relaxed.

It is also worthy of note that the literature mentions that Murakami was, "the official European delegate of [the] Japan Karate Association as well as being Founder/President of [the] European Karate Federation."

The BKF grading register shows that the following people from a variety of *dojos* successfully graded on the 2nd August 1963, on completion of the Chigwell Summer School: 6th kyu – P. Hart, D. Havies, R. Merrick, G. Stephenson; 5th kyu – J. Bounds, J. Clark, N. De Silva, E. Whitcher, R. Williams; 4th kyu – T. Astley, L. Barnett, G. Bryant, A. Chuntz, J. Green, R. Mills, S. Moore, G. Thompson, F. Vernon; 3rd kyu – J. Chialton, J. Chisholm (H), A. Dewar, K. McCaldron (H), A. Sherry, A. Smith, R. Woolfall (H). Interestingly, 6th kyus, P. Hart and D. Havies were from Nottinghamshire, though a BKF Notts branch wasn't to be formed for another two years.

In 1963, Vernon Bell established a *dojo* at the 2nd Parachute Regiment, based at the Guillemont Barracks in Cove, near Aldershot, Hampshire. Records still exist for nineteen members of this *dojo*, who were: Ronald Barker, Richard Bond, Peter Butcher, James Castle, Terence Duke, Ralph Griffin, Reginald Hassall, Roger Jenner, Edward Jones, James Lamon, Robert Marsh, George McKay, Michael Ovenden, Peter Parker, Leslie Peacock, David Powell, Leslie Singer, Colin Vance and Gordon Winks. Ranks were up to Lance Corporal, and the average age of the students was 21.84 years, the youngest being eighteen years old, the eldest twenty-six. Vernon Bell and Terry Wingrove taught at the base at weekends for several months before the regiment was posted to Bahrain with the job, it is believed, of protecting the oil wells. As Major W. Young of the 2nd Paras noted to Bell in a letter dated January, 1963: "The introduction of any new sport to the battalion will be invaluable out there."

The remaining three letters, out of six in English available from Master Murakami, come from 1963. He wrote to Bell on the 2nd October: "Thank you very much for your letter [now lost] dated September 27th. I just send these words to make you know that I agree about everything you said in your letter. I have just caught a cold last week and I think I will be alright next week." He wrote to Bell again on the 15th October: "I write to you this letter so lately because I thought it was able for me to go and see you on October the 18th. It seems now that I have to stay in bed for a week because I caught a very cold. I'm very, very sick. I beg your pardon for I think I shall not be able to go to London on the 18th October. I'm very sorry. Instead of this broken stage [training course], would you like me to come to London on the October the 25th? I'm looking forward to hear from you soon." It seems fairly obvious that Murakami's "cold" had developed into something else.

Bell replied, in a sympathetic manner, on the 16th October 1963. Murakami replied on the 25th October 1963. "I have received your letter [also lost] and the work permit and I send you some words to tell you that the dates of courses proposed to me seem alright. I shall be in London

Richard Bond   Gordon Winks

Reginald Hassall   Robert Marsh

George McKay   Edward Jones

Six members of the 2nd Battalion, the Parachute Regiment *dojo* – early 1963

on Friday, November 8th, in the afternoon. Now, I have to tell you that Mr. Harada is a friend of mine and he is a real 5th Dan. We have the same way of teaching and he is very good. I never mind if he was recognised by JKA, so I don't know exactly. I have to ask him for that." This letter is very interesting bearing in mind what appears to have happened to Master Harada in France. Murakami's address at this time seems to have been, 69, Rue du Cardinal, Lemoine, Paris 5. This information was obtained from a passage card from Paris to London.

PART VI

Jacques Delcourt, President of the Karate Section of the Fédération Française De Judo et Disciplines Assimilées, wrote to Bell (and the chairmen of karate organizations in other European countries) on the 14th May 1963, suggesting that, "The time has come to engage into friendly and sportive relations with your Federation," and had proposed a meeting of teams towards the end of that year. On the 20th August 1963, Bell received another letter noting the programme, which showed the planned events were to be in the following order: the international meetings, the French National Cup for Technique (*kata*), inter-club competitions, and finally, demonstrations by Japanese experts then present in France – and in particular Hiroo Mochizuki. On the 28th August, Bell received yet another letter announcing the venue – the Stadium Pierre de Coubertin – and a request to know if a British team was to be sent.

Any letters between Bell and Delcourt from the end of August to the 11th of November on this, the first European karate meeting, are lost. On the 12th November, Bell received a letter from Delcourt announcing that Belgium had confirmed its participation, and that the main attraction would be the meeting between France and Belgium, if Britain decided not to take part. If Britain, who was yet to give an answer, decided to participate, then a triangular tournament would be organised.

In another letter of the 13th November 1963, discussing proposals for the event, some interesting details emerge on the French karate scene. Delcourt wrote: "At the moment, I can point out that our Federation has at present 80 clubs all over France (organised in district leagues) and having about 3,800 to 4,000 members (altogether about 90 to 92% of French karate exponents). Two small private little groups exist: one with the Vietnamese, Nam (Autonomous Federation of Karate) and one with the Japanese Murakamy [*sic*] (National Sportive and Cultural Federation of Karate). These associations have a limited activity and have no representation on the national scale; as I have already pointed out in a circular, only our Federation has the support of the French governmental authorities."

Bell replied on the 21st November 1963, accepting the invitation to visit Paris, and then again, reiterating the BKF's position, on the 27th November. Delcourt's address was 12, Rue Lecuirot, Paris 14. Bell would act as team manager.

A letter from Bell to intending BKF team members has survived, undated, but late November 1963. As the event is of great historical interest, this letter has its place, and the entire contents will be reproduced here, with the original emphases given. At the top of the letter, a note in red biro read: "Have you got your passport up to date?" Bell wrote: "Further to the recent circulars sent to you regarding the forthcoming proposed visit to Paris, I wish you to know that a positive reply in writing from you, in duplicate, one reply going to the General and Commercial Agency, Ley Street, Ilford, and the other to myself [is expected]. These two replies <u>MUST</u> be received by Monday next, the 2nd December at the latest. By now you have heard from the travel agency with full details of travelling arrangements, and as your name was given to them as a definite party having expressed a positive desire to go on this trip, then the agency replied with full details last week. I am told by the principal of the agency that he has booked a definite return flight on the B.E.A. for you for Friday night, 13th December, returning late evening, Sunday 15th. This flight reservation must be confirmed by you in writing enclosing [a] substantial deposit, and this confirmation reserves hotel accommodation for Friday and Saturday. So kindly adopt a business-like attitude and obey this request for much embarrassment is caused to the agency and the BKF by your not complying in this manner. I regret that I take a serious view of BKF members who delay their obligations when having expressed a firm desire for this trip, so kindly do not bring discredit to the BKF by any lackadaisical attitude in this matter. I shall expect the courtesy of an early reply.

"Re[gards] the Paris visit, we are all travelling as an official BKF party on the same planes and staying in the same hotel. There will be about eight or nine in number and the programme takes in a private karate course at the *dojo* of Mr. Murakami on Saturday the 14th in the morning and afternoon – his *dojo* being reserved all day for BKF members only, and those wishing to participate may join in optionally, giving their names to me on the day, and charge for instruction will be according to the number practising and the number of hours tuition. Hours proposed for tuition: 10 to 12, and 2 till 4, and maybe 5 p.m., and again on Sunday 10 a.m. to 1 p.m., and Sunday evening 7 to 9, subject to slight alteration in time as may be found necessary according to events effecting the programme. We are responsible for paying Mr.

Murakami, and with eight people participating all the time, the maximum fee for tuition would be in the region of £2. 15s to £3, being the price off a normal weekend course. These figures are liable to be altered either way, slightly, according to numbers decided on the day. If you wish to attend for tuition to Mr. Murakami's *dojo*, it is necessary that you apply at once by the 1st December, in writing, stating the times of sessions you wish to attend at his *dojo*, with a deposit, which secures a definite vacancy on his course. I must insist in no uncertain terms that you realise full well that close co-operation is necessary, for Mr. Murakami is opening his *dojo* particularly on Saturday and Sunday as a private course for our members only, and he wishes to know for certain by the end of next week how many people are attending, who they are, and times, and I must confirm this to him no later that the 6th December, giving him time to make his own arrangements. PLEASE REPLY DEFINITELY STATING YOUR PRECISE REQUIREMENTS AND CONFIRMATION NO LATER THAN THE 1st DECEMBER OR ELSE THE PROGRAMME WILL BE IN JEOPARDY.

"Also on the programme will be our attendance as the official British contingent at the French Federation of Judo, Karate Section, Annual Championships and Display at the Coubertin Stadium in Paris at 9 p.m. on Saturday, where there will be exhibitions of karate by the Master Mochizuki, 4th Dan, who is the official legal instructor to the French Federation appointed by the Government. Our contingent will have friendly practise with the master and all our graded members will take part in a 3-team match between France, Belgium and Britain, which will be on a very friendly and non-committal arrangement, and will provide valuable experience to our members. Remember that you are representing the BKF, and your name has gone forward as a team member, so do not create any bad feeling at [a] top-level, official basis, by any failure to keep your expressed obligations or crying off at the last minute. Also, do not worry about your grade, for this is not a full international match of all black-belt grades, and we have it on written authority that the French and Belgian Federations have had little or no Japanese tuition over the past few years until very recently, so their technical standard may not be as high as ours. So just go in, do your best and have a go and ignore the result and circumstances. After the evening's display, [the] BKF has arranged a private gathering for its party at 10.30 p.m. with Mr. Mochizuki. On Sunday afternoon at 3 p.m., the French Federation has invited our party to attend, as witnesses, their black-belt gradings, which should provide valuable experience for us all. On Sunday morning, I am attending, as official British delegate, a private conference with the Belgian and French and other delegations present, to establish a new European Federation, with the prime object of establishing karate on a European level more than a national level, which should be to the advantage of all. The whole weekend should be of great interest and benefit to all concerned, and has been specially arranged to be a full weekend of karate, which should be very profitable for everyone. It has taken much hard work and time to organise and we require your fullest co-operation in making it a final success. We are arranging for Mr. Mochizuki to visit England to teach at our Branches in January or early February, and we hope to hold a large display in London on the occasion of his visit.

"I am pleased to say that the French Federation has agreed to pay for our hotel and two meals for one night, in return for our doing the same when they visit England, and I have requested that they allow us a refund for two nights hotel and two meals each day and I now await their confirmation. All we do is pay our fare (return), and as we are going as a party through an accredited agency, we must naturally pay for our fare and hotel combined before we go and the French Federation will reimburse us during our stay.

"I trust this meets with your full approval and I shall expect the favour of an early reply without delay, but PLEASE read this letter carefully. Further leaflets regarding the French Federation's programme have just been received and are being translated, and copies will be sent on to you at the end of this week."

On the 12th December 1963, Bell wrote to Delcourt, replying to the latter's letter of the 9th December (now lost). Terry Wingrove, as BKF representative, had been in negotiations with Charles Palmer, 5th Dan, Chairman of the British Judo Association, at the Budokwai, the same day as Bell wrote his letter. Bell noted that following, "Mr. Palmer's telephone conversation with your good self [Delcourt], then we are pleased to hear that all difficulties and most problems have now been settled between our organisations. I am now pleased to confirm that our Federation will be attending your display on Saturday, 14th Dec., as the official British Team and we look forward to a very successful evening." The BKF team then, left London on Friday, 13th December 1963, arriving in Paris at midnight. Precisely what Mr. Palmer's and the BJA's role [unless Palmer was acting independently in some way] was in all this is unknown, but a similar situation arose a few months into the New Year (see later).

On the 11th March 1963, a certain J.D. Parker of Carleton, Blackpool, had written to the BJA regarding karate. This letter is now lost. A J.L.

Capes had replied on the 13th March, and noted: "Generally speaking, the Association does not encourage this, though there is no written rule about it. The reasons being that as far as we know, there is nobody in this country who is fully qualified to teach this rather dangerous pastime, but many seem to set themselves up as teachers after taking a weekend course. I would certainly try to establish the authenticity of the British Karate Federation, and in particular the qualification of your member. We have been trying to do this for years, but with little result." Presumably, one of Parker's members had graded under the BKF. Bell took up cudgels, and on the 4th April, wrote to the BJA: "I have been shown the letter you sent on the 13th ulto., to Mr. J. D. Parker of Blackpool in response to his letter concerning karate, and I must inform you that I am most surprised at the incorrect statements and insinuations contained therein, so much so that I must call upon you to refrain from broadcasting such misleading information. Firstly, your statement that there is no-one in this country qualified to teach what you choose to call "this dangerous pastime" you know is incorrect, although I admit there is not one in your Association, and this is doubtless your sore point … [Bell then gives details of his credentials] It is obvious, therefore, that the statement in the third paragraph of your letter that you have been unable to establish the authenticity of the BKF after trying for years is a gross untruth and is so obviously prompted by resentment that a member of your Association was not granted such authority by the Japanese official authority in karate, and savours of a most unsportsmanlike and despicable attitude by one who holds a responsible position in promoting sport ... [more of Bell's credentials]. Finally, should any further suggestions or insinuations of a detrimental nature to myself be circulated, I shall have no hesitation in seeking legal advice."

Capes, as BJA General Secretary, replied on the 11th April: "May I refer to your letter of the 4th April 1963, in regard to the authenticity of the British Karate Federation, and may I confirm that the points you have raised were noted by the Executive Committee." Perhaps, then, the BJA took notice of Bell, for any other letters are lost, but why the BKF found it necessary to contact Palmer is a mystery, unless it was just good politics, or of concern to the French.

A final interesting point was contained in Bell's letter, for he had applied to an advert in the March issue of *Judo* for a qualified karate instructor, and wondered the outcome of his application. Capes replied that *Judo* magazine was an entirely separate entity, and therefore he was unable to help in this matter.

But back to the intended triangular international championships! The first ever British karate team to take part in an international event was captained by Terry Wingrove and, supposedly, would be composed of two 2nd kyus, four 3rd kyus, two 4th kyus, two 5th kyus and one 6th kyu, with one reserve (as noted by Bell in a letter to Delcourt on the 27th November 1963). The event, held on Saturday the 14th December 1963, at the Stadium Pierre de Coubertin, was in fact the first-ever karate international competition to be held in Europe.

Terry Wingrove recalled: "Three weeks before we went, Murakami [who had apparently fallen out with Plee] said, 'If you go I will disown you. You're not capable of fighting – none of you.' Vernon Bell said, 'We're going as Britain,' and there was a big disagreement. On the Friday we arrived, all in our new tracksuits, Murakami asked to see us. He said to Vernon, 'They're not to fight.' Eventually, Murakami said it was okay for Neal and me to fight because we were 2nd kyus, but not the others, because they were too low a grade. He said it was ridiculous. Murakami came to the stadium, but instead of sitting with the VIPs, he went and sat up in the audience."

The competitions were held on a marked-out (in red or white) floor, forming a square, with equal sides between eight and ten metres. All competitors were required to wear a clean white *gi*, shin-pads, forearm pads, knee and elbow pads. Elastic bandages were forbidden unless under the advice of a doctor. The wearing of a protective box was optional. The rules for this competition were really quite comprehensive (twenty Sections on six quarto pages), and things had been thought out. However, the best laid plans can go awry.

Events commenced at 9.00 p.m. Terry Wingrove recalled: "There was Jimmy Neal, Alan Smith, Andy Sherry, Brian Hammond and myself. It was televised, and went all over Europe. When we arrived the French National Championships were going on. Everybody ... [was really worried]. It was bad for me as well, even though I'd been to France before. They were knocking the hell out of each other – no boxes. There were stretchers piled up on the side – man on a stretcher, carried off; man on a stretcher, carried off – and so on. That's all it was. Knock a man down and get a point, and we looked at each other and thought what the hell had we let ourselves in for. Then came the international, the team event. The first match was between Belgium and England. Leo Aarts, who is now a top man in Europe, captained the Belgian team. They were all black-belts, and there we were, brown-belts and a lower kyu grade, if I remember correctly [Sherry and Smith had been 3rd kyus some four months, while Hammond was, according to the

The first European Karate Championships – British team members, from right to left: Brian Hammond, Andy Sherry, Ron Mills, Jimmy Neal and Terry Wingrove (1963).

BKF grading register, 4th kyu, a grade he had been awarded in 1961]. I went up first as captain against Aarts who was a 3rd Dan I think, and I got in a *chudan mae-geri*. Hiroo Mochizuki was the referee and said, 'No point. Not hard enough.' Within four seconds I hit Aarts again, same technique. Back he went. Mochizuki said, 'No point – harder.' I thought, 'God!' Within another few seconds I hit him a third time with *mae-geri* and he went down on his back. '*Ippon!*' Aarts stood up and said, 'This is not karate,' and I said, 'Sorry, Leo. You heard what he said.' Aarts said, 'You won. You won. You're quite correct,' and bowed.

"Then Jimmy went up and we wiped them five to nil. I remember looking up at Murakami and he just looked away. Then it came to Switzerland [if so, then it was no longer a triangular match] and we wiped them out five to nil also, and then it came to France – the hard one. This was the European Final and I'm telling you it was a blood bath. Every member of our team was injured. Jimmy Neal had his nose split from here to here. I think it was Barroux, who subsequently became European Champion and was really agile, went against Alan Smith [from Liverpool]. Within twenty seconds Barroux had split Alan Smith's nose from here down to here and I was there with the towel. Vernon was on the edge shouting, yelling, swearing at everybody, trying to stop the fight. I held Smith's nose and asked him if he wanted to continue. He said, 'Yes! Yes! Just wipe my face and I'll have him!' I wiped his face and he went out and kicked Barroux with a *mae-geri* to the groin. This man went up in the air in pain and agony and as he came down Alan Smith kicked him again in the same place. Smith got on top of him, grabbed him by the throat and brought his fist back. I thought, 'Christ, he's going to kill him!' Mochizuki jumped in and grabbed the fist. Barroux was out of it; he didn't know where he was. Neal lost and Smith lost because of lack of control. I think Sherry and Hammond lost too, but we were all against black-belts, up to 3rd Dan. Then it was my turn. I was the last to go up, and I was against Szpirglas who was built like a heavyweight boxer. He was the French captain. He was hot. He'd just won the *kumite* title. He put them in hospital. They thought Szpirglas would kill me. I knew I had little or no chance. I ran around for a minute, backed-off, until everybody booed. I got him out of breath and he was getting annoyed. The technique I was best at was *Uraken,* and as he came in I jumped up – I was only ten and a half stone – and hit him on the bridge of the nose. I didn't pull it. I hit him as hard as I could. He just stood there and shook. I thought, 'My God, he'll kill me now!' He was angry, very angry. I jumped again about five seconds later, jumped and tucked my legs up, and did the same technique to the same spot. This time he went down, and he'd never been down in his life before. Mochizuki just looked at me. I remember turning to Vernon and the others. 'He's getting up! He's getting up!' I kept saying, and he did, and there was an eruption. He really came after me, I'll tell you. I really thought he was going to kill me. I thought the only chance I had was to hit him again in the same spot as I'd done before. I went for it and hit him. I almost broke my hand. He went down this time and didn't get up. There was another eruption. They stopped the contest. Mochizuki pulled me off. Vernon shouted out, 'He's won! He's won!' Vernon was swearing at the French. We needed that, a real diplomat. You know, 'All w—s begin at Calais.' Mochizuki said, 'Void contest.' I said, 'Void? I beat him!' Mochizuki told me to leave the mat and Vernon went up to him and did his, 'Now you listen here' routine. And it was on television. Szpirglas got up and came over to me. I asked the lads to stand between us because I thought he was going to hit me. Szpirglas said to me, 'You won.' I said, 'Thank you very much. That's very nice.' It was an absolute blood bath. I've never seen so many people injured."

A Belgian newspaper clipping of the event has survived, and the results reported are somewhat different from those described above. The surnames of the members of the French and Belgian teams are given, and are: Barroux, Sauvin, Bernard, Bahu, Szpirglas, and, Aarts, Coppieters, Rubenska, Melis and Nevejans, respectively. The results show that France beat Belgium 4-0, with one match drawn; that Belgium beat England 2-1, with two drawn; and, that France beat England 3-1, with one drawn. The report, entitled, 'Belgium 2nd in Paris,' is written in Flemish, and notes that karate is still a young sport in Belgium, whereas some four thousand students practice the art in France. The brief report confirms the event as the first European competition of its kind.

At 9.30 a.m. on the morning of the 15th December 1963, Bell attended a special conference of the European Congress for Karate, concerning the establishment of a possible European Union for Karate. Delcourt and Sebban acted as the French representatives, Leo Aarts and Jean Stas, the Belgium representatives, with Augusto Basile, Bernard Cherix and Karl Heinz Kiltz acting for Italy, Switzerland and Germany (Hamburg) respectively. Mister S. Garcia of Spain sent an apology for absence. Reading the four and a half pages of minutes to this meeting, they conclude with some interesting figures with regard to practising *karateka* for four countries. Germany was estimated to have between five to seven thousand karate students, Belgium between twelve and fifteen hundred, France some four thousand, and Great Britain, five thousand (this, presumably should have read '500.' It is the author's opinion that some of these figures are on the optimistic side, and differ considerably from figures given six months on (see later). Certainly, the German Karate Federation, on the 15th December 1963, had only ninety-six graded members (letter to Bell from Uwe Fullgrabe), arranged so: 1st Dan – 1, 1st kyu – 0, 2nd kyu – 10, 3rd kyu – 9, 4th kyu – 28, 5th kyu – 48. The author is unaware of the whereabouts of the remaining 4,900 – 6,900 students, unless they were all novices!

The BKF members trained under Murakami the day following the international meeting. Terry Wingrove recalled: "I was full of the evening before, you know, I'd beaten the champion. Murakami put me in my place. He said that it wasn't a question of a brown-belt beating a 3rd Dan, rather the 3rd Dan was equal to a brown-belt, otherwise I wouldn't have beaten him. He then rammed that home by knocking me out. I'm a one hundred per cent Murakami man in ideology and application. He was my teacher. I have always been very grateful to him for the way he taught me, because it's always easier to get easier."

After the meeting and training, the team watched the FFJ black-belt gradings at 3.00 p.m., and left Paris that evening at 10.00 p.m. Candidates for the French karate black-belt were required to provide the following information prior to grading, as given in an FFJDA – Karate Section note: "a written authorisation from their teacher; evidence of brown-belt 1st kyu; justification of two years of karate practice, certified by two consecutive years' licences; to have their federal licence up to date; and, to have a competition card."

Another document exists showing what was required for Dan grade. Whether the contents that follow is complete is unknown, for a single page in French survives, and rusty pin marks on the top left of that page reveal that perhaps there was more to the grading. However, as a copy of this document also exists in English, and this translation has rusty marks in exactly the same location, it is highly likely that one was clipped to the other. The contents of the first part of the grading, under the heading, 'Technique,' was: "*Kihon* – the competitor must be able to execute all movements required (under their Japanese name) with skill, speed and strength. Mark: out of 40; *Kata* – one *kata* chosen from the five *[H]eian;* one *kata* as requested by the panel of judges. The *kata* will be executed according to the candidate's conception of them, and with speed, strength and spirit. Mark: out of 40." The contents of the second part of the grading, under the heading, 'Competition,' was: "*Sambon-kumite* (fight in three attacks) to be executed with a member of the Technical Committee or a partner assigned by the T.C., following the rules formulated below. Mark: out of 40. Furthermore, candidates will be requested to answer all questions asked by a member of the Committee, concerning technique or spirit of karate, and the general behaviour of a karateist. To pass the examination, candidates will need a total number of marks of 80 out of 120."

The 'Rules to Practise *Sambon-Kumite*' were given as follows: "Adversaries will attack each other successively (starting with the lower ranks). The attacker will make three attacks followed by *oi-zuki* at a predetermined and precise level. The attacker has the right to strike his opponent at each attack. The latter blocks or avoids the attack following his own judgement. He must counter-attack at once after his 3rd blockage (or avoidance), but without touching his adversary. Then the partner attacked becomes the attacker, following the same rules. The attacker takes the position of attack starting from the position *shizentai* (*Yoi*), and moving back one of his feet to take the position of *zenkutsu*. Note: *Sambon-kumite*, though following strict rules which turn it into a conventional fight, must be practised with the utmost sincerity of which participants are capable."

In a letter to Art Malia, dated the 31st January 1964, Bell recalled the international event: "The BKF recently sent a National Team including Messrs. Wingrove and Neal to Paris in December for International matches against Belgium and France, and we only lost by the odd contest in each match under non-Japanese rules. This was an excellent result and valuable experience considering all their other members of the Belgium and French teams were all black-belts and our team members were 5th to 2nd kyu only [perhaps the 5th kyu was the reserve? Robert Williams and Ronald Mills (from Harrow, who, the author understands, later trained in Shukokai) were also part of the British team]. Our technique was far better to watch and superior, but we did not understand their contest rules and some decisions against us were ridiculous." Unlike Wingrove, Bell does not mention a match with Switzerland.

Leo Aarts and Bell corresponded quite a bit after their initial meeting at the 1963 tournament. This correspondence lasted until 1965 at least. Writing to Bell from Minderbroedersrui 35, Antwerp, on the 29th May 1965, Aarts, who worked in a bank, referred to the lack of honesty in some of the judging decisions at this first European international.

Whilst the BKF were working up towards this tournament, Bell had received a letter, dated the 3rd October 1963, from Robert Regnier, a 3rd Dan *judoka*, President of the Japanese Martial Arts Section of Inter Activités, based at 54, rue d'Aboukir, Paris 2. The letter concerned bringing Master Hiroo Mochizuki to England. Bell replied to this letter on the 16th October 1963, and then again on the 14th November 1963, in reply to another letter by Regnier of the 6th November 1963, which stated that Mochizuki would be pleased to visit England as long as travelling expenses and lodging was paid by the BKF and a fee of one hundred Francs be paid to him per day. Bell was keen to get Mochizuki to Britain, and had originally proposed that the master be part of the (now famous) demonstration of martial arts held at the Albert Hall on Saturday, 23rd November 1963. However, this was not to be, and Bell proposed a meeting in Paris with Mochizuki during the two days of the above international competition.

Regnier replied to Bell on the 6th and 20th of November 1963 (letters now lost) and in an undated letter by Bell, a meeting was arranged in Paris. Regnier replied on the 10th December 1963 (letter now lost), and Bell noted in his final reply on the 12th December 1963, that he was pleased that a large table at a Chinese restaurant at 42, rue Pancelet, had been arranged for the meeting after the display on the 14th (the 15th December 1963, is referred to in subsequent letters, and presumably refers to the meeting after midnight, unless plans were changed).

On the 23rd January 1964, Bell received a short letter from Regnier to which Bell replied on the 28th January. Bell wrote: "I have definite confirmation of his [Mochizuki's] services to teach his system of karate at our branch in the City of York on all day Sunday, 23rd February. Also, I have arranged for him to teach on Friday evening and all day Saturday on the 21st and 22nd February at our London HQ. I am endeavouring to arrange for a display to be given for our members only, in one of our *dojos*, on the Saturday or Sunday evening, in which we would like *Sensei* to perform his favourite *kata*. For this, kindly inform me what would be his fee separately from the course. I very much regret that it will not now be possible to arrange for a very large display for Mr. Mochizuki on this visit at a large public hall in London, as we had originally planned, for the reason that we have been totally unsuccessful in being able to book in advance, and it is not possible to arrange booking at two months notice. Accordingly, we will attempt to arrange for Mr. Mochizuki to return to England in May, and we will try to fix him to perform in a public display in association with another organisation whom we will not name at this moment [JKA] (in case negotiations break down)."

A famous visitor to the London BKF Horseshoe pub *dojo* in the last week of November 1963 was Master Mitsusuke Harada. Born on the 16th November 1928, in Manchuria, Harada had shown an interest in the martial arts since an early age. One of the few students, still alive, who actually trained at the Shotokan during the war (the famous *dojo* was destroyed in the dreadful fire raids of the 10th March 1945), under such greats as Motonobu Hironishi, Wado Uemura and Yoshiaki Hayashi, Harada had actually known the legendary Yoshitaka Funakoshi, who died a few months after the Pacific War ended. As if this lineage wasn't impressive enough, Harada trained as a private student to the founder of Shotokan karate, Gichin Funakoshi, at the master's eldest son's house, in 1946, when Funakoshi was seventy-eight years of age. Harada also practised under the great master at Waseda University, where he was to train, and in some cases teach with, virtually all the other great Shotokan masters, including Hiroshi Noguchi and the extraordinary Tadao Okuyama. Harada also taught American airmen with Masatoshi Nakayama, Chief Instructor to the Japan Karate Association. But the greatest Shotokan master to influence Harada was undoubtedly the fearsome Shigeru Egami, and Harada trained with the famous master on a private basis, seven days a week for one and a half years. Harada had introduced Shotokan karate to South America (Brazil) in 1955 and came to France in early 1963. He was invited to Britain from Belgium

Master Mitsusuke Harada in 1963

by Kenshiro Abbe, and performed his first demonstration at the National Judo Championships, Royal Albert Hall, on Saturday, 23rd November 1963, already referred to. Bell was therefore eager to attend his demonstration. Bell knew Harada's situation from a letter from Delcourt of the 13th November, already alluded to. Delcourt, writing of rivalry between Harada, Murakami and Mochizuki, wrote: "As among other things, M. Harada had expressed doubts on the power of our federation. We obtained his expulsion from France to make him realise the position ...!"[For a thorough understanding of Master Harada's life, and his contribution to British karate from 1963 (bearing in mind *Shotokan Dawn* is following the BKF line), see the author's books, *Karate Master: The Life and Times of Mitsusuke Harada* (Bushido Publ., 1997), and, *Reminiscences by Master Mitsusuke Harada* (KDS Publ., 1999)].

It must be said that Murakami/BKF karate and Harada's karate had different emphases. In his 27th November, 1963, letter to Delcourt, Bell gave his rather negative impressions of Master Harada, having watched the master's Royal Albert Hall demonstration, which Bell considered "not very professional or of high technique." In truth, Master Harada no doubt felt the same way. In *Karate Master* ... the author wrote that Harada remembered "the demonstration well, but was rather disappointed, as it did not go as he had planned. He performed his favourite *kata*, *Enpi*, but the *kumite* demonstration was badly flawed because his assistant [Julien Naessens] didn't turn up until the last moment. A new assistant [Mr. Vanderdonckt] had to be found, and nothing seemed to go as planned, in front of the audience of 8,000, due, quite simply, to insufficient practice with the assistant. Master Harada recalled that when he performed *gedan-barai*, his opponent fell over – which, of course, he wasn't supposed to do!" [For further information on the Royal Albert Hall demonstration, see *Karate Master* ..., pp. 131-133]. Harada reflected: "The venue was packed out and people from far and wide came with their wives and families. It was a big occasion. Few people had seen karate in Britain and the comments I received were encouraging, and the event overall was very successful" [*Reminiscences* ..., p. 119]. Master Harada subsequently became the first Japanese karate instructor to reside in Great Britain.

Despite his initial views, Bell was, nevertheless, quick off the mark to invite Master Harada to teach at the London *dojo* of the BKF. In the above letter to Delcourt, Bell wrote: "The BKF has engaged him for two evenings in our own *dojo* as a visiting instructor for the only purpose of experiencing his techniques. The impression from all our members at our London *dojo* last night under his tuition was not very good and we are all very disappointed with his over-talkative manner, his high voice, and rather failing in hard training. Our Federation is most disappointed in the claims of this high-ranking karate teacher whom we feel there is much lacking in performance, technique and teaching ability from such a high grade. But it has served the BKF as a useful experiment in assessing this man of whom we have heard so much and have never met until now. We are all most disappointed to say the least." Much of what Harada taught at the Horseshoe pub must have been way above the heads of virtually all the students at that time, and he wasn't invited to teach there again.

However, one of the two highest BKF grades at the time (other than Bell), Terry Wingrove, reflecting, remembered at least one evening of Harada's visit well, and differently. "It was a really nice night. He was a real gentleman – a very nice man." Apparently, in the course of the evening in question, Master Harada had got the students to practise a technique that had the effect of bringing the proprietor running upstairs, as the ceiling downstairs was threatening to collapse!

A notable divergence was occuring amongst the leading exponents of Funakoshi's style of karate after his death. Egami, a true disciple of Funakoshi – and the only *karateka* to be at Funakoshi's bedside when the old master finally passed away aged eighty-eight/eighty-nine (Funakoshi did not know his month of birth) – believed he had developed Funakoshi's style in the manner and direction that the old master would have wished. Harada was a student of Egami's and followed this line at the time (he later reverted to 1950s Shotokan training). Harada, in 1963, was teaching what might be loosely described as 'Egami Shotokan,' which later developed into Shotokai. Bell was comparing this with the hard Takushoku-type JKA Shotokan of Murakami, and Harada's emphasis of technique and higher-order abstraction were alien to BKF students.

More than thirty years on, Vernon Bell remembered Harada so: "Following Harada's display at the Royal Albert Hall, he did a number of courses for Abbe, in fact several close to my home at the time, in Chigwell, Essex, at the National Playing Fields Association Annual Summer Camp at Grange Farm. For want of appearances, Kenshiro Abbe and Mitsusuke Harada were very similar [?], and there was great respect between them. Harada knew who I was and always treated me with the greatest respect, through those horn-rimmed glasses and large white teeth of his. I found him to be a very gentle little man. I was told by my karate *sensei*, Tetsuji Murakami, that he had spent a lot of time with Harada in Europe and they were friends. Murakami would often ask me about my relationships with Harada and the British Budo Council.

"I remember Harada had a secretary called Len Hazard from Harlow, who later became secretary to the British Karate Control Commission [of which Vernon Bell was a founder member in 1966]. I went to Harada's *dojo* through the medium of Len Hazard. I will always remember two things about Harada *Sensei*. Firstly, he would always start the class from a kneeling, *rei* position, and get everybody to jump up and perform a *chudan mae-geri* and a *jodan oi-zuki* at the same time. Secondly, he would tell students that the power of karate was in the fist – and the little grin that went with it! We'd been conditioned to the Japanese smile during the war. A Japanese would smile at you, then kill you! I couldn't forget that. I remember him saying, 'This is my karate. No competition – only techniques, movement and *kata*.' He was honest and straightforward – I liked him."

Master Harada recalled the two evenings of training that week at the Horseshoe more than thirty years ago: "Many people came, but Bell didn't practise. Bell wasn't there to watch. He just organised it. I was very disappointed. Practice was for two hours. At the end of the practice he came in and said, "Thank you." They practised like Murakami's students. The class practised *kihon* and *gohan kumite*. You weren't able to practise much because you couldn't move as there were many people watching." Master Harada also remembered the pillars in the centre of the *dojo* and how they got in the way of training.

The first BKF grading of 1964 was held by Master Tetsuji Murakami on the 26th January, at the Blackpool *dojo* – it was to be Murakami's last for the BKF in Britain. Bell booked the train tickets through Commercial and General Travel Service Ltd, based at 12, Masons Parade, Ley Street, Ilford, on the 24th January. Bell and Wingrove travelled, 2nd Class, alongside Murakami, and the return fare for all came to £17 2s. Another invoice shows that Wingrove, at least, and one assumes Murakami and Bell, stayed at the Gables Hotel, Osborne Road, Blackpool, on the nights of the 25th and 26th, at a cost of £1 5s 6d per night. A loose slip of paper records that on the 26th, Murakami taught from 9.30 a.m. to 1.30 p.m., from 2 p.m. to 4 p.m. and from 4.15 p.m. to 6 p.m. at a rate of £2 5s per hour.

The following Blackpool students, of whom not all their first initials are known, were promoted on the 26th: 8th kyu – C. Ashley, D. Burle, (?) Canton, (?) Greenhelch (BKF grading register entry is unclear), R. Leary, S. Leary, R. Lodge, F. Lovis, G. Parkinson, A. Pyrah; 7th kyu – R. Bell, J. Connolly; 6th kyu – R. Fishwick, P. Harley, F. Lumas, J. Taylor; 5th kyu – W. Ellwood, E. Hutchinson, A. Stewart; 4th kyu – J. Green.

Michael Randall described his first encounter with Vernon Bell and his first lesson at the Horseshoe pub *dojo*, situated at 24, Clerkenwell Close, EC1, in January 1964: "I worked with Ray Fuller at Union Cold

Storage. The head office was in Smithfield and the workshop was in Blackfriars. I met Ray Fuller at Blackfriars and we got quite friendly. I was a carpenter and joiner; Ray Fuller [then twenty-nine] was a painter [and decorator]. He said to me, one day, would I like to do karate, and I said I didn't know what it was really. He said that whilst in the Middle-East with the army [between 1952 and 1954 with the Paratroop Regiment] he saw some martial arts, and his wife had bought him a book – Nishiyama and Brown's, *Karate: The Art of 'Empty-hand' Fighting* – last Christmas and it had whetted his appetite, and he asked me to join with him. I said I would, and then started the long search for a *dojo*, and believe me it was a carry-on. In the end we telephoned the Japanese Embassy in London and they gave us a number. It was Vernon Bell. He lived over Ilford way. We got his address and drove down to his house [on Ray Fuller's motorbike and sidecar] but had no luck. Eventually we contacted him. He was a strange man, rather eccentric, and we had to write to him officially and send him ten shillings, which was quite a sum of money in those days. Then he sent us back a large envelope full of literature."

Bell sent out duplicated sheets on behalf of the BKF containing all the necessary information required by potential students. Once individuals had joined, they were given further details and occasionally, in those early days, translations and extracts of various relevant articles, most notably from a certain continental magazine. These articles were, "for distribution and private circulation only to B.K.F. licensees and must not be loaned or given away to non-members." Some of these articles have survived and include the following titles: 'What is Karate?' 'How to Make a Fist,' 'Beginners Be Careful,' 'Who Lives by the Sword Shall Perish by the Sword,' 'Body Control in Karate,' 'Muscular Control,' 'Sports and the Martial Arts,' 'The *Shiai* of *Kata*,' 'Combat Rhythm,' 'The Meaning and Spirit of Budo,' 'The Age of Budo,' 'Respect Towards the Master,' '*Pinan* No. 2,' 'Description of No. 4 *Heian kata* (Yoseikan Style),' 'No. 2 *Sanbon Kata*,' 'Hokkaido *Shodan Kata*,' 'Styles of Karate in Japan,' 'Practical Advice for *Kumite*' and, 'Karate-Do.' These pieces often contain some classic *Zeitgeist* lines. The author's favourite appears in 'Karate-Do,' where it is stated that, "Soft drink bottles can be halved by a healthy swipe." The information in these articles is generally very sketchy, as one would expect, and often incorrect, as one might expect. However, good intention is always present, though the English grammar and syntax often leave much to be desired – no doubt partly the result of too literal a translation.

Hyperbole was sometimes stressed in membership application form material. In information on the benefits to be gained from being an Associate Member of the BKF, one leaflet regularly sent out to prospective students read: "If you are converted and wish to practise it [karate], remember that only real teachers can really make you invincible..." Such 'spirit of the time' lines are brought home when, on the same leaflet, Bell refers to, "Britain ... [and] the Empire."

Michael Randall continued: "The requirements were, basically, that we had to have a doctor's certificate of fitness of health and two recommendations from professional people, one of which we got from the solicitor upstairs in our company. We had to fill out numerous forms (which Randall and Fuller did on the 17th and 20th January 1964, respectively). Everything was a put-off. I liked that. The interesting thing was that this literature was talking about this man who had done all these things and it was quite good. We read all about this certain person and the last line said [in effect], "Gentleman, this is myself." I really wished I'd have kept that. We were extremely impressed. We sent back all the literature, and I think he wrote back. We went to the *dojo* [climbing the single flight of seventeen stone stairs with a wrought iron banister to a small landing] and knocked on the [swing] doors. We were really nervous. The doors opened, and he had a way of calling you 'Laddie.' 'Come in laddies and sit down,' he said. I remember two pillars in the middle of the *dojo* that made training difficult, the brown linoleum floor, a small stage to the right and a table by a window where Vernon Bell used to sit. Jimmy Neal was taking the lesson. We sat down [on some chairs to the right as one entered the *dojo*] and watched. At the end of the lesson [which lasted about one and a half hours], Vernon Bell came over, and I can't forget it, said, 'What do you think, laddie?' I said, 'I really like it. I want to do it.' He said, 'What makes you think you can?' He just took the wind right out of my sails. And I said, 'Well, I'd love to try,' and he said, 'Okay. Come back next week, laddie.' And that was it."

Randall and Fuller, both of whom were to become famous Shotokan instructors, trained twice a week at the Horseshoe pub and then began training at the St. Mary's *dojo*, Upminster, on Sunday mornings, with Ray Fuller providing the basic transport, picking Randall up on the way from the Elephant and Castle. At this time, the lessons in London (which Randall would get to on his moped from Stoke Newington) were being taken by Jimmy Neal and Terry Wingrove.

"This most important *dojo* in the history of British karate," as Vernon Bell called the Horseshoe pub, is still there, but no longer used for

The Horseshoe pub, Clerkenwell, in 1994

training. Mercifully, little has changed, and one can still sense an atmosphere despite the passing of more than thirty years. A small bar has appeared in one corner and the room is now used for recreational purposes and houses two small-size snooker tables. The *dojo* is rectangular, measuring approximately twenty-two feet in width by thirty-eight feet in length. The two rectangular central pillars, where the very

An unchanged view looking out from the Horseshoe pub *dojo*

early *karateka* would practise leaning upon their fists and dodging attacks, are still there, and form a little bit of British karate history. The old dumb-waiter is also still there – to the left as you enter the *dojo*. The Horseshoe pub is well worth a visit, and the landlord, Richard Tucker, is a friendly and agreeable chap.

Randall remembered training with Hiroo Mochizuki, as does Gordon Thompson. Mochizuki had returned to Paris to study veterinary medicine. Randall noted: "He was only young, very nice, pleasant-natured and modest in his attitude. He was polite and dignified. I think he had a better bearing than a lot of the Japanese. I remember distinctly that we were always told, in *zenkutsu-dachi*, bolt upright, that the back foot should be flat on the floor, especially the heel, and that you 'pushed' from the back heel straight to the punch and to raise the heel was a sin, a weak point. Mochizuki said, 'That's allowed now,' and we were all quite amazed that that was acceptable, but that's just what he said. I remember him doing that. [Mochizuki had returned to Japan after his initial visit to Paris and then came back (in March 1963?) a 4th Dan in Wado-ryu – hence the problem!]. I recall, also, he did *Heian Shodan*, and we'd never seen anything like that before. We were totally impressed with the power and speed of it. We were only beginners, and Jimmy Neal was a brown-belt. Though we were terribly impressed with Jimmy Neal as a teacher, Mochizuki was that much higher and it showed, and that was very inspiring. I remember Terry Wingrove took Mochizuki up north and was very impressed with his modesty. He said he couldn't believe it. On the train going up he asked Terry what he would like him to teach. For a man of his calibre to ask ... Terry couldn't believe Mochizuki's modest approach."

Gordon Thompson recalled how Mochizuki would punch with his fist held vertically on striking, rather than horizontally. He also remembered that the training was very basic.

Both Michael Randall and Gordon Thompson's recollections of Hiroo Mochizuki's only visit to Britain for the BKF, relate to a trip that Mochizuki made between the 21st/22nd to the 24th February 1964. On the 22nd February 1964, he stayed for one night in Room 101 at the Mount Pleasant Hotel, 53, Calthorpe Street, London, WC1, at a cost of £1.10s.3d. On the 23rd February 1964, he stayed at the Arran Guest House, 7, Argyle Road, Ilford, at a cost of one guinea, and then on the 24th February 1964, he stayed in Room 169 of the Skyway Hotel, Bath Road, Hayes, by London Airport, at a cost of £3.15s. The air ticket cost £14.12s.

On the 23rd February 1964, Mochizuki conducted a grading at the York *dojo*. The BKF grading register reveals that the following people were promoted: 6th kyu – A. Aydon, S. Cattle, J. Coatis, P. Cooper, D. Douthwaite, J. Feldman, G. Gill, J. Kay, P. O'Donovan, S. Olsson, K. Stones, P. Walker; 5th kyu – J. Ashton and M. Dearney.

Bell had written to Charles Palmer, at the BJA headquarters at Chandos House, Palmer Street, London, SW1, prior to Mochizuki's visit on the 17th February, presumably about the master's trip. This letter is now lost. The contents of Palmer's reply, on the 28th February, are interesting and startling, for he wrote: "Please accept this letter as official confirmation of the fact that I have already given approval to the FFJDA in France by telephone for the visit of Mr. Mochizuki to London to teach karate." The letter thus post-dated the visit, for Palmer had been in Berlin. Palmer also noted that: "I trust that your weekend was successful and I am only sorry that I was not able to see Mr. Mochizuki whilst he was here." Why Bell wrote to Palmer, and why he apparently needed his approval, as two months before, is unknown.

Randall continued: "I remember my first grading under Vernon Bell at Upminster. Ray and I were working together as I've mentioned before, and had access to the whole building as we were on maintenance. We went on to the very large flat roof, and drew out the line of movement for *Heian Shodan* [the first *kata*]. Every lunch-time we went up on that roof and trained after we'd had a couple of cheese sandwiches and a cup of tea. We did that for a long time. We practised *kata* five days a week on that roof. I knew *Heian Shodan* backwards by the time of my first grading. It was the only one I knew in any case, so I couldn't get confused. I remember in the grading getting to the last age-*uke*, and looking, I just saw Vernon Bell sitting in front of me at the table, and I *kiai*'d and I froze, catching Vernon Bell's eyes. And he had his black-belt rolled up on the table and threw it at my head, as I was only a few feet away from him, and he said, 'Sit down laddie.' I thought, 'Oh no! I've fluffed it!' I was so terribly disappointed. At the end of the grading he said, 'Laddie, one more time,' and I sailed through it and that was my first taste of gradings. Now, when I act as grading examiner, if I see people freeze I know it's nerves and I think to myself it happened to me. So I fully understand that." The grading and belt system under Bell and the BKF at this time, from 9th kyu to 1st kyu was as follows: red, white, white, blue, purple, purple, brown, brown, and brown.

Although the BKF grading register does not show his name – in spite of the date being recorded on Randall's BKF licence – the grading that Michael Randall referred to was held on the 4th May 1964. It appears that Bell did not record red-belt gradings, which were sometimes referred to previously as "novice." It seems likely, given the next London grading

Michael Randall blocks Ray Fuller's *oi-zuki* and counters with *chudan-yoko-geri* – Epping Forest, 2nd August, 1964.

(see below) that a number of students attempted red-belt that day. Records actually show that the following people graded on the 4th May: 6th kyu – (?) Isenberg, A. Nightingale; 5th kyu – B. Harper, H. Peters; 4th kyu – J. Bounds, N. De Silva, R. Merrick, E. Whitcher.

The next grading Bell held for the London members was on the 4th July 1964, when twelve students graded to 8th kyu, so: D. Ashead, P. Fisher, R. Fuller, J. Lassey, P. Bindra (Laville), P. Lebasci, N. Malley, P. Metcalfe, M. Peachey, M. Randall, K. Roebuck, K. Sayles.

The 4th July 1964 must have been a very busy day for Bell, or otherwise there is an error in the BKF grading register, for Bell held a grading at the Blackpool *dojo* the same day. Records show that the following Blackpool students were promoted: 8th kyu – F. Catchpole, D. Draper, A. Humble, S. Leary, J. Morgan, J. Revill, W. Warren, H. Watson; 7th kyu – D. Burle, R. Lodge, F. Lumas.

By this time then, Pauline Bindra had travelled down from Middlesbrough. She recalled: "Walter Seaton had given me the address where to go to train ... I said to him, 'Are there any women there?' and he said, 'No. You won't find any women [training in karate], anywhere.' I remember the first time I went to Vernon Bell's *dojo* [The Horseshoe

Pub in Clerkenwell]. That was an experience. I went in there with a girl from the hostel, a foreign girl, because I wouldn't go by myself because I was so nervous. I walked in and it was, 'Hello girlie. Who are you?' [Bindra always remembers Vernon Bell wearing, "an old raincoat and driving an old car. He always wore this dirty old mackintosh, and he always came in that old jalopy"]. So I produced my licence and said, 'I've come to join.' Everybody laughed and tittered and said, 'Oh yeah!' But they just humoured me. 'Oh yes, you can come back next week,' said Bell, which I did. [Bindra's (presumably second?) application for BKF membership was dated the 2nd March 1964, when she was nineteen years of age]. I went back with this girl, but she couldn't take it – one lesson was enough. I went back and joined. It was really strange. Whenever there was a person who didn't have a partner, my partner was taken off me because I was the lowest of the low. If anybody was late it was, 'Go in the corner and teach her.' That was the punishment, to teach me. In some ways I was segregated from the class on certain things even though I was just starting, even though there were other beginners there. Ignored, because I was a female.

"After about two weeks the novelty wore off and they thought if they treated me badly, I'd leave. But the worse they treated me, the more I was determined to stay. I think if they hadn't treated me so badly I would have left, but they got the opposite reaction. Virtually all the men treated me badly in a way. You know, you have two lines, and you bow to one another. They'd by-pass me, so there would be a gap, so they'd push the next one out of the way so I never had anybody opposite me. And then sometimes the instructor would shout, 'You opposite her – stay with her.' Jimmy Neal was very fair. I liked Jimmy Neal. After a while they began to accept me." [After Sunday morning training at Upminster, Bindra would go back to Vernon Bell's house to complete some BKF typing].

"I always remember, I was so shy," Bindra continued. "I used to go to the Horseshoe club, change in the ladies' toilets, and look through the keyhole to see when the lesson started, so I wouldn't have to go out and talk to anybody. I'd hear the instructor say line up, and I'd go out. I was really shy. There were no women and the men, you know, thought, 'What is this thing amongst us?' Oh! It was terrible – a real male domain. It wasn't like that for one lesson – I was doing this for a year."

Bindra stayed because, "They tried to get rid of me, nothing else. Then it [karate] appealed to me – even with my religion. I'm a Seventh Day Adventist, which is a very strict religion, and I didn't go to missionary college, I couldn't fit in, because all that was at the back of

The Prince of Wales Baths, Kentish Town, in 1994

my mind was karate and training ... The Adventists didn't like me doing karate – they didn't understand it ... I don't know why, I just wanted to do it. After a while it just got hold of me. It was an escape, an escape from reality really; an escape from mundane things. It was a good release ... Karate gave me confidence. I used to get depressed, really depressed – very bad – and the only thing that brought me out of it was karate.

"Later [in 1965], I went to work at Butlins, and I stopped training for a while. I could have stayed longer but I missed karate, so I came back. I was in Minehead for two months and I taught karate to the kids. I think they only took me on because I said I'd done judo and karate. Once a week we did karate. Of course the kids hadn't seen it before and they asked about clubs, but there weren't any."

Bindra continued: "I was always being asked out, and I went out with a lot of members – but nothing else, because I knew that if you had a liaison, something like that, with one of them, my karate was finished. I made a point right from the beginning not to get into bed with anybody, because they would all have talked about it, and I couldn't have done karate. So, I always went out, had a good time, and nothing else."

It was during the Horseshoe pub *dojo* days that the numbers of students began to grow noticeably, as has been noted before, though it was finally replaced by another *dojo* located at the Prince of Wales Baths, on the corner of Prince of Wales Road and Grafton Road, Kentish

Members of the London BKF *dojo* at Kentish Town Baths - 1964. From left to right, standing: unknown, Jasper Lassey, Ray Fuller, Vernon Bell, Jimmy Neal, Mick Randall, Mick Peachey; kneeling: Eddie Whitcher, Royston Merrick, Terry Wingrove, John Chisholm, Rob Williams, Brian Harper.

Town, NW5, in 1964. This change had become necessary because, as Pauline Bindra recalled: "The landlord used to complain about the racket upstairs at the Horseshoe." The club was at the new *dojo* for something like one year when, as Michael Randall noted, "A man came to tell us to leave. Our time was up in the evening. Vernon Bell took great exception to the fact that he walked into the hall, and he chased him down the corridor, and that was the last day we were there." The man Bell pursued may have been a Mr. Dias, the caretaker at the baths. But this was no great loss, for the floor was stone, and very cold. Terry Wingrove, who instructed there along with Jimmy Neal, recalled: "The floor was cold, yes, but I liked the Kentish Town Baths *dojo* because it had length and breadth, and it had good lighting too. It was much better than the stuffy old pubs we'd had in the past, which tended to make the karate somehow a bit sleazy." Nothing really remains of the Kentish Town Baths *dojo*. Sure enough, the impressive red brick exterior to the baths, built in 1900, survives, but where the *dojo* stood is now a shallow teaching swimming pool. The club then moved to Lyndhurst Hall, a five-minute walk away, in Warden Road. The Lyndhurst Hall *dojo* was to become famous in the annals of British Shotokan karate (see later).

The BKF had given many demonstrations (the author has concentrated on the earliest) to the end of 1964, but these had created relatively minor or local interest. Without a doubt, the real cause of a surge in public interest in karate was as a result of the cinema. There had been, prior to the early Sixties, a number of feature films that showed snippets of karate or karate-like techniques. A particularly influential film from the Forties has already been noted. There is little doubt that during the Fifties the most famous and inspiring of encounters showing karate technique was to be found in John Sturges' 1955 classic, *Bad Day at Black Rock*. Spencer Tracy, at his subdued and thoughtful best, played the one-armed stranger, John J. MacReedy, and Ernest Borgnine memorably played local small-town thug, Coley Trimble. *Bad Day* ... was notable also, in a martial arts sense, for its economy of word and action. Tracy's performance, as a man looking for his Japanese friend, Kamoko Smith, was good enough to rate an Academy Award nomination for Best Actor, as indeed was John Sturges' direction and Millard Kaufman's script. Many critics regarded it as a milestone film in the history of the cinema. The much respected film critic, Leslie Halliwell, for example, wrote, "The moments of violence, long awaited, are electrifying." Indeed, the fight sequence is, given the context of time, probably the finest of its kind ever filmed.

Tracy enters the town café/saloon to be shortly followed by Borgnine, who is accompanied by his boss, Robert Ryan. Borgnine tries to goad Tracy into a fight and Tracy attempts to leave, but Borgnine spins him around and issues insults, whereupon Tracy delivers a *shuto* to Borgnine's neck. The blow has such force that Borgnine crashes into a wall gasping for breath. Recovering, Borgnine throws a circular punch, but before contact is made Tracy strikes him in the stomach, and follows this up with a *shuto* to the back of the neck and a convincing upward knee strike to the face. Again Borgnine crashes into the wall. Borgnine then delivers another circular punch which Tracy side-steps and delivers a *shuto* to the back of the neck and then another *shuto* to the lower back, which sends Borgnine crashing through the establishment's front door. Recovering slowly, Borgnine swings a final punch, which is side-stepped, and Tracy catches the arm and throws his adversary, who screams. Throughout the fight there are no words spoken. Ryan, and other heavy, Lee Marvin, are taken aback. The scene ends with the town doctor, played by Walter Brennan, standing over Borgnine's body exclaiming, "Man, man, oh man!" as Tracy leaves the cafe. The whole scene lasts for five minutes and thirty-four seconds of which the actual fight sequence lasts one minute and five seconds. It is a brilliantly handled piece of filming in terms of camera work, editing, timing and choreography. Ironically, Borgnine got his own back though, at least in real-life, for it was he who pipped Tracy at the post for the Academy Award of Best Actor that year for his role in the film *Marty* – though the two shared the Cannes Film Festival prize.

Another film worthy of mention in the Fifties, as representative of showing a karate-like snippet and because of its star, was *The Left Hand of God* (1955). Humphrey Bogart, a WW II DC3 pilot shot down over China, disguised as a priest, punches a bandit in the stomach and *shuto*'s him to the back of the neck, which sends the bandit plummeting like a stone. There is also a classic line Bogart directs at Gene Tierney, "Violence wasn't quite what you expected from Father O'Shea!" Described as a real curio in Bogart's career, the film, directed by the much-respected Edward Dmytryk, is worthy of mention for another reason also. A forty-four year old actor named Philip Ahn played a Buddhist monk. It was Ahn who played Master Kan in the television series *Kung Fu*, which of course had a tremendous influence in popularising the martial arts from the time of the pilot episode in 1972.

In Britain, Honor Blackman, from 1962, in the immensely popular *The Avengers*, co-starring with ex-Etonian Patrick Macnee, seemed to combine judo with touches of karate in her weekly portrayal as Cathy Gale. Her character was, in many ways, a first for British television. Sexually alluring, intelligent, refined, dressed in a leather utility suit and the infamous boots, she added a strange, almost bizarre element to the series that later was reflected in decidedly surreal episodes. Blackman gave up this lucrative role to play Pussy Galore in a 1964 film that probably had more influence than any other at that time in bringing martial arts to a wide western audience – the third, and probably best James Bond movie, United Artists' *Goldfinger*, directed by Guy Hamilton. The film was made in England, and grossed nearly twenty million dollars in one year, making it one of the all-time money-making movies, and allowed Sean Connery to enter the Annual Top Ten Box Office Stars' list.

Blackman, sure enough, had a judo encounter with Sean Connery (playing Bond), but it was Goldfinger's seemingly invincible bodyguard, Oddjob, played by Harold Sakata, with his razor-edged bowler hat, which he used to deadly effect, that many wanted to identify with. As Bond kneels by a fridge in search of Dom Perignon champagne, an open hand menacingly comes up and across screen and strikes across the back of Bond's neck with a *shuto*. The strike lays our hero out cold, and nothing but a bowler-hatted shadow on a wooden wall is seen. So Oddjob entered film lore. Oddjob, a villain in the classic tradition, strangely did not play a Japanese, but a Korean, and relied chiefly on his obvious wrestling skills – karate, as such, was kept to a minimum with one rising type block, a few *shuto* and one back-hand to Bond's stomach. But it was Oddjob's obvious power (he crushes a golf ball in his hand, and a hefty gold bar thrown at him merely bounces off his chest) and his sense of invincibility (though Bond ends up electrocuting him in Fort Knox) that spurred many to search out unarmed combat and self-defence, perhaps in preparation for one day encountering their own Oddjob! Whereas Bond was obviously comic strip, there was something undeniably powerful and permanent about the inscrutable Oddjob. Born in 1920, Sakata, in real-life, was a much-respected weightlifter, having won the silver medal at the London Olympic Games of 1948. In fact, he tied for the gold medal, but was one pound heavier than his opponent, so took second place. He became a professional wrestler under the fighting name of The Great Togo, and fought in this country a number of times up until the Sixties. In 1952, Sakata, along with karate master Matsutatsu Oyama and *judoka* Kokuchi Endo, made a famous tour of the USA, which some say led to the karate movement in that country being founded. Harold Sakata died of cancer in 1982.

Honor Blackman (who also appeared in an episode of *The Saint* with Roger Moore, an effective and very popular series made from 1962, emphasising Simon Templar as a character on the edge of the law – a role that invariably appeals to prospective martial artists) was replaced in *The Avengers* by Diana Rigg, who, dressed in a PVC catsuit, played Emma Peel. Rigg appeared no less impressive on the martial arts front, incorporating more karate techniques.

Probably the best of the Blackman/Rigg episodes, regarding karate, was in *The Cybernauts,* when Steed and Peel investigate a series of broken necks from devastating blows. Though described as very secret, we are nevertheless treated to an inside view of karate practice in a *dojo* and hear the sounds of karate practice in the adjoining room, on two occasions, lasting five minutes and forty seconds in total, which is approximately twelve per cent of the episode, excluding title sequence – and that's a lot! Some of the karate is awkward and cumbersome, though one individual clearly has trained in the art and performs *mae-geri* and even an *ushiro-mawashi-geri.* The most impressive of the *karateka*, however, is, supposedly, Oyama, "5th Dan judo, 4th Dan karate," played by Bernard Horsfall. The instructor, played by actor John Hollis, head shaven, notes that, "Oyama, the Tall Mountain, can shatter a door with a single stroke," and Oyama, to show his power, breaks a thick piece of wood with a palm-heel strike (in the delivery position of a *gyaku-zuki*) for the class, of which Emma Peel is a new member. In fact, Peel has to fight a woman black-belt ("3rd Dan judo, 1st Dan karate"), in order to be able to enrol as a student! Hollis notes to Peel, "Karate, unlike judo, is not a sport. It is a science, an art, a discipline ... The hands, though empty, can become more deadly than any weapon. It is the concentration of force and the development of courage."

The whole image of the martial arts continued to grow more popular though this unusual series. Men and women alike were impressed by the way Blackman and Rigg disposed of the villains. It may have been way-out fiction, but it was new and entertaining, and people liked it.

'James Bond? Wouldn't Stand A Chance...' was the title of an unknown newspaper piece by Peter Simmonds, on the 20th August 1964. With an eye-catching, "He Can Break Bricks With One Hand..." Simmonds gave the usual details about Bell and the BKF. However, it is noteworthy because of the following. Simmonds wrote: "Karate will be coming into the public eye shortly with the release of James Bond's latest film, *Goldfinger*. But Mr. Bell is scornful of the 'James Bond type of karate.'" Simmonds quoted Bell as follows: "It gives the wrong impression of the art ... and we rarely admit people who apply for membership having seen it in films or read about it in paperbacks. We carefully vet every application. We have to be sure our pupils want to learn karate for the right reasons. It takes a mentally adjusted and stable individual to complete the rigorous training."

Bell always gave the impression that the above remarks were true. In the above newspaper article, Simmonds noted that karate had not grown very large, and that Bell did not want it to. Back in 1961, Bell had written a long letter – seven quarto pages of single-space type – in reply to Martin Stott, already referred to, which was full of quotes about the type of student he wanted in the BKF. Bell wrote: "It is not our intention, nor is it the policy of the Yoseikan, to establish karate in any country on a massed scale with thousands of clubs and hundreds of teachers ... we have quality in our organisation which is far better than quantity ... we are not interested in promoting karate on a National scale by letting everyone do it, doing hundreds of displays, masses of advertising etc. We are only interested in the true pupil who seeks us and who will be an asset to karate rather than having dozens of would-be pupils who we do not know ... there is no need as yet for a further TV appearance and it is not the policy of the BKF to seek commercial publicity nor do we intend to seek to laud karate from the housetops for every Tom, Dick and Harry to take up as a five minute wonder. We are only interested in the keen, enthusiastic, sincere seeker who comes to us through the usual medium of self-enquiry."

Although it was Oddjob who gave the martial arts a tremendous boost in 1964, in that literally millions of people went to see the film, the first two Bond movies, *Dr. No* (1962) and, *From Russia with Love* (1963), were both very influential in that they really set up the genre. *Dr. No* is the least noteworthy in a karate/judo context, as this type of action seems to have developed through the early Bond films, but in one scene Bond is held from behind as a knife-wielding Quarrel (John Kitzmiller) approaches. Bond kicks the knife from Quarrel's hand, and then follows this up with a *mae-kekomi* to Quarrel's stomach area using the same leg. Quarrel is sent reeling backwards, and Bond then disposes of the man clasping him, who has the odd name of Pussfellow, with a judo throw. Near the end of the film, when Bond disposes of Dr. No (Joseph Wiseman), the hero of the British Secret Service performs a stamp-kick on the arch-villain's chest. All Bond's punches are circular however.

In *From Russia with Love*, on SPECTRE Island, we see wood-breaking, knife-fighting, judo and the like, but what is of particular importance is that *makiwara* are shown (for the first time?) in a western film. There are five *makiwara*, and we see a rather poor *shuto* and a kick delivered against two of them. In this film we get the obligatory assassin's (Robert Shaw) *shuto* to the neck.

The fourth Bond movie, *Thunderball*, the last to fall in the remit of this book, appeared in 1965, and, being concerned mainly with underwater action, martial arts interest is minimal.

In 1967, of course, *You Only Live Twice* hit the big screen. This film, the second highest money-making movie of that year, was set largely in Japan, and made the most of various martial arts. This subject will not be gone into in any detail, as 1967 falls just outside the parameters of this book; however, sumo is featured, though the best is reserved for Tetsuto Tamba's ninja school. We see demonstrations of sword, stick, *shuriken*, and self-defence. The most notable karate moments are Kyokushinkai-type breaks – *nukite* through a water melon and a head-break through ice – and a five-way display of *tameshiwari*, each break being of two, one-inch boards, in the sequence: *gyaku-zuki, empi, mae-geri, otoshi-shuto*, and *yoko-tettsui*. The author has heard it said that Keigo Abe, the well-known JKA instructor, performs the breaks, and it may well be so.

On 30th January 1965, the *Daily Mirror* ran what is believed to be the newspapers first article on karate, after its representatives visited

Terry Wingrove performs a *yoko-geri-kekomi* upon *Daily Mirror* reporter, John Smith – Kentish Town Baths *dojo*, 30th January, 1965.

the BKF London *dojo*. The piece that followed was to have quite an impact. Reporter John Smith, and a photographer, visited the Kentish Town Baths, and although the author does not wish to jump ahead too much, the relevance of the news item here will become apparent. Under the somewhat sensational title of, 'This is Murder – Britain's Most Secret Sport,' the article is accompanied by a first-rate picture of Terry Wingrove performing a *jodan yoko-geri kekomi* on the tall Smith, who is standing upright in a suit and tie. In the background, one can see Michael Randall and (the author believes) John Chisholm, who is kicking. Behind Smith, to the rear, is Mick Peachey. Vernon Bell can just be seen in the top left of the picture talking to a group of white belts. The article follows the usual format, but one point is of interest here, concerning the power of film and of the Bond films in particular. Smith wrote that Bell's "biggest battle is keeping karate away from anyone who wants to learn it just so that he can look like James Bond when it comes to a punch-up in a pub on Saturday night." It may seem fanciful, simplistic, not to say even childish today, but it reflected the innocence of the time. The article is also worthy for the following, as Smith quotes Bell as saying: "I've only once had to use karate in an emergency ... A boxer assaulted me in a dance hall. I dislocated his kneecap."

Bell's admission might be fine, but this air of make-believe, so common at the time, continued. In another article, unremarkable save for the quote that appears below, that was published around the same time, perhaps a little later, in an unknown newspaper, by an unknown reporter, under the title, 'Trained to Kill – With One Blow,' Bell is quoted as having told his karate class: "If you are assaulted in a dance hall by a fisticuffs merchant, tap him two or three times on the knee. He will remember it to his dying day – and he won't walk for six months!" Of course it didn't say what the no doubt enraged fisticuffs merchant would be doing while you were tapping him on the knee!

A year later, in the *Times* (25th July, 1966, p.13), it was noted that, "a single glancing blow with the hand can kill a man," and then, a karate maestro "might for example split thirty bricks with his head." Today, thirty years on, the myth still continues.

The notion of a kind of natural or developed invincibility that Oddjob epitomised so well (remember, Bond used guile to overcome the Oriental and would almost certainly have lost in a man to man confrontation – somehow we feel that Oddjob's death lacked sufficient dignity), and that such newspaper articles no doubt unintentionally fostered, was highlighted, perhaps best of all, by the highly influential Clint Eastwood/ Sergio Leone trilogy of so-called spaghetti westerns, that completely revitalised the genre. *A Fistful of Dollars* appeared in 1964, *A Few Dollars More* in 1965, and *The Good, the Bad and the Ugly*, in 1966. They were less popular than the Bond films of course, but in terms of getting into the minds and hearts of future *karateka* they were truly unbeatable. Eastwood's mysterious, avenging stranger, the 'Man with No Name,' a bounty hunter, was appealing to many a young man, who could picture himself in that independent, maverick role. It was an escape from the seeming futility and complexity of modern living, back to a more simple time, where a man could be a man in rugged, natural surroundings, and where a kind of uncomplicated natural justice prevailed – you knew where you were. This had been done before in film of course, albeit less violently, that was, after all, the western's prime appeal, but what really struck home, in the psyche of the audience, was the way these spaghetti films were written and directed by Leone. *A Fistful of Dollars* was based on Akira Kurasawa's famous 1961 film, *Yojimbo*, and from the sparse, uncomplicated, mostly dubbed dialogue and simple storyline, emerged a distant kind of existential Zen-like quality, and it was this that many prospective *karateka* subconsciously aspired to. Young men could not perhaps become invincible with a handgun in mid-Sixties Britain, but the impression gained was that such an invincibility was available through the 'new' martial art of karate – they could become a real Oddjob, if you like. The spaghetti westerns set the notion of an individual alone, and a certain kind of person empathised with them. Of course, Ennio Morricone's strange, and now famous musical scores, added to the exceptional nature of the movies at the time.

One sequence stands out perhaps more than any other in the above westerns, with reference to the invincibility of the 'Man with No Name,' and with particular relevance for budding *karateka*, for instead of using a gun, Eastwood uses his body in a cleverly choreographed fight sequence. In *For Few Dollars More*, we are introduced to the Eastwood character as he encounters his prey in a saloon. We are given the strong sense that Eastwood has only one arm, his left (though a momentary glimpse of his other arm is available prior to the encounter in retrospect). At a card table, an unfortunate outlaw goes for his gun, but his gun arm is grabbed, twisted behind his back, and he is then pinned to the table by Eastwood. The outlaw clasps Eastwood's neck, but his hand arm is *ude-uke'd* away, and this is followed by a *shuto* to the outlaw's neck. Eastwood then blocks a swinging right punch to the head with an *age-uke* type block, then delivers a swinging punch immediately afterwards. The outlaw then falls down a small flight of stairs and, undeterred, throws two more swinging punches to Eastwood's head. A left arm is blocked by an *ude-uke*, the right arm by a kind of *haiwan uke*, which Eastwood immediately follows up with a left punch to the outlaw's face. The man hits a pillar and Eastwood follows up with (what looks like) an *uraken* to the chest and a *shuto* to the side of the neck. The outlaw goes down and is hauled up by Eastwood. Throughout the entire fight, Eastwood uses only his left arm. From first punch to haul up, twenty-three seconds have elapsed, and no words are spoken. With his back to the saloon door, the man Eastwood is really after (Eastwood has been given false information), and two other outlaws make an entrance. Realising that he has the wrong man, Eastwood swings around and shoots all three dead using his right hand, which he had under his poncho all the time. The outlaw that Eastwood had beaten up then goes for his gun on Eastwood's side, and the Man with No Name calmly shoots him before collecting a large bounty for the four men. It's marvellous stuff. During Eastwood's opening sequences (to the shooting of the last outlaw), four minutes and fifty-one seconds have elapsed. Eastwood speaks only twenty-seven words, and only forty-eight words are spoken in these impressionable introductory sequences in total.

Of course Leone was not the first to transfer a Japanese film about samurai to the old west. In 1960, John Sturges', *The Magnificent Seven* appeared, based on Akira Kurasawa's 1954 masterpiece, *Shichinin no Samurai* (The Seven Samurai).

John Saxon is thought to have visited the BKF Kentish Town *dojo* in 1964. The twenty-nine-year-old Brooklyn-born actor was in this country, filming (it is believed) *Nightmare*. Terry Wingrove recalled: "He walked in and said that he was a student of Nishiyama's and asked whether he could join the class. I said he could. He was good, much better than we were. He was a Shotokan *Shodan*, I think, [another source suggests brown-belt] and a very nice man." Saxon, of course, was to feature prominently in the 1973 Bruce Lee martial arts actioner, *Enter the Dragon*. Saxon played Roper, a man on the run from the Mob. *Enter the Dragon*, along with the television series, *Kung Fu*, were largely responsible for the enormous surge of interest in karate and other martial arts in the Seventies, and, in the film, Saxon shows off his martial skills to good effect. [More about karate in films is to be found in Volume II of this work].

Vernon Bell and his London students also had their opportunity to contribute to karate film history – in a big way. Around seven o'clock on the evening of the 6th November 1964, a film crew from Pathé Pictorial arrived at the Prince of Wales Baths to arrange their lighting equipment and so on, for a prompt start at eight o'clock, when the karate lesson commenced its usual Friday night practice. Requesting the possibility of an extension of time from a Mr. Austin, Town Clerk of St. Pancras Borough Council, David Williams of Pathé News hoped not to go beyond the ten o'clock limit, but explained that it would help the cameraman if he were not governed by too rigid a completion time. The result of the evening's endeavours was two minutes fifty-two seconds of classic archival colour film. The author is fortunate enough to possess a copy and will relay its contents.

The film, which is accompanied by the buoyant 1964 Tokyo Olympic Games theme tune, and male voice commentary, begins with the class of about twenty students performing warm-up exercises, including the impressive leg behind head pose in yoga, with a close-up of Terry Wingrove performing this. Then follows *ippon kumite* and *sanbon kumite* with Wingrove shown instructing John Chisholm and Robert Williams. Eddie Whitcher (blue-belt) is paired-up with Michael Peachey (white-belt), and Whitcher finishes proceedings with a knee strike. Basics then follow with close-ups of Michael Randall (white-belt) and Chisholm (blue-belt). The basics shown are *gedan-barai* followed by six punches (two *jodan*, two *chudan* and two *gedan*), and *mae-geri/oi-zuki/ gyaku-*

zuki from the *kamae* position. Wood-breaking is demonstrated by Ray Fuller (white-belt) with a *chudan* reverse punch, Terry Wingrove (brown-belt) with *chudan mae-mawashi enpi*, and Robert Williams (blue-belt) with *yoko-geri*. Then Vernon Bell, standing behind a table, presents brown belts to Terry Wingrove and Jimmy Neal (this was merely for the cameras, as both were brown-belts prior to this, of course), and the short film concludes with a freestyle demonstration between Brian Harper and Royston Merrick with Jimmy Neal acting as referee, and then Harper and Merrick are pitted in a freestyle environment against Wingrove. The colour film, which was shown to cinema audiences the length and breadth of Great Britain, has acquired that lovely aged quality about it. As in the case of Bell's 1957 film, Shotokan *karateka* are incredibly lucky that such a film should have survived. If readers wish to secure a copy of this vintage footage on video, they should write to British Pathé News, Pinewood Studios, Pinewood Road, Iver, Bucks, SL0 0NH for further details. The charge for the service/video at the time of writing was £50.

A slip of paper has survived to show that two weeks after the crew of Pathé Pictorial had filmed at the Kentish Town Baths, a substantial fifty-three members were training at the London BKF *dojo*. They were (although sometimes the writing is far from clear): Adamou, C., Adamou, N., Alexander, Barclay, Bayliss, Berrington, Burgin, Chisholm, Copper, Court, Dunne, Firlej, Foster, Fuller, Gander, Geday, Gentry, Glenister, Goodbody, Granditer, Green, Harper, Hunt, Johnson, B., Johnson, J., Judge, Lassey, Laville, Lear, Lebasci, Lewin, Longstaff, Mannion, Marcjak, Martindale, Merrick, Mille, Munday, Nightingale, Nolan, Parsons, Patterson, Peachey, Peters, Price, Randall, Statham, Stone, Tipping, Watson, Whitcher, Widdick, Williams. Of these fifty-three, fifteen paid by cheque, twenty-nine by postal order, eight by cash, and one is unrecorded. The training fee, for three months (in advance), was £15.00 per person.

Another, longer list, undated, but probably early 1965, of Bell's Seimeidokwai (which Bell translated as 'Way of Life Society') had the additional names: Adshead, Bounds, Brown, Cutting, Evans, Fisher, Gale, Gardiner, Garland, Green, Hagon, Man, Manning, Mercer, Metcalfe, Midgen, Moffat, Neal, Newman, Parker, Pressman, Rabner, Rivett, Russell, Shoesmith, Vincent, Wingrove and York. Neal and Wingrove had been made Honorary Life Members of the BKF, and that is probably why their names had been excluded from the earlier list, rather than there having been an oversight. Bell probably just put their names down without thinking in the later list.

It was in early December 1964, that the Adamou brothers, Christopher and Nicholas, who were also to become famous Shotokan instructors, actually began their karate training at the Prince of Wales Baths. Both were living in Wood Green. Nineteen-year-old Chris worked as a clerk and had interests in ancient history and archery, while Nick was seventeen and a solicitor's clerk at the time of joining, with interests in classical music and reading. They completed their BKF membership application forms on the 14th and 26th November 1964, respectively. (It is likely then, that the above London BKF *dojo* list of the 20th November 1964 was compiled retrospectively and slightly in error.)

In the summer of 1964, immediately following his 'O' levels, Nick Adamou had been passing the college notice-board with some fellow examinees, when he noticed a poster advertising karate. Two *karateka* were pictured, one in a low *zenkutsu-dachi*, the other performing a *yoko-tobi-geri* – the classic photo. After enquiries at the Tottenham library, the brothers were put into contact with the BKF, but they had to wait some four months before being allowed to train, as there were no vacancies. During this time, the brothers practised techniques from Nishiyama and Brown's, *Karate: The Art of 'Empty-hand' Fighting*. Nick Adamou recalled his first visit to the Kentish Town Baths *dojo*: "This was the first karate class I had ever seen. In that class was Eddie Whitcher who I remember performing *mae-geri*, stepping down, other leg *chudan kekomi*, stepping down, other leg *jodan mawashi-geri*. He did this coming towards my brother and myself. Other people in that class were Ray Fuller, Peter Lebasci, Royston Merrick, Robert Williams, Mick Peachey, Michael Randall and Pauline Laville (Bindra). Mister Bell walked into the *dojo* wearing a drab green chequered jacket, dark green waistcoat, light green shirt and dark green tie. He referred to all of us as 'Gentlemen' and gave the impression that he couldn't care one way or the other if we joined or not." Nick could remember quite clearly what grade each of the above students had reached at that time, and so strong was the impression gained that on December 13th 1964, less than one month after he and his brother had first seen karate, they were travelling the near two-hour trip (a bus journey, followed by three underground tube trains and a walk – Ah! those were the days) from their home to the Upminster *dojo* to train under Jimmy Neal and Terry Wingrove. Nick remembered that, "Jimmy Neal always used to train in a judo suit [which he may be seen wearing in the Pathé film], and I noticed on many occasions that he would teach and train gripping small hand weights." Nick also recalled that Jimmy Neal advised him, "to always press my tongue into the roof of my mouth just behind the top teeth so as not to cut or bite the tongue [when training]."

Nick Adamou had several recollections of the training at the St. Mary's *dojo* in early 1965 with Vernon Bell, who always seems to have been eating Cadbury's Fruit and Nut chocolate. "The week before, Bell told us to bring a piece of wood ... two foot long, four inches wide and half-an-inch thick. On the Sunday morning, most of us, including myself, brought the wood, and Bell made us place it at a forty-five degree angle against the wall [resting on the floor] and attempt to break it. No one could, and he went around to several pieces and performed side *fumikomi* to them and broke all of them." Another incident involved Bell demonstrating resuscitation on an unconscious student by punching the unconscious man's heel with a middle-finger fist. As Nick recalled, "the man groaned and changed from white-faced to a slightly better complexion as he awoke."

The last grading held in 1964 was conducted by Bell at the St. Mary's *dojo* on the 6th December. The BKF grading register reveals that the following people were promoted: 8th kyu – R. Burgin, J. Firlej, R. Gale, C. Gardiner, A. Garland, D. Hagon, D. Hart, R. Lee, S. Longstaff, W. McGuire, M. Mercer, R. Moffat, C. Patterson, I. Shaw, E. Stone, J. Vincent; 7th kyu – K. Roebuck, K. Sayles; 4th kyu -J. Ashton, B. Harper, H. Peters, F. Williams.

At this time (to 1966) there were a very limited number of books on karate in English generally available in Great Britain, though a considerable number of books on judo, and to a lesser extent ju-jitsu and self-defence were obtainable. Karate books being advertised at the time included: E.J. Harrison's, *Manual of Karate* (1959), priced at 19s.0d; Nishiyama and Brown's, *Karate: The Art of 'Empty-hand' Fighting* (1960), priced at £3; Plee's, *Karate by Pictures* (1962), priced at £1.0s.10d; and, Oyama's, *What is Karate?* (1957), priced at £5.5s. In America, many more books were available prior to 1966, and whilst some of these did reach the bookshelves in Great Britain, they appear to have been mostly available through American magazines and direct from publishers. Most of the following books were, consequently, rarely read in Great Britain at this time. Among the American karate titles available then were, with the date of publication in brackets: Edmund (Ed) Parker – *Kenpo Karate* (1960) and, *Secrets of Chinese Karate* (1963); Moja Rone – *Super Karate Made Easy* (1960); Hank Siegal – *Karate Techniques, Advanced Super Judo: The Oriental Art of Foot and Hand-Defense* (1960?); Tim Yuen Wong and K.H. Lee – *Chinese Karate Kung-Fu* (1961); George E. Mattson – *The Way of Karate* (1963);

Bobby Lowe – *Mas. Oyama's Karate as Practised in Japan* (1964); and, Craig Lomack – *How to Protect Yourself with Karate* (1966).

The two most prolific authors of that time appear to have been Donn Draeger and Bruce Tegner. Draeger's six *Practical Karate* books were published by Tuttle and comprised of: (1) *Fundamentals* (1963), (2) *Against the Unarmed Assailant* (1963), (3) *Against Multiple Unarmed Assailants* (1964), (4) *Against Armed Assailants* (1964), (5) *For Women* (1965), and (6) *In Special Situations* (1966). Among Bruce Tegner's karate books published by Thor Publishing of Los Angeles were: *Karate: The Open Hand and Foot Fighting, Vol. 1 – Self-Defense* (1959), *Karate: The Open Hand and Foot Fighting, Vol. 2 – Traditional Forms for Sport* (1961), *Bruce Tegner's Method of Self-Defense* (which included karate) (1960), *Judo – Karate for Law Officers* (1962), *Bruce Tegner's Complete Book of Self-Defense* (1963), and, *Instant Self-Defense* (1965). Although the Draeger and Tegner books seem to have been more readily available in Great Britain compared to some of the above American titles, few interviewees for this book recalled having seen them at the time.

As a matter of historical interest, Master T. Okazaki wrote a series of truly excellent articles for the American magazine, *Strength and Health*. The first of these, *Introduction to Karate*, appeared in April 1962; the second article, *Fundamentals of Karate: Use of the Arms and Legs*, appeared in May 1962; the third article, *Fundamentals of Karate: The Blocking Hand*, appeared in February 1963; the fourth article, *Fundamentals of Kata*, appeared in May 1963; the fifth article, *Fundamentals of Karate: Technical Explanation of Kata*, appeared in an issue unknown to the author, whilst the last of the articles appeared in January 1964, entitled: *Fundamentals of Karate: Makiwara*.

Vernon Bell had started BKF club representative meetings at his home every few months or so by this time. As Gordon Thompson recalled: "This seemed a good idea at the time and would have been fine if they had served any purpose. What they boiled down to was a long monologue from Mr. Bell about his trials and tribulations, his personal sacrifices, the pressures on him, how he found it difficult to get new clubs to conform, etc. Some of the things he told us passed all understanding. For instance, he was visited at his *dojo* by some council members who had heard about karate and wanted to find out about it. To us, that seemed a reasonable thing to do and something to take advantage of. Not Mr. Bell – he would not even let them into the *dojo*! The things he taught, he stated, were secret, and could not be divulged to non-members. He did not want his training ideas stolen, and he saw no reason why he should satisfy their curiosity. So they stood outside and talked about karate and some of the things he told them were incredible like some of the things he told us ... Eventually he would run out of steam, end his monologue, and we could start discussing one or two relevant things – but it was a waste of time. He still went his own sweet way. One meeting I remember quite well ... the ridiculous membership forms and the oath of allegiance were discussed. We all agreed on sweeping changes and made something half-way sensible out of them. One step at a time we thought, get this done and we could modify them again later at another meeting. Well I thought, at last we have achieved something, but the very next day – he must have written the letters as soon as we had left – we all got a letter from him stating that he did not agree with our modifications, that he had looked at them again, revised them himself and would use these revised forms in the future. He enclosed a sample of them and they were exactly the original forms without any modification whatsoever ... We wrote back saying that the meeting had no purpose if the decisions made could be overturned by him alone.

"At one of these meetings however, a truly momentous decision was made. He told us that he had been in touch with Japan and for the first time we heard about the Japan Karate Association. He wanted to bring over a Japanese instructor for a year or so. He told us about some of his letters and indeed he had been quite busy. Mister Kanazawa had been suggested and the choice was strongly supported by Mr. Nicol who was training in Japan at the time. He told us that we could hardly make a better choice and that he had spoken to Mr. Kanazawa about it, and assured us that he wanted to come to England. Well, Mr. Bell laid it on quite thick about the responsibility he was taking on, the financial commitment and so on, so we felt worried about biting off more than we could chew. It was Terry Wingrove who really swung it. He spoke for some time and showed us how the fund for his [Kanazawa's] support could be maintained. I will always remember him saying, 'We just keep pumping up the fund a little at a time, a little at a time, like going through the motions of pumping up a bike tyre.' Anyway, we decided to go ahead, as is well known, and that was the meeting which changed the whole course of karate in England ... Kanazawa completely changed the direction of karate in this country. Before his arrival we seemed to be dominated by France and the French way of doing things. From this time on we took our direction from Japan..."

(Continued in *Volume II* of *Shotokan Dawn*)

INDEX OF SURNAMES

ABOUT THE AUTHOR

Clive Layton was born in Hertfordshire in 1952, the son of an architect. He began his martial arts training with judo in 1960 under Terry Wingrove, and started Shotokan karate in 1973 under Michael Randall and the Adamou brothers, Nick and Chris, gaining his black-belt from Hirokazu Kanazawa in 1977. Originally studying environmental design, he later read for M.A and Ph.D degrees from the University of London, and is a Chartered Psychologist and teacher. Doctor Layton has appeared on both BBC television and radio in connection with his academic work. A prolific writer, with ninety publications, including eighteen books on karate (some in press), and numerous learned research notes, including those co-authored with famed Goju-ryu master, Morio Higaonna, and Kyokushinkai master, Steve Arneil, to his credit, he has emerged not only as one of the most productive, but, arguably, the finest writer on the Way of Shoto in the world. His biography of the early years in the life of Master Hirokazu Kanazawa has recently been published to much acclaim. He has also acted for many years as a consultant reader to the journal, *Perceptual and Motor Skills*, on experimentation into the martial arts. Any spare time is taken up researching new books, pursuing his love of history, film and fine clarets, and enjoying the peace of rural life, by the sea, with his wife, daughter and labrador. A highly innovative and deep-thinking *karateka*, in 1997 he was awarded the rank of 6th Dan.

NOTES

NOTES

NOTES

NOTES

NOTES